Montgomery Clift

MAURICE LEONARD

SCEPTRE

First published in 1997 by Hodder and Stoughton
A division of Hodder Headline PLC
A Sceptre Paperback

10 9 8 7 6 5 4 3 2 1

A CIP catalogue record for this book is
available from the British Library

ISBN 0 340 72860 4

Typeset by Palimpsest Book Production Limited,
Polmont, Stirlingshire
Printed and bound in Great Britain by
Mackays of Chatham PLC, Chatham, Kent

Hodder and Stoughton
A division of Hodder Headline PLC
338 Euston Road
London NW1 3BH

CONTENTS

ACKNOWLEDGEMENTS

Doris Barry, Patricia Bosworth and her biography 'Montgomery Clift', Chili Bouchier, Laura Brockbank, Ian Brown, Jack Clareman of New York, Pat Cox, Rosalie Crutchley, Cheryl Finney, William R. Fitts of Los Angeles, John Graham, Robert Guenette, Dr Geoffrey Handley Taylor FRSL, Christina Hatt, Olivia de Havilland, Brian Klein, David Kossoff, Robert LaGuardia's biography 'Montgomery Clift', Nell and Tony Liddell, Ethel McGinnis, Pat Marmont, David N. Mason, Gary Raymond, Mira Rostova, Dr William Russell MB MRCGP, Bernard Taylor, Phyllis Thaxter, Susan Tiplady, Gordon Thomson, Mark Torrender, Alexander Walker, Rowena Webb, Tom Wettingell, the late Michael Wilding, Colin Williams, Susannah York, the late Fred Zinnemann, and special thanks to Monty's nephew Edward M. Clift.

While every effort has been made to obtain permission from the photographers and copyright holders of the marvellous pictures used in this book, I apologize to anyone who has not been contacted in advance or credited.

ACKNOWLEDGMENTS

Part One

1

One evening in 1959, at about 7.30, I was luxuriating in bed, revelling in the splendour of a suite of a luxury hotel in London. I had spent most nights there now for about two months or so. My clothes were chucked all over the room. Some had landed on the floor, others hung where they had fallen; my underpants dangled from the arm of a velvet couch. I'd always admired that couch – it was moss green with a buttoned back. Very elegant.

Monty was still asleep. The sheet had slipped, exposing his chest. The chest had been shaved for *From Here to Eternity*. In that film he had played Private Prewitt, a man who had refused to box for his regiment, and who had to look vulnerable. Hairy chests were not vulnerable, according to the Hollywood demographs of the 1950s, so it had had to go.

But it was I who was vulnerable at that moment. Time was ticking by and I had a job to hold down. I went to the bathroom, showered, shaved, gathered my clothes and put them on. My shirt was a disgrace. Originally white, it was now filthy, yellow under the armpits and torn. It didn't smell, but was only one step away from it. The separate wax collar was revolting. Monty had fallen about when he had first seen it. I was still wearing it. It was part of a ploy on my part. I was twenty years old and rebelling against the world. My blue socks were part of that rebellion. They looked horrible with the uniform.

Dressing was hazardous as I was drunk, having downed several large vodkas and orange before falling into bed. I was not rolling drunk but almost. I was just in control. But my head thumped. The sleep after the alcohol had brought that on.

The dirty glasses greeted me in the sitting room. One was on a table and the other on its side, where it had come to rest after rolling across the floor. The residue of the orange drink had seeped into the carpet. That looked nice.

I lit a cigarette and knotted my threadbare tie, making it fit into the throwaway collar. It took some doing as the whole thing was held by a single stud at the front. I had lost the back stud. But as long as I didn't move too quickly the ensemble stayed more or less in place.

Monty was in England making *Suddenly Last Summer* with Elizabeth Taylor and Katharine Hepburn. Elizabeth was staying at a nearby hotel, and they would often talk on the phone in the evenings even though they had been working all day together. They were great buddies. Miss Hepburn was not staying at a hotel, but had rented a cottage where she could potter about in the garden. She enjoyed things like that. She had invited Monty to spend a weekend with her, in an attempt to discourage him from drinking, but had wasted her time.

I woke Monty before leaving. This was dicey, as he had a habit of hitting out when disturbed – not just an instinctive punch but the full flailing screaming attack. He didn't know the meaning of a peaceful start to the day. Nor a peaceful end to it, for that matter – he was a chronic insomniac.

'I'll see you later,' I told him when the panic had faded from those amazing light green eyes. 'I'm late. Don't forget to leave the door unlocked tonight.'

Sometimes he did forget, and it was like raising the dead if he did sink into unconsciousness. Sleep was too gentle a word for what happened to him when he finally closed his eyes. It took forever for him to get asleep so he took pills, and then an atom bomb could not wake him, even though his sleeps never lasted for long. It was usually well after midnight when I got back and I couldn't yell out for him to open up. It might wake Maria Callas in her nearby suite. She wouldn't like it.

I lurched out, meticulously circumnavigating the table and colliding only with the doorpost. Not bad.

I could not leave without reconnoitring the corridor. There were too many enemies about and I had to watch out for them. Most were employed by the hotel. Word was already about, among the staff, that I was living with him. I did not want anyone actually to be able to prove this. To be seen leaving his suite, clearly drunk, could only fuel gossip. Not that I feared for my reputation – I enjoyed the notoriety – but I didn't want to lose my job.

I stubbed out my fag as I nipped down the staff exit which would take me down to the front hall where I worked. It was all I could do to keep myself on an even keel as I manoeuvred those steep stairs. But I was in a good mood. Booze was a new discovery to which Monty had introduced me, and I had taken to it.

When I got to the ground floor I went to the alcove of telephone booths where I worked. I did a job that no longer exists: if guests in the hall wanted to make a call, I put them through. In addition I took messages, which I wrote out by hand, for guests who might be out or were not accepting calls. I was also the hotel's International Operator, which meant I rang INT, as it then was, and placed long-distance calls. In order to blend with the decor of the place I was kitted out in a patrol jacket uniform, rather like the best blue I was later to wear in the RAF.

Each night, when I finished my shift and went back to Monty, I would tell him the gossip of the day, enacting the antics of the various stars I had seen. So much for those who suggested he lived in a maelstrom of unrelieved depression. I never saw him depressed – worried occasionally and sometimes annoyed – but not depressed. I learnt later that he was anxious about his career during that time, but he certainly kept it from me. It was not all-pervading. We laughed a lot while he was making *Suddenly Last Summer*.

2

I had been working at the hotel for some months when Montgomery Clift checked in. I was loving the celebrities and the escape from a dreary home life. 'Film star Montgomery Clift tip-toed into London yesterday from America,' the *Daily Mirror* reported.

> His arrival was all terribly hush-hush. He came into London airport guarded like a diplomatic secret. Although ringed by film officials somebody managed to ask him if he was thinking of getting married. Pale-faced, he said, 'If I were, you would have heard about it long ago.' He took a fast car [to his hotel] and a fast lift to his suite on the 7th floor [sic]. He slept most of the day. At 6pm a dark-haired woman secretary opened the door of the suite exactly 4 inches and said breathlessly: 'He's not asleep now. He's having a shower. Oh NO, he's not seeing anyone.'

The dark-haired secretary was Marge Stengel, his personal assistant, who guarded him with the ferocity of a tiger. He later saw a reporter from the *Daily Herald*:

> To ask him why he isn't married, and if he intends to marry, is to hit the jackpot of unfriendly reaction. And still get no answer . . .

Kindly, amusing and very much alive. But edgy, restless and often withdrawn and unhappy. A perfectionist in his work, an honest and courageous artist, and an exciting and likeable man. That's how I see Montgomery Clift – a genuine non-publicity-seeking star. And THAT makes a change.

The reporters, of course, knew exactly why he wasn't married, and he knew they knew.

Each morning the hotel circulated a guest list to staff with the names and room numbers of everyone staying there. There he was in black and white. Just a few floors above.

I soon learnt his routine. He was the Invisible Man. The studio sent a car for him each day at 6a.m. He was long gone by the time I arrived. He came home late and went straight up to his suite. Whenever I tried to ring him, on some pretext or other, the phone was answered by Miss Stengel. No one got past her. Whatever the excuse, she fielded off calls with rigid courtesy.

I had mugged up on his films. He had had three Academy Award nominations (later four) but no Oscar. *A Place in the Sun*, which he had made in 1951 with Elizabeth Taylor, was already a classic.

I had glimpsed him one evening, on his way through the foyer to the lift. A woman had been with him, I presumed Miss Stengel, but only got a long shot. He was nondescriptly dressed in an overcoat and wearing glasses. *Glasses! Montgomery Clift!* That was a betrayal for a start.

This was the new face, of course. Presumably the glasses went with it. The old one had been smashed up in a terrible car accident he had had in 1956 while making *Raintree County*. The headlines had shrieked the news all over the world. I remembered it. I longed to look at that face close up, see for myself what damage had been done, trace the scars with my fingers, but time slipped by and I never managed to get to him.

I had almost given up when I finally spoke to Monty on a Saturday evening in May. I was alone on the switchboard and he had been making a huge number of international calls. I waited until things died down and then rang up. I expected Miss Stengel to be fielding the call.

Eureka! It was not Miss Stengel – it was him. I recognized the voice at once. The patter I had rehearsed, should I ever get to him, flooded out. It was a little speech all about telephone efficiency. He listened in surprised silence.

'Was the reception clear?' I fussed. 'Sometimes it's not so good.'

Transatlantic calls had been via cable for years and the reception was excellent, just like a local call. My voice was a caress.

'You're very kind,' he said, after assuring me he had heard perfectly.

'Well,' I said. 'I'm in the hotel and I like to know things are right for you. I'm such a fan of yours.'

'You're in the hotel?'

'Just downstairs.'

'I'd like to buy you a drink – you've been so kind.'

I told him I would be happy to come to his room.

'I can't tonight,' he said. A bomb dropped somewhere in my soul. 'I've got some people here.'

'I'm here tomorrow morning,' I said brightly. Desperately.

'Tomorrow morning? Do you want to come up about eleven?'

'I certainly do.'

'Come up at eleven. I'll expect you.'

'Shall I ring first?'

'No. Just come up.'

My eyes shone brighter than his in *Red River*. Brighter than Mitzi Gaynor's in *South Pacific*, for that matter. *South Pacific*, in which Mitzi starred, was currently slaying them in the West End. She was staying at the hotel with her sexy husband Jack Bean.

I was euphoric that night as I walked to the tube station. I had a date with Montgomery Clift. Please God he wasn't too drunk to remember. I got home to my parents and spent the night fretting that Marge Stengel would be with Monty in the morning. She would be, I knew – she always was. As I couldn't sleep I read my old copies of *Picturegoer*. I had a stack of them and could never bring myself to throw them away.

Picturegoer kept me in touch with the doings of Natalie and Bob, Elizabeth and Eddie Fisher, Zsa Zsa, Tab and Rock, plus my special favourites like Yma Sumac, Ralph Meeker and John Ericson. I looked through the pages and, sure enough, there were Elizabeth and Monty together. I couldn't believe I had just been talking to him.

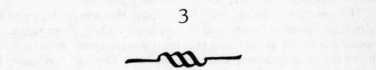

3

I washed my hair before leaving home in the morning and shaved meticulously. No way did I wish to appear at less than my best. But as I walked through the West End streets a breeze struck up and a piece of grit lodged in my eye. That was it, I thought – finished. My eye would be red and it would put him off.

I went round to the staff entrance and clocked in. If I failed to clock in on time a quarter of an hour's pay was docked. Then I made my way through those myriad, scruffy corridors backstage to the porters' changing room.

I had arranged to see Monty at eleven and that presented a problem. I was working by myself, so there was no one to take over my duties while I was away. I could nip down to the canteen for a quick bite of lunch, and put up the PLEASE APPLY AT ENQUIRIES sign, but there was no way Enquiries would wear that at 11 a.m. Why should they?

One thing was for sure: I was going up at eleven. Out came the sign – there was no alternative. There were international calls connected to a few of the rooms which could have lasted for hours, so I ignored them. I disabled the switchboard so that no one could make further calls, and, most importantly, locked the little cash drawer where we stowed the money. Our tips were in there, and if they went my boss would hang me. The main switchboard could handle international calls if I wasn't there. They had to at night.

Heart pumping, I went up the staff stairs to the fifth floor. I didn't dare take the lift. I didn't want the Swiss lift-boy to blab where I'd gone when there was trouble, as there would be, when my absence was detected. As far as the hotel was concerned my booths were the *Marie Celeste*. I had been transported to another planet.

I knocked on the door and he opened up. He had clearly just come out of the shower and looked fresh in a dressing gown. His hairy chest showed at the neck and the shortish hair of his head was still damp. I was conscious of my eye, now a strawberry jam red.

There was a scar on his neck; I later learnt this was the legacy of a glandular operation he had had in Germany as a boy. There was still something boyish about him – perhaps it was the quick, nervous way he smiled. His eyes were clear and sparkling like Asti Spumante. I later learnt this was from the effect of something in a bottle he kept in his expansive medicine chest. He always gave the impression of being amused. On this occasion it was probably because I was trying to be at ease.

He was not neurotic, not tortured and not out of control. What he was, was charming, friendly and decent. Despite the accident, he was still a good-looking man. So much for the magazine twaddle – which, of course, I fed on – which said he was a ruin.

He was also in fine spirits. I suppose that was the sight of me. He hadn't known what he was getting after all. I could have been Quasimodo. Here I was, good-looking and gift-wrapped, although admittedly with a red eye.

'Come in,' he said. 'What's your name?'

'Maurice.'

'That's a hairdresser's name.' The shy smile that had flashed from a million screens lasered me.

'Sit down,' he said. 'I'll get you a drink.'

Ella Fitzgerald was singing 'Old Devil Moon' from a nearby record player. He always hired a record player when he travelled.

He didn't ask what I wanted, which was just as well as I didn't know. I only drank the odd pint in the Fountain. I'd never had anything else, apart from my mum's home-made parsnip wine. I'd decided I'd say scotch, if asked, but I didn't have to now.

He came back with what I thought were two tumblers of orange juice. It was clearly laced with something subtle. A pleasant drink. Aside from the orange, what taste there was hinted at forbidden pleasures.

Whoopee. It went down a treat. I was soon floating on pink clouds. Ella sounded divine.

I then offered him one of my Craven A's and he accepted. This, I thought, was a breakthrough. I believed that movie stars must surely have special cigarettes and could never enjoy the plebian Virginia we all puffed on. Yet he had taken my Craven A. What a gent.

'Where do you live?' he asked.

'Tooting Broadway, actually.' I'd never used 'actually' in my life. But I had to have a new image, sitting here in a suite supping with a star.

He laughed for some reason. 'So you work here?'

I nodded and flashed a grin. He made a relaxed atmosphere. Although I was anything but relaxed, my stomach was churning. But the booze helped. It was a delightful discovery and I swigged more down. I had never been drunk in my life and didn't recognize the symptoms. I loved it. He refilled my glass.

'What's this I'm drinking?' I asked.

'Vodka.'

Vodka was not as popular in England then as it is now. Even if it had been, it was hardly the thing one asked for in the Fountain. Definitely not a man's drink.

'It's really nice,' I said, swigging more. Then I rubbed my eye. 'I've got something in it.'

'Let me have a look.'

He bent over me and opened it up. I was not too sure I wanted him to do that. An inflamed eye is not a pleasant sight in close-up.

'I've got something that'll soothe it for you.'

He went to the bathroom. I could see through the open door from where I was sitting. There were medicine bottles everywhere. Even accepting he was a hypochondriac, which I soon discovered, this was ridiculous. He came back with a sort of small paintbrush. Dipping the brush into a pot, he opened my bad eye again and painted it. The irritation went at once. I don't know what was on that brush, but it helped.

About an hour later, my clothes were all over the floor and the bottle and brush had been chucked. I think the goo from the bottle was seeping into my trousers. Frank Sinatra had taken the place of Ella. I looked at the scene of carnage with satisfaction. This was depravity. I'd always fancied it.

It was to become a pattern that I would always throw my clothes on the floor when I was with him. It was a symptom of abandon. Two fingers up at convention. I don't know why I couldn't have put them neatly on a chair – I was quite a neat person, really. It wasn't as if there was a panic.

It was as much a part of being with him as were Ella and Sinatra. He had quite a few LPs and they were all Sinatra or Ella – he never played any other artist. Whenever I now hear Ella doing 'That Old Devil Moon' it takes me straight back to that Sunday morning at the hotel.

I believe, although I'm not sure, that I might have kept my shirt on that Sunday – minus the detachable collar, of course. I know I spent ages afterwards trying to find the stud that attached it to the shirt. It had rolled across the floor when I had wrenched it off. Whereas I could keep it on with the one stud, with no stud at all I had no chance. It would have looked like a choker, or one of those rings African women wear round their necks to stretch them.

I certainly had my shirt on at some time, when I was lying on the bed smoking a cigarette. He was moving about the room doing something or other, because that was when he said: 'For Christ's sake take that shirt off – you look like an infidel.'

'I am an infidel.'

He laughed. So I laughed too. Well, it was funny. Particularly when you're pissed.

Our tryst came to an abrupt end when I got panicky. Now the whirl of excitement was over it came to me, through my veil of drunkenness, how irresponsible I had been to leave the switchboard unmanned.

I must have been missed by now – God knows what was going on. He laughed again when I told him what I'd done. I could see the funny side of it myself. He thought I was old enough to sort out my own problems. One half of me did not give a damn what the hotel thought, but the other half did not want to lose the job.

Before I left he told me to come back at eleven that night. I couldn't believe things were working out so well. Neither, of course, could he. Here was trade on the doorstep, just for the asking. Grateful trade, at that. Who could ask for more?

I ran down the five flights of stairs to the foyer. By some miracle perhaps I hadn't been missed. I staggered to the booths. If I had been blind I would have found them because all the phones were ringing. The manager was waiting for me, too.

'Where have you been?' he snarled.

'I've been ill,' I said. My face backed me up. By now the vodka was getting its own back. Everything has to be paid for. The excitement, coupled with the exercise, had made me queasy.

'Ill!' he echoed, Edith Evans-style.

'I've had to sit in the toilet. I've been sick. I had to go – I couldn't be sick here.' That was clearly true. 'I've vomited four times.'

I could see he believed me. And I was nearly in tears – I could act a bit.

'Why on earth didn't you tell someone where you were going?' There was a hint of compassion in that. I latched on and played the injured party.

'There wasn't time. I thought I was going to throw up on the floor. I did put up the Enquiry board.'

'Well, you look ill, I must say. For heaven's sake, next time you decide to vomit kindly tell someone at the Enquiry desk.'

'Yes,' I said, 'I'm sorry.'

His tails nearly caught me in my recently doctored eye as he left.

4

Monty went out during the day and I didn't see him return. When I rang at eleven there was no answer. I half expected Miss Stengel to be there, and if she answered I was going to say I had a personal call to Monty from Dr Silverberg, his psychiatrist. I don't know what his reaction would have been to that, as Dr Silverberg was important to him.

I realize now that I needn't have worried. I was actually doing everyone a favour by looking after him, keeping him out of trouble. While he was with me he wasn't scavenging the streets looking for anyone else. Columbia Films should have put me on the payroll – I was saving them a lot of possible aggravation.

I kept ringing and the phone remained unanswered. By this time I had a headache. My first hangover. The minutes ticked away and it was a worry. The last tube went at 12.30 and I really did not fancy walking the twelve miles home. I couldn't stay the night with him, even if he wanted me to, of which I was by no means certain. I took certain liberties at home, but there was no way I could stay out all night. If I wanted to see him, however, I had no alternative other than to stay spinning at my loom. At the back of my mind was the thought that he might have forgotten about me. I was just a knock-off. He might have dragged back other trade. I couldn't bowl up to his door and wait.

My wonderings got darker as time ticked on. Finally, however, I rang up yet again and the phone was answered. I was taken aback as an imperious female voice demanded:

'Who's that?'

'Is Mr Clift there?'

'Who wants him?'

'It's the international telephone operator.'

'And what do you want with him?'

'It's about his call to Chicago.'

'What call? Are you mad?'

I stammered and tried to explain it was about an earlier call. 'Listen,' she butted in. 'Just fuck off!'

He fell about. It was him.

He was good at impressions and often put on strange voices to talk to me. It never amused me. Invariably I was strung out, dodging the house detective or trying to hoodwink the phone operators. What made it particularly irritating was that I was always fooled by it. I thought he was playing with me – not according me the dignity I deserved.

I bunged up the Enquiries board and bolted up the staff stairs, then stopped dead. A horrible thought struck me. My clocking-in ticket was lodged at the staff entrance, which was closely guarded. There was no way I could brazenly clock out when I left Monty. I shot down the five flights again. I would have to clock out and then sneak back in. Not easy, because I could not re-enter the hotel through the front in full view of Reception and Enquiries.

In fact, it did not prove too difficult. I just waited until the security guard was talking to someone and clocked out, moving my ticket to the appropriate section. Then I threw up my hands as though I'd forgotten something and went back up the staff stairs. I needn't have bothered with the histrionics – the old man hadn't even noticed me.

When I got to the fifth floor I reconnoitred for enemies, then did a bolt to the door. It was, of course, locked. I gently knocked. Nothing. I knocked louder. Nothing. I knocked again. Nothing. I knew he was there. He wouldn't have gone out again. In the end I kicked. Not once but several times, viciously. He opened the door. It was a dull buff colour which I had augmented with grotesque scud marks.

'Were you asleep?' I said as I nervously skulked in, looking over my shoulder for anyone who might have been attracted by the noise.

'Yeah, I fell asleep.'

That was flattering.

'I was knocking out there for hours.'

'You couldn't have been there hours.'

'It seemed like it.'

The light was out in the sitting room and there was just a lamp on in the bedroom. It had an amber shade. He handed me a vodka and orange which I downed like a trooper. I'd forgotten I had a hangover and felt fine again. Then we got into bed and he fell asleep.

That was nice. Now what did I do? I couldn't stay the night. As it was, I wouldn't be home before four even with a good wind behind me. I could try hitching. There were no muggers about in those days, and people would sometimes stop if thumbed.

He looked so peaceful, in the glow of the amber light, that I didn't like to disturb him. But he could get peace any time. Perhaps I should just slip out, but that seemed churlish. Besides, I wanted to know when I would see him again. I hadn't got this far to chuck it all down the drain. Something had to be done.

I stroked his cheek. No response, so I gave him a brisk shake. His yell nearly stopped my heart – I'd never had that effect on anyone before. He shot bolt upright, his eyes mad. He shouted again, as though I'd stabbed him. If Judy Garland, who was then in town and staying with us, was near she was certainly getting a cabaret that night. I was trying to conduct a discreet affair, we were only one day in, and so far I'd nearly kicked the door down and he was screaming at one in the morning.

'It's all right, it's all right,' I whispered frantically. I don't know why I was whispering when he was shouting. 'It's me – the telephone operator from this morning. Remember?'

'Oh God,' he said, holding his head in his hands. That, too, was flattering. Wherever he was, it wasn't here. He was totally disorientated, the eyes seeing things invisible to me.

'I'm here,' I said, as though that were the panacea for everything. It certainly wasn't. His eyes were glazed and he was clearly troubled. He went to the gram and put on Ella.

'Shall I get some drinks?' I said.

'Why not?'

I padded to the fridge which was in the sitting room, obviously by special order. I opened the door and there was the vodka and a jar of orange juice. There was also a syringe peering at me. The stories were true! He was a drug fiend. I had once seen a young man heat up opium in a dessertspoon and then inject it, so I knew about these things.

I knew less than nothing. I later found out the syringe was for Demerol, which had to be injected to quell the pain in his jaw and shoulder – a legacy from the accident.

I hastily mixed two drinks. I did not know how to make drinks, which was apparent as he spat his out. I had poured in Tizer-sized portions diluted by just a slop or two of orange. I'd nearly emptied the bottle. He put matters right, moaning about the waste. I don't think it was the money – more the terror of running out.

He couldn't free the ice-cubes from the tray. I'd not put ice in the drinks, but he was cheerful again by now – he had swings of temperament. In high spirits he chucked the ice-tray hard at the wall. That did the trick. The cubes ricocheted about and sounded like a sten gun. Poor Judy.

I giggled.

He asked me to stay the night.

'I'd love it, but my Dad'll kill me.'

He was understanding about it. 'Is Tooting near here?'

'Is it fuck! It's miles away, and all the buses and trains have finished by now.'

'So what you going to do?'

'Can you give me the money for a taxi?'

'No problem. How much do you want?'

'I don't know, I've never taken a taxi home. I think it'll be about £10. Give me that. If it's more I can walk from where he drops me. If it's less I'll give you the change tomorrow.'

I didn't want him to think I was a hustler, which I was in a way. It was his world I wanted, not his money. Also I liked him.

He gave me £10 which I stuffed in my pocket. I promised I'd ring him tomorrow. After six, when he got home from work.

'Now, how do I get out?' I spoke aloud but the question was rhetorical. 'The only exit's the main one and I can't use that. Everything else is closed.'

'Jump out the window,' he said. We were five storeys up.

By the time I'd got my clothes on he was fast asleep again. Since I'd met him my clothes had gone on and off more times than traffic lights. Ella had finished and the arm of the gram was jerking about in the middle of the record. I released it, turned off the machine and left the suite, stepping over the melting ice-cubes.

Now, how *was* I to get out? The security guard was sitting at his high desk reading the paper, like something from Dickens. It was tomb-quiet now. I crept towards him, but he had no idea I was there. I ducked so that I could not be seen from his desk and crawled silently through the open door.

Out in the fresh air I did a little dance to celebrate.

What a full day I'd had.

5

PREFERS OLD CLOTHES TO SMART BLONDES

Hollywood and one of its top stars – Montgomery Clift – don't like each other at all. Because Monty likes to lead the life of an average American man . . .

He is, Hollywood declares, a male Garbo . . . shy and unfriendly. The fact that he seldom dates film actresses and that he shuns cocktail parties and premieres add to his legend as a mystery man . . .

Monty, in return, says he prefers not to let success turn him into an artificial person . . . When he dates a girl he takes her to a quiet out of the way restaurant because he feels it is an intrusion of their privacy to be seen and written about in the gossip columns . . . He likes his dates to be dark, soft and feminine types like Jean Simmons, Pier Angeli or Audrey Hepburn. He says he doesn't like women who are 'blonde, brittle and driving and who have had to struggle hard for success, because this always shows in their faces and makes them hard' . . .

When he's in New York he likes to spend his days reading play and film scripts. While doing this he usually chain smokes and continuously drinks cups of coffee. Most days he goes to a local gymnasium to exercise and keep in shape and when he wants entertainment he goes to the cinema . . . As far as Monty's appeal is concerned one girl

*fan sums it up by saying: 'He's got such expressive sad eyes that
he arouses terrific maternal instincts in women.'*
                              Bridget Jones, Reveille

We slipped into a routine. I would ring him just before I was going
up, after finishing my duties. That way I could be sure he would be
awake. He would leave the door ajar so I could sidle in. It saved all
that banging and kicking.

He liked leaving booby traps for me. One day he piled a stack of
cushions over the door so that when I pushed it they fell on me.
Another time I found the place in darkness. I groped my way in
and fell flat on my face over another pile of cushions, this time in
the middle of the floor. He was pleased with that one – it was a great
success. I thumped straight into the door jamb, which made my head
bleed. He had a lovely sense of humour.

Nowadays I was able to spend some nights with him by telling my
folks that I was working nights, which obliged me to live in. Sometimes
he would have wake-up calls as early as 5a.m. He'd answer the phone
and go straight back to sleep, almost deliberately. Columbia rang back
to remind him. Sometimes they could ring half a dozen times.

I usually had a shower first. Then, while I was dressing, he would
shower. Sometimes I would sit on the edge of the bath and talk to him
– not often though, and he turned the shower on me once. I was ready
to go downstairs to work, and next minute I was dripping.

Usually I left the suite before him. Then I snoozed in the porter's
changing room until it was time to start work. If he was late leaving
I went straight to work and I'd get downstairs in time to start taking
messages for him. I would speak to the same luckless man who had
been ringing the suite. 'He's on his way,' I would say. 'I've just seen
him leave.' Just seen him leave? I'd just slept with him. Oh, if only
they knew the truth, I naively thought. Now, I realize, they probably
did and couldn't have cared less.

Sometimes it would be as late as 9a.m. before he left for work. I
was staggered at what he got away with, particularly when he might
be keeping Elizabeth Taylor and Katharine Hepburn waiting. I would
not have kept my partner at a switchboard waiting intentionally. But
then, people like us didn't.

6

'Which movies of mine have you seen?' he asked me one night.

'None.'

'Then you're not much of a friend.'

My face blazed with humiliation. I had replied in a Smart Alec way, as though I was saying something clever. I had, of course, seen *Red River*. But he had taught me a lesson and I was never quite that flip again. He didn't pursue the matter; he was too kind.

'What's your best film?' I asked a bit later, trying to backtrack. We were sitting in the middle of the floor. It was cosy. Ella was playing.

'*Lonelyhearts* and *The Young Lions* are on release now. You can see them. *Lonelyhearts* is an embarrassment, but I like *The Young Lions*.'

'Better than *From Here to Eternity*? Everyone says it's wonderful.'

'I prefer *The Young Lions*.'

'But you don't like *Lonelyhearts*?'

'No.'

His friends Myrna Loy and Maureen Stapleton were both in *Lonelyhearts*. Myrna Loy was an elegant actress who, in the 1930s, had been voted 'Queen of Hollywood'. A housewife on a radio show once asked her how to live a happy life. 'Don't try to be Myrna Loy,' she had said. Maureen Stapleton was a fine, Method-schooled actress. It was her first movie. Monty always seemed to have friends with him when he was making movies, so I couldn't understand why he hated making them. She was nominated for an Academy Award for it.

But he did hate making them. He told me he would not have come back to movies at all but for the fact that he was broke. He had done both *Lonelyhearts* and *Suddenly Last Summer* purely for the money. 'I hate it,' he told me.

We did not speak a great deal about movies – what would a bellhop know about them? He didn't want to talk about them, anyway. He had enough of it at work all day and he was no gossipmonger; he never mentioned anybody famous to me – only Elizabeth, now and then, if something had happened that had amused him, and Hepburn not at all. Part of my charm for him was that I had nothing to do with movies.

He was better looking off-screen than on. He, who had been the most photogenic of actors had, by some malicious fate, become the reverse of photogenic after the accident. But I think he no longer cared about how he looked – or about anything much at all. There was no great will to live. Yet he did not inflict this on me; he was excellent company.

But he did rue the loss of his sexual potency. The spirit was willing but the flesh was weak. 'There's no oil in the well,' he had wailed miserably one night. Couldn't be helped.

We used to lark around like two wide-boys. He loved fighting and swearing. I would get the evening off to a good start if I came in and, without a word, pushed him off the chair or bed. He'd grab a cushion to belt me, and so it went on.

He also loved running about naked, especially down the corridor. We would get the kegs off, surreptitiously peer through the door until the coast was clear, then dare each other to run a certain distance naked. If someone came round the corner and caught a glimpse of the arse of one or the other of us he was in ecstasy.

One night he gave me the £10 for the taxi but refused to let me go. I was in my uniform but he was naked.

'Come on,' I said. 'Don't muck about.'

'Stay,' he pleaded. 'I'm not going to let you go.'

'Try and stop me.'

He lay in front of the door like a draught-excluder so I couldn't open it. I just dragged him by the arms and pulled him away – he didn't weigh that much. When the door was free I wrenched it open and shot into the corridor. With an Indian whoop he charged after me, bollock naked. As I darted through the staff swing door he shoved me with all his might between the shoulder blades, sending me flying.

At that time Eartha Kitt had a single out called 'Monotonous'. It contained a verse that fascinated me:

> For 30 days salt air I sniffed,
> While I was shipwrecked and cast adrift,
> With a guy who looked like Montgomery Clift.

I used to adore it when I heard it on the radio.

One of the newspapers carried a story that the cast of *Suddenly Last Summer* was feuding. Monty spoke to Elizabeth on the phone about the report while I was in the room; clearly it had upset him. He was always upset by hostile press reports.

Now and then I would amuse him – or at least I hoped I did – by telling him some of the things I got up to when I didn't see him.

'Why can't I do things like that?' he once moaned. 'Where can I go? If I set foot out the door I'm recognized. You can go out and get drunk and fall down and that's fine. If I do it everyone reads about it.'

I would have swopped places. You think being a movie star's hard? Try getting to work in the rush hour, then working the phones for eight hours in the front hall.

The filming of *Suddenly Last Summer* was coming to an end. I didn't want to think about it. I was going on a week's holiday to Cornwall with Rita, who was a girlfriend, and her mum and dad and their Alsatian dog Tina. I was nervous that the film would be finished while I was away and he would leave for New York without saying goodbye. But he assured me this would not happen.

'I'll ring you every day,' I promised. He humoured me.

In fact I did ring every day, reversing the charges. 'Who's calling?' the hotel operators would ask. 'Ralph Richardson', I would say. It was my pseudonym for his purposes. Silence. They knew it was me but they put me through.

Standing in the red phone box, at the end of the road our rented flat was in, I told him about Tina, about her mum Vi, and about how we got the car jammed in a river.

'When in doubt, back out,' he told me.

Rita gave me the elbow when we got home. I had told no one the nature of my friendship with Monty and had simply told her I had met him and spent time with him, but she had sussed it out.

'You're in love with Montgomery Clift', she had told me one evening. That was news.

7

I was beginning to look a sight.

Monty never slept for long, which meant I didn't either – the longest period he went without waking was about two hours. When he did sleep it was fitful and he would thresh about, sometimes landing on the floor and staying there. I left him where he landed; he got so little sleep he might as well nod off where he was. Anyway, the carpet was soft. Plenty had worse beds.

So I lay there in the small hours, cramped and sweating if he was jammed beside me. My body heat freaked him out – probably the reason he flung himself on the floor.

When he did wake he would pad about, play Frank or Ella, or drink. He'd wake me anyway. I never minded but he would apologise and say he mustn't do it as I had to work in the morning. So did he for that matter. He'd sometimes sit, then fall asleep at once, and we'd have peace again for a few hours.

This nightly routine, coupled with the booze to which I was fast becoming accustomed, and the constant fags – I was up to fifty a day, very sophisticated – was leaving its mark on me. My face was green and my eyes sunk in grey circles. 'They look like two footballs,' my mother said as I crawled in one Saturday morning.

The day dawned when Monty had to go back to New York. He was pleased, for New York was his life and I was only ever a diversion. But not even Lucille Ball could divert me, and she had just checked in. *I Love Lucy* had been shown on British television for years and I used to watch it sometimes on a Sunday night with Rita at her house.

Lucille Ball wasn't exactly timid. I was a great fan, which didn't wash at all. She was not interested. She looked just as she did on the screen – scarlet hair, Siamese cat eyes, carmine lips, figure like a model, but the difference was she never smiled or, if she did, I never saw it. Laugh? Forget it. I was in the lift one day with her and her three henchmen.

'Cigarette,' she barked.

Three open packets were waved at her.

Could this be the zany Lucy the whole world loved?

Sir Thomas Beecham, Britain's celebrated orchestral conductor, was waiting for the Swiss lift-boy to take him upstairs when I finished my shift on the last day that I saw Monty. A luscious young lady with long blonde hair was with him. They went upstairs – not, I'll wager, to discuss the finer points of a Delius score.

By the time I got to the suite, at around 7.30 that evening, I didn't look much like a bellboy. I had changed out of my uniform and arrived in civvies, new black jeans and all. It was a special occasion.

While we were sitting on the floor in the gloom, with Ella and our vodkas, an elderly woman came into the facing suite and started to change her clothes. She had no idea we were watching. He was choking with laughter as she wandered about in her knickers, not knowing she had an audience. He kept punching me in ecstasy.

This was not quite the candle-lit end to a relationship that some might have envisioned. But everything was out of my control; it all just happened that way. I was upset he was going, but gave no hint. This, I knew, was the end. He was a film star and I was a bellhop who took messages. No one could have been more decent. He was delighted to be going back but trying not to rub it in. We joshed along all evening. Then I had to go.

I thanked him for everything. I meant it, too. He had given me memories I still treasure – a glimpse into a lifestyle beyond my grasp.

'Can I ring you?' I asked.

'Of course you can.' He gave me his New York number, which I wrote on the message pad and shoved in my pocket. It had started with messages and it was ending that way. Messages were my life.

'It'll have to be collect. Is that all right?'

'Ring when you want.' Then he took out his wallet.

'I can get the tube tonight.'

'Buy yourself a yacht.' He took a wodge of fivers and jammed them in my pocket. The trousers were so 1950s' tight he couldn't jam them in, so they stuck out like feathers. I had never had so much cash in my life.

'Have some more,' he said. Another wodge was jammed in the jeans. I laughed and he laughed.

The money did ease the pain, and the image of a pair of black suede shoes I might buy flickered into my brain. Then I was in the corridor putting the money away. I was giddy from it all.

Next day, when he had gone, I was sitting at the board when a American man's soft voice asked if I could get him a number. For a minute I thought he'd come back. I spun round, all expectancy.

It was Gary Cooper, immaculately dressed in a light blue suit, hair neatly groomed, elegance personified. I leapt up and wrenched open a booth door, almost bowing him in. Gary Cooper. Wow!

He was dead two years later. Monty survived him.

I did ring him sometimes, and I must have been a pain in the neck. I had been fun to be with in London: scampering into his bedroom at night, dodging the house detectives and waiters, and diving underneath the clocking-in machine – all that had appealed to him.

But what use was that three thousand miles away, particularly when he was paying for the call? And, really, I had nothing to say. I would talk to him about bits and pieces that had happened, and tell him I missed him, but was only flannelling. I wanted to stay in contact. Wanted to know Montgomery Clift.

How, I wonder, would I have behaved if the boot had been on the other foot? Probably I'd have accepted the first call, then left word I was out. He never did that. He was always friendly and affectionate. Always accepted the charges.

I kept abreast of him via the newspapers. *Wild River* came out in 1960 – he had left me to make that. He had expected it to be a chore and was dreading it. Another job done for the money. *The Misfits* and *Freud* followed. I devoured every word of the copious publicity.

Then there was silence for a while.

I learnt of his death through the *Daily Mail*. It was on Monday, 25 July 1966, two days before my birthday. By this time I had left the hotel and my parents' home in Tooting, and was living in Crystal Palace and working for Harlequin Records in the City. I was strap-hanging on a Southern Region train and saw his picture in a newspaper which someone was reading further along the carriage. I pushed my way through the other strap-hangers, and read the caption: 'MONTGOMERY CLIFT FOUND DEAD'.

As soon as I got to Victoria I bought the paper and read it for myself. My hands were shaking. He had died of a heart attack at his New York house on East 61st Street, where I used to ring him. It was seven years since I'd seen him.

He had made just seventeen films, yet at the time his fame was as widespread as that of John Wayne or Joan Crawford, who had each made dozens of films. 'He was one of the finest actors of our time. He was a fine human being and a good friend,' Frank Sinatra was quoted as saying. The *Observer* noted: 'His presence in a film was a sort of guarantee of quality. There are not so many people of similar talent and independence in the American cinema that it can afford to lose him. In private life he was retiring . . .' Later, *Paris Match* gave us what we really wanted, 'The Curse of Montgomery Clift'.

Meanwhile I stood against W.H. Smith's news-stand and read the *Daily Mail*. Then I folded it up and put it in my pocket. It was rush hour and the station was crowded. I had to open up the record shop I now worked in, so I pushed my way on to the tube. There was no one to talk to about it.

Part Two

1

He was a sensitive child with a face too beautiful for a boy. He was prettier than his twin sister Roberta and prettier than his brother Brooks. It was as though Sunny, his mother, had poured all her beauty into him alone. He was easily wounded and his face betrayed the pain. The lips trembled with hurt and the big, light green eyes, which three decades later would glitter from the world's cinema screens, readily filled with tears.

His delicate mental equipment was not the best armour to fend off the rigours of one of the toughest professions in the world, but at the beginning of his career it helped. It gave him a vulnerable look. Here was a different type of hero. Audiences longed to soothe his agony. It was the image that launched a thousand orgasms.

He was born on 17 October 1920 at 2101 South 33rd Street, Omaha, Nebraska, into a spacious middle-class home which boasted both a maid and a nanny. There was no theatrical blood on either side of his family.

That birthday was shared with the gorgeous Rita Hayworth, Love Goddess of the 1940s; and the libertine John Wilkes, who was a member of the notorious Hellfire Club and is entitled to remembrance for sneaking a baboon into the club and releasing it as the members were calling upon Satan. There were several near heart attacks – Monty would have loved it. It was also the birthday of chaste St Audrey, who founded a monastery at Ely. The abandoned and the chaste always battled in Monty's soul.

On the actual day of his entry into the world two other misfits were discovered. At respectively three and five years old, the wolf-children of Midnapore were dug up from their lair by the Reverend Joseph Singh. They were found among a litter of cubs being brought up by a she-wolf. She was doing a good job and they were fit and happy, loping along on all fours like the wolves. This soon altered. Under the pious administration of the Rev. Singh their adoptive mother was killed and the children put in an orphanage where they survived in utter misery for a few years, constantly pining for their wolf mother, until they mercifully died – untamed creatures who could not fit into society.

Monty's mother and father, William Brooks and Ethel – Bill and Sunny – had an unorthodox marriage. Bill doted on her, but she ruled the roost and was too busy for him. Sunny, nicknamed for her bright laugh, put all her formidable energy into bringing up her children and Bill was shoved to one side. 'Do as your mother says', he told his children. He worked his fingers to the bone for his family, and Sunny kept him at it, for she needed the money he earned to bring up the kids in a manner she thought befitting. This was expensive.

Sunny was complicated. Monty inherited that from her, as well as his looks. She was brought up, for the first year of her life, by the doctor who delivered her, Edward E. Montgomery, then fostered out to the family of Charles Fogg, an alcoholic foreman in a steel factory. Fogg was a brutal man and Sunny grew up detesting drunks. Her beautiful son was to develop into a notorious drinker, although far from brutal – he seldom hurt anyone except himself.

The Foggs brought up Sunny to believe she had been conceived in sin. It was drummed into her that she must be severely corrected when naughty or she might become a bad woman like her mother. The Foggs did not know who her mother was, as Dr Montgomery had been sworn to secrecy and promised not to reveal this information to Sunny until she was eighteen.

In fact, Sunny was not illegitimate but the clandestine daughter of Maria Anderson and Woodbury Blair, an aristocratic couple who had secretly married in the 1880s. The marriage had been annulled but not before Maria became pregnant. After Sunny was born Maria was kept a virtual prisoner and Blair not informed he had a daughter. Unaware of Maria's sad fate, Dr Montgomery had written several times to her suggesting she acknowledge her daughter. His letters were returned unopened. Maria would never have seen them.

Although Sunny was not told the identity of her mother she was told she was a grand lady. She spent her entire life striving for social recognition for herself and, more importantly, for her children. She was over ninety when she died and still vainly writing letters to try to prove her aristocratic origins, determined her children should not suffer the purgatory of rejection that she had known. The fact that by this time they could not have cared less did not deter her.

Bill was thirty-four when Monty was born and Sunny thirty-two. He was five foot eight (Monty grew to become five foot ten), no great looker, with thinning hair, and inclined to give way rather than fight. He was Vice-President of the Omaha National Bank, a well-paid position for which he had worked hard.

He came from an established Presbyterian Southern family: his father was a judge with a large house and several black servants. Bill was brought up to believe that blacks were inferior to whites, something that stayed with him all his life and which caused him grave discomfort towards the end of his life when Monty was virtually living with a black man on whom he was totally dependent. This, coupled with his son's homosexuality, was a bitter pill for Bill to swallow.

Although he became an investments consultant, Bill started his career studying mining at Cornell University. Shortly after he had started his course, however, his father lost most of his money and Bill had to work his way through college, which he did by selling advertising space for the college newspaper. He found he was a natural salesman.

Sunny was also at Cornell, where they met in 1910. She was studying law, racy for a lady at that time, but she had a determined spirit. Bill was instantly infatuated by her beauty, notably her mass of fine hair which, coupled with her zest, made her one of the most attractive women on campus.

They married in 1914, the year of the outbreak of the First World War. The Clift family did not bless the union. Sunny was thought to be an orphan, and this was a stigma. It was a Quaker wedding – Sunny was a staunch Quaker and Bill converted. She brought up Monty to be a Quaker. Her religious belief was reflected by her demeanour. She preferred plain clothes and no make-up, although progressive women were beginning to experiment with tinted powders. But even when fashions changed she wore a minimum of make-up.

Sunny exuded confidence, but there was another side to her. She was a mass of insecurities which she passed on to Monty. She was frightened of spending nights alone, and when Bill had to travel would insist that a bodyguard slept in the house. It was not unknown for her to wake him in the small hours and make him search the place because she thought she had heard an intruder.

In 1918, when the war was over, Sunny encouraged Bill to switch from mining to banking. He had never been interested in mining and made no money out of it, but she had recognized his flair for finance. He started working for the First National City Bank of New York, which sent him to Omaha to open a trust company. While there he transferred to the Omaha National Bank, which he persuaded to open an investment department. He was then created Vice-President of the newly formed Omaha National Trust Company. He flourished but had to spend long hours at work to do so. A fourteen-hour day was not unusual.

When he was not at the office it was sometimes necessary for him to entertain at home, where Sunny came into her own. She gave elaborate dinner parties with the accent on culture, and dazzled guests with her wit and erudition. Few realized the desperation that lay beneath.

In 1919 Sunny gave birth to her first child, William Brooks, named after his father, but always called Brooks. The twins, Edward Montgomery and Roberta, followed eighteen months later. It was a difficult confinement; Roberta came first, Monty several hours later. Although Sunny chose the name of Roberta she soon discovered it was also the name of a relative whom she grew to hate, and from then on Roberta was known as Ethel, after Sunny, a name she still uses although both she and Sunny detested it. Edward was always Monty.

Summers in Omaha could be boiling, with temperatures of up to 45°C, and Sunny decided to take the children to the cooler climate of New England. Sunny taking the children away and leaving Bill behind became an accepted part of Monty's childhood.

The children had a nanny, the formidable, big-boned Emma Wilke, never accorded the familiarity of her first name and always referred to, dismissively and often curtly, as 'Wilke'. There was a strange bond between Wilke and Sunny. Wilke had been a nurse at the hospital where Brooks was born. Sunny had also had difficulties giving birth to Brooks but had borne the pain stoically. It had grieved Wilke to see her suffer. A co-dependency grew, and Wilke promised Sunny that she would never allow her to suffer alone again. She offered her services as nursemaid and stayed on. This had suited Sunny, as she believed it proper her children should have a nurse. Wilke was to remain until Brooks went to college.

Wilke and the children did not particularly like each other but she was devoted to Sunny and dutiful towards them. In photographs, and the early home movies Sunny arranged when they were visiting Europe, the dourly dressed Wilke can be seen hovering in the background rather like a crow. She is not part of the family, always the hired help. She would have killed for Sunny. It was a doomed and unreciprocated love.

In 1924 the family moved to Chicago, where Bill had accepted a position with the Ames, Emerich Investment Co. Within a year he was renting permanent accommodation in New York as he was commuting there so often.

Of the children, Ethel and Monty were particularly close, although they did not look much alike. Brooks often felt an outsider: 'I had a feeling that the twins were pushed up and I was pushed down,' he recalled in an article that appeared in the *Washington Post* on 6 August 1979. Yet all three were 'tripletized', as he put it – dressed identically in short trousers with the same style overcoats and Dutch bob haircuts. Ethel looks like a little boy, Monty sometimes like a little girl. They could have been either. Both had devastating smiles.

Brooks and Monty actually had quite a lot in common. Both were later bitten by the stage bug. When Monty became a star, Brooks did his best to become one, too. He studied drama and even worked for one season in stock as an actor, but he did not shine. Later he was to become a television director, with which he had more success. In *Beautiful Loser* Barney Hoskyns quoted Monty as saying later about his own career, 'I wouldn't know why I wanted to act, but someone said it had to do with competing with my sister and brother.'* Clearly there was competition between all three.

Brooks and Monty had another thing in common: the same timbre to their voices. Monty's voice became one of his greatest assets. Dark, husky and expressive, with a uniquely reticent delivery, it added immeasurably to his roles. Brooks's voice was uncannily similar, even following the same cadences, so much so that the boys would play pranks on the telephone, each pretending to be the other.

'Monty and I shared confidences,' Brooks said in the *Washington Post* piece of 6 August 1979. 'There was some kind of solace we could give one another.' They had similarly pliant physiques, although Brooks was more chunky and had a ruddier complexion. Monty was always trim and never became flabby. Brooks became an athlete, developing,

---

* *Beautiful Loser: Montgomery Clift* by Barney Hoskyns, Bloomsbury Publishing Ltd, 1991

while still a boy, into a figure-skating champion. Monty was nearly as good. Both developed highly sexed libidos, labouring for satisfaction with a variety of partners.

In the same article Brooks stated, tellingly, about their mother, when she was ninety, 'She could be very cruel – but this was her way of showing love. Love plus ambition for her children to excel . . . There is a lot I could say – but, well . . .'

There was something unnerving about these immaculate, precocious-seeming triplets with the twins' inter-blending sexuality. A touch of Jean Cocteau's *Les Enfants Terribles*.

As Dr Montgomery had promised, he kept the identity of Sunny's mother from her until her eighteenth birthday. Not knowing of Maria Anderson's circumstances she had written immediately to her but, like Dr Montgomery, received no reply. In 1925, when she had taken the children on an extended vacation to Bermuda, she heard from Dr Montgomery that her mother had died. She sent lilies to the grave. No acknowledgement was forthcoming.

The death of her mother made her even more desperate for recognition and she spent hours on genealogical research, trying to track down previously unknown members of the Anderson family. She urged Bill to do the same, and eventually an elderly aunt was located in Washington DC. This was Sophie Anderson, her mother's sister, who lived alone in the Hotel Wyoming. Sunny bombarded her with letters and finally received one back. What was not apparent from the letter was that her aunt's powers of reason were imperfect.

Sunny was summoned to the Hotel Wyoming in 1926 to meet her Aunt Sophie. Her excitement may be imagined: this was the fulfilment of a dream, and she arrived trembling. The old lady received her cordially, heard her claim to kinship sympathetically, and gave her presents for the children. She was aware of the circumstances of Sunny's birth – indeed, she had assisted in the elopement of her parents. It was Aunt Sophie who told Sunny that her father never knew he had a daughter.

She agreed to see Sunny again and invited her to bring the children. In keeping with many older ladies, she found Monty 'delightful'. Sophie seemed inclined to dismiss matters there, but Sunny beseeched her to fight her cause and act as intermediary between her and her grandmother in order that she might be accepted as part of the rich Anderson family. Sophie told her she must not hurry things: formal introductions would take place in due course. When Sunny suggested that she herself would approach the family directly, and even contact her father, Sophie became hysterical and threatened to commit suicide. She insisted she must handle things in her own way and in her own time.

It was a ploy. Sophie had no intention of ever introducing Sunny to any members of her family. Presumably it was her unstable mental health that had brought about this vindictive behaviour. But for Sunny, acceptance by Sophie was a triumph in itself. It turned her head. She believed Sophie because she wanted to, and was convinced that it was just a matter of time before the Andersons accepted her and, more importantly, her children.

She would not allow her children to mix with others of their own age. She had never been keen on it, but now became fanatical. She wanted them educated privately, and was already teaching them Latin from a correspondence course. Monty had a natural flair for languages and later became fluent in both German and French. Another reason for this exclusivity was that she did not want the children questioned. If they were so well connected, where were these wealthy relatives?

Sunny's exclusion of the unsuitable included the Clift family. The Clifts were middle-class but not in the same league as the Andersons. When her mother-in-law once tried to cuddle the twins Sunny flew at her, snatching them away.

She took the children to Sophie again the following year. Again, Sophie thought them charming but not sufficiently polished to be acceptable to her family. Sunny was desperate enough to swallow this – the rest of the Andersons, of course, had no idea what was going on.

Sophie suggested that a foreign education might be a good thing. The children could broaden their knowledge of languages and absorb some culture. It would also keep them away for a while.

In May 1928 Sunny, with Wilke in tow, took her children on a nine-month European 'culture' tour, one of several such tours. Bill had to stay in Chicago to finance them. They left on the *Ile de France*, one of the most luxurious liners of its day. The attractive young mother and her three identically dressed children, in the care of their nurse, became a curiosity on board.

Seven-year-old Monty loved the cruise and was thrilled when he caught a glimpse of Buster Keaton, the silent screen star, who was also on board. His fun was brought to an abrupt end in the ship's pool when another lad held his head under water. Monty, thinking he was drowning, struggled so violently he burst a gland in his neck. He was taken to the ship's hospital. Within hours an infection set in which did not abate. When the ship docked in France he was critically ill.

Sunny went to the American Embassy for advice and was told the best gland surgeon in Europe was in Munich. By the time they arrived Monty was nearly at death's door and was immediately operated upon. He responded to treatment, but was forced to lie still for days with a brace around his neck. His neck bore the livid operation scar for the rest of his life; it can be seen in his movies. When Sunny first saw it she rounded on the surgeon, blaming him for disfiguring her son and accusing him of cutting too deeply.

Bill was kept abreast of these dramatic events by letter. He missed his children and wrote telling them they would all be together again soon. He wrote specially to Monty, telling him how much he loved him and how concerned he had been about the operation.

From Munich they returned to Paris where, in addition to Latin, they were taught French and German. The Diaghilev ballet had taken Paris by storm and Sunny made sure they had the finest seats in the house. She also took them to art galleries, to plays at the Comédie Française and to the opera. Monty saw the celebrated French star Yvonne Printemps and fell in love with her warm soprano voice; he played her records on a gramophone Sunny hired for him. On the rare evenings when they were not at the theatre Sunny would read to them from great works of literature. Ethel remembers that sometimes Monty cried at the stories.

Sunny moved them on to Switzerland, where they learned to ski and ice-skate. In Montreux Sunny found to her delight that Lady Astor was staying in the same hotel. Occasionally they had dinner together, and Lady Astor gave Brooks a book as a present.

They went on to St Moritz, where Sunny intended to stay for several weeks. She rented the top floor and staff of a spacious villa, converting one of the rooms into a classroom for the children and hiring a blackboard and desks. She also engaged the services of a Monsieur Helman, a teacher at a nearby school. Lessons started promptly at 8.30 every morning except Sundays.

One evening, Sunny found Monty preoccupied cutting out shapes from coloured paper which he had asked her to buy for him, making costumes for a little play he had devised and wanted to act out for her. He thought he might like to be an actor. Sunny smiled indulgently. He called the play *The Conversion of King Clovis* and there were parts for Sister, as Ethel was called, and Brooks as well as Monty.

They performed the play in the villa, in front of Wilke, Monsieur Helman and Sunny. There was enthusiastic applause afterwards. Then Sunny gave Monty her notes. He rather resented it.

He had his eighth birthday in Switzerland: he and the other children spent part of the day with a new friend, Kate Billings. A breezy geologist in her twenties, fresh from an expedition on the Gold Coast in West Africa, she had seen the family in the hotel and, like many others, was intrigued by the children and their perfect manners. She introduced herself and Sunny permitted her to take them on sledge outings. However, she soon put a stop to it. Miss Billings was pleasant enough but not an aristocrat. Sunny was determined that Aunt Sophie would have no grounds for not introducing them to the Andersons when they returned to America.

From St Moritz the family went to Vevey where Monty was allowed to play with Edward Foote, a boy of his own age, who was on holiday with his grandparents. Edward had an uncle who was a senator, so that was all right. Once Sunny had established his acceptable credentials, which she did by directly questioning his grandmother (so directly that she later recounted the questions with amusement) the Footes could not get rid of her.

Edward did not much care for Monty at first, finding him 'conceited and self-involved' according to Patricia Bosworth in *Montgomery Clift*.* They stayed in touch, however, until Monty became a movie star, and then moved in different circles.

---

* *Montgomery Clift* by Patricia Bosworth, Harcourt Brace Jovanovich, 1978

2

America seemed a different world to the Clift children when they returned in February 1929. With their European clothes and courtly manners they no longer blended in, which was exactly what Sunny wanted. They were like characters from an Ivor Novello musical comedy. The boys bowed when introduced, kissed hands and almost clicked heels, sprinkling their conversation with French and German phrases. Monty was the most courtly of all.

Bill did not care for it and wanted to send the boys to a military academy to toughen them up. Sunny, however, would not hear of it. They were coming along superbly – fit for the Andersons. She did, however, agree to send them to a school rather than continue with their private education, which, in Bill's opinion, was a step in the right direction. They were enrolled at the Highland Park Public School in Illinois, not far from where they lived, so they were able to cycle to and fro.

The boys had a hard time adjusting, though Ethel coped better. Both Monty and Brooks were bullied mercilessly – their European veneer inflamed the other boys, and the fact that they knew nothing about popular American culture, such as baseball or dance crazes, was even worse. But their gravest sin was that Sunny insisted they wear short trousers, even though the other boys were in long ones. This was asking for trouble. On several occasions they only escaped being beaten up by grabbing their bicycles and fleeing. They were strong cyclists.

Fortunately they only had to endure this torture for one term. By the autumn Sunny had them back in St Moritz where their private tuition continued. By now music was heavily on the agenda: Monty had piano and singing lessons and Brooks learnt the violin. They were also instructed in physical culture. Sunny not only wanted them to sound right, she wanted them to look the part too.

Monty, who later became fascinated by his well-proportioned body, had an affinity with physical training. He could do most of the exercises comfortably and continued to train all his life. To him, it was a form of yoga.

There is much home movie footage of the children in Europe. In those days, home film-making was an almost unheard of luxury. Mary Pickford and Douglas Fairbanks did such things, of course, in their mansion in faraway Hollywood, as did royalty, but private individuals rarely indulged. It was an expensive and laborious process.

There is film of the children, in matching white clothes, being guided through the Paris traffic by their tutor, and there are shots of Monty standing in snowscapes with the Alps towering behind him. But Sunny had started filming them long before they travelled to Europe and there is footage of them, while little more than babies, cavorting through meadows, always looking immaculate.

Monty's personality already shines through in these baby films. In one he is balanced on a rolling log with his arms outstretched, his eyes sparkling, as he tries to remain upright. In another he is sailing a toy boat, totally absorbed in what he is doing. 'Mother was very interested in giving us the broadest education she could,' Ethel told film-maker Robert Guenette in 1989 for his TV documentary *His Place in the Sun*. She added that Sunny took them travelling because Bill was also travelling, on account of his job, in America. Rather than go round America with him, or wait at home without him, they might as well broaden their education in Europe.

Meanwhile, Bill took a mistress. Ironically, he had met Marie Sermolino on a ship in 1925 on his way to rent accommodation in Bermuda for Sunny and the kids. Had the family been together, in all probability the relationship between Maria and him might never have gelled. Maria lived in Greenwich Village and, as Bill frequently had business in New York, they were able to spend time together. He was not discreet, and when Sunny returned to America he introduced them. He was clearly making a stand.

Sunny may have had a cosmopolitan veneer but she was American enough to resent a mistress. Not surprisingly, the two women did not take to each other. Even so, Bill remained close to Marie for the rest of his life. Eventually Sunny had no option other than to accept the situation.

But by 1930 there were changes all round. America was in the grip of a recession. Wall Street had crashed, leaving thousands bankrupt and financial affairs in chaos. Shares became worthless and millionaires were made paupers overnight. Suicide was rampant. Farms turned into dust bowls and beggars lined the city streets, but those from whom they begged were often just as badly off. Queues at soup kitchens stretched for blocks. The newspapers were full of tragedies.

Investors were badly hit, but Bill survived better than most. Sunny was not over-concerned, and it was with some irritation that she cut short her stay in St Moritz and, in response to her husband's urgent summons, returned to Chicago.

Money was now in shorter supply, although the children were unaware of it. They still attended important cultural events, including a recital by Yuhudi Menuhin at the Civic Center. Sunny took them to Washington DC again for a further visit to Aunt Sophie. The demented old lady informed Sunny that she and the children must return to Europe for further grooming because they were still not fit to meet the Andersons. Sunny swallowed it all.

Bill was aghast – he did not have the money for another expensive trip to Europe. He pleaded with her to stay in America but, determinedly, she set sail with the children in June 1930 on the SS *Bremen* bound for Germany, where they stayed in splendour at the Hotel Bristol in Berlin. Bill reluctantly gave up his New York apartment, which he could no longer afford. The family visited Oberammergau, then toured the Rhineland before the money ran out. Bill had no more to send and, feeling she had been betrayed, Sunny had to return to Chicago.

She continued to have the children privately tutored and by the spring of 1931 decided that the family finances had recovered enough for further travel. She took the children to Bavaria and Austria, where they visited Garmisch, Salzburg, Innsbruck and Vienna. Bill frantically tried to recoup his investments but failed. He lost his job. Again Sunny was forced to return to Chicago sooner than anticipated. This time things were worse.

Bill thought his prospects might be better in New York, so they sold most of their possessions and moved to a tiny furnished apartment, little more than a room, above an Italian restaurant

on West Ninth Street. At least he had the consolation of being
near Marie.

Sunny ensured that things ran smoothly. If the children queried why
they now lived in reduced circumstances, they were told it was none
of their business and to carry on as normal. Meals were still presented
on silver dishes laid on starched napery. The bed sheets were silk. The
apartment shone like a new pin.

But Bill could not carry on as normal. He could not find another
job and slumped into a comatose state of shock, staring into space or
out of the window for hours on end, his elbows on Sunny's polished
furniture.

It was easier for Sunny to find work, because she was not seeking
skilled employment. Anything would do as long as it brought in some
money. She found not one but two jobs, the first as a medical secretary
at the Mount Sinai Hospital and the second as a cleaner in a public
library. She who was fighting for her children's birthright went out
scrubbing floors in order that they could be bespoke tailored. She
could not cover the entire household expenses with what she earned,
of course, but had no objection to running up debts that Bill could
clear when he found work again. Meanwhile, what she did bring in
helped, and she never complained. The children rather liked her going
out to work. For one thing, it saved them having to traipse round art
galleries and exhibitions, of which they had had more than enough.

Hardship brought out the protective side of Sunny's nature. Rather
than berate Bill for their misfortune she gave him hope, encouraging
him to look for work rather than sit at home. Whatever their differences,
and despite the existence of his mistress, he always loved her.

Eventually, after nearly two years of unemployment, Bill did manage
to land a job as an insurance policy salesman. It had none of the kudos
of his former status, but it was employment. Sunny refused to give up
work: constant money was needed, as the children still had a tutor. She
even took an additional job as a part-time secretary, although Bill warned
her she might kill herself through overwork. 'A thoroughbred goes on to
win,' she replied, as quoted by Patricia Bosworth in *Montgomery Clift*.

She must have decided, by autumn 1932, that she was well on
course, as she resumed her nomadic habits and took the children to
Florida. There was a method in her madness, for Brooks had developed
asthma and the warm climate would suit him better, whereas a winter
in New York could bring dire complications. She also reasoned it was
cheaper to live there than in New York.

She rented a house in Sarasota and the children resumed their luxurious lifestyle – which Sunny assumed was enjoyed by all aristocrats – as though the Depression had never happened. They went riding most days – all three rode superbly – played formidable tennis and even indulged in croquet before tea on the lawn. Some might have considered this a trifle extreme, but not Sunny; it was how she wanted things and expected them to be.

Sunny had brought their tutor with them from New York (as she had brought Wilke, who never left them throughout their hardships) and with him, that autumn, they studied the entire works of Shakespeare. It opened a whole new dimension in Monty, instilling a love of the playwright that never waned. All his life he wanted to play Hamlet. It was his tragedy, as well as the theatre's, that he never did. He was tailor-made for the part.

Sarasota had a thriving theatrical tradition, both amateur and professional, and Monty's tutor, Walter Hayward, liked the theatre. He had a friend who was an amateur producer and who was putting on the comedy *As Husbands Go*. A twelve-year-old boy was needed and Hayward thought Monty might enjoy doing it. Even more importantly, he thought that Sunny might enjoy him doing it.

She, indeed, seemed tickled by the prospect of her favourite son appearing on stage, and he himself leaped at the idea. He was already a good mimic and did a wicked impersonation of the dour Wilke, parodying her walk superbly. Brooks would crease up.

When Sunny took him for his audition the director took one look and give him the part. Monty was at home on stage, relaxed, confident and betraying no signs of awkwardness. Sunny brought him to rehearsals and got herself a job as prompt.

Opening night was 30 March 1933, and everyone was excited. Acting was all the rage, largely due to the talkies which had arrived during the late 1920s. By now, Hollywood was producing an era of stars that was to last into the 1950s. The big studios all had their own stars. MGM, king of studios, was run under the despotic supervision of the brilliant Louis B. Mayer. Garbo was his supreme star – the supreme star of all stars. The careers of many silent actors had crumbled with the advent of the talkies, but Garbo's had blossomed, her husky tones matching her exotic image.

Mayer's sex symbol was platinum, wise-cracking Jean Harlow, then in her early twenties and doomed to die before reaching thirty. Her husband, studio executive Paul Bern, had been discovered with his brains blown out, immediately after their marriage. It was said he had undeveloped genitalia. Why had the world's most voraciously sexual female married a sexually inadequate man? Was the shooting suicide or murder? Was Mr Mayer involved with a cover-up? Rumours still persist. At the time Monty was taking his first steps on a Florida amateur stage, Harlow was being sued by claimants to Bern's estate. On top of all else, his marriage might have been bigamous. Clark Gable was another of Mayer's problems. The macho actor had run down a pedestrian while drunk, and a mammoth cover-up was in full swing. The truth was not uncovered for years.

At rival studio Paramount, Adolphe Zukor was boss. His top money-maker, the audacious Mae West, over-blown and nearing forty when making her first film, had defied censors with her outrageous burlesquing of sexual promiscuity. The press had demanded that questions be asked in Congress, and Zukor prayed these would not be too probing. West's films had saved Paramount from bankruptcy, and he did not want her association with New York gangsters to become common knowledge. West had discovered a handsome and gifted young actor whom, against advice, she cast as her leading man. After that, Cary Grant had never looked back. Another Zukor star was Marlene Dietrich, imported from Germany. She electrified audiences with her first American film, *Morocco*, with Gary Cooper.

Warner Brothers Pictures Incorporated had the benefit of Humphrey Bogart, Edward G. Robinson and James Cagney. They were also enjoying a run of successful musicals starring Ruby Keeler and Dick Powell.

Monty had not seen many of these stars as Sunny had not included films in the children's curriculum, but the stage was different. The classics were performed there. It would not hurt him to take part in a tasteful amateur production.

The whole family were there to cheer him on opening night, together with Wilke and Hayward. They were not disappointed. He was precisely the hit everyone predicted he would be. Poised, elegant and handsome, he brought the house down.

He received applause for the first time in his life. Although Sunny was there, in her role as prompt, his performance had nothing to do with her. When he was on stage, he alone was master of the situation. She was out of it. Young as he was, it gave him great satisfaction.

3

Referring to that first performance, Brooks was quoted by Patricia Bosworth as saying that Monty 'carried his own spotlight'. Most amateur performers are highly praised – that is one of the reasons for amateur performances – but even so, he obviously had something special. He was curiously detached, though, smiling politely but aloof and unswayed. Sunny was more affected. A seed took root, and from then on, virtually overnight, she became that fearsome phenomenon, a stage mother.

When the family returned to New York they moved to a more spacious apartment, in a block called The Chateau in Jackson Heights. They were still in debt and it was far from luxurious, but it was certainly an improvement on the single room they had shared before.

The children were in their teens, and Sunny conceded to Bill that they could go to school – but only to very special schools. Ethel was sent to the 'experimental' Dalton School, where pupils were unsupervised and literature emphasized, after which she went to the exclusive women's college Bryn Mawr. Brooks went to the Quaker Friends' School in Germantown, Pennsylvania, followed by Harvard.

Monty, however, did not go to school, for Sunny had a future mapped out for him on Broadway. The Florida applause had shifted her perspective. He continued to work with his tutor in the mornings;

in the afternoons, while his brother and sister prepared for university, he and Sunny haunted the Brill Building, which housed the offices of casting directors, agents and producers. They trudged Broadway in traditional fashion, looking for work.

They did better than many. Producers were not prepared to take a chance with him on stage, but he managed to get highly paid modelling work. His face was photogenic and featured in magazine advertisements for Arrow shirts and Steinway grand pianos. But Monty was indifferent at seeing himself in magazines. It was no more than he expected, Sunny had always told him he was special, and he believed her. But she loved it. Everyone could now see that the makers of those quality products had chosen her son to endorse them.

She did not allow herself to bask in glory but got yet another part-time job, this time as a filing clerk at the Metropolitan Museum. She could do that in the mornings while Monty was being tutored. Then they could visit agents together.

In the summer of 1934 Bill went to Chile on business – he had given up insurance sales and had become involved with a goldmine. Against some opposition from Sunny he had insisted on taking the fifteen-year-old Brooks with him. Brooks, who had not been looking forward to another cultural tour with his mother, was delighted. Ethel went to summer school, which left Sunny free to devote her energy to Monty.

Although he loved his mother, he was by now resentful of her unrelenting attention. It was unhealthy for any mother to be so close to her teenage son, and he envied Brooks in Chile. Sunny had already arranged their summer holiday, and had rented a house for the two of them in Connecticut. The scenery was spectacular and Monty could indulge his latest passion, photography. Sunny had bought him the most up-to-date equipment, irrespective of her overdraft. Although he was becoming increasingly tetchy with her, his camera did bring him solace. He would spend hours looking for a subject and the right lighting in which to shoot it.

He remained a keen photographer throughout his life. Actress Phyllis Thaxter, whom he nearly married, remembers him obsessively taking photographs when they were on tour with the Lunts in 1940, six years later. 'Don't forget the photography,' she said in a telephone conversation with the author. 'He was a wonderful photographer.'

The house next to the one that Sunny had rented was occupied by a theatrical producer. He told her that an acquaintance, Theron Bamberger, was producing a comedy called *Fly Away Home* in nearby Stockbridge.

She knew of Bamberger. When Bill had been on his way to Bermuda, on that eventful trip during which he had met his mistress and Sunny had subsequently learnt of the death of her mother, Bamberger had been on board ship. It was he who had introduced Bill to Marie.

Bill had stayed in contact with him and, at Sunny's urging, had mentioned his son to him. Just as a boy had been needed for As Husbands Go in Sarasota, so Bamberger needed four teenagers for Fly Away Home. There was still a vacancy for one of the boys. Fortune was on Sunny's side. Bamberger auditioned Monty and was charmed rather than impressed. Monty had done so little that no one knew if he had talent or not, but it was clear he had poise.

Fly Away Home, by Dorothy Bennett and Irving White, starred Thomas Mitchell. At fifty-two the former reporter was an experienced Broadway star of impressive range from sinister to saintly. He had already appeared in one movie, the 1923 silent Six Cylinder Love. In 1936 he was to star with Rosalind Russell in the hit movie Craig's Wife. After that he made nearly a hundred Hollywood films and starred in the TV series O. Henry Playhouse. He was an exemplary actor, and a dyed-in-the-wool professional. Monty was fortunate to have such an experienced artist with whom to appear in his professional debut. And it was professional – although he did not receive a fee, his expenses were fully covered.

He took to the professional theatre like a natural and Bamberger and his wife Phyllis were delighted by his application – he knew his lines well before opening night. According to Phyllis Bamberger, quoted by Robert LaGuardia in Montgomery Clift: A Biography, 'He gave Theron and me the impression that he was having a great deal of fun being around all these theatrical people, and that he hadn't had much fun before. He was such a charming child and his performance made that play.'* He delighted the Bambergers with his European manners and by chatting uninhibitedly about the capital cities he had visited, peppering his conversation with French or German phrases as Sunny had encouraged him to do. Some might have found him insufferable, but his spontaneity overcame that.

He had a flair for comedy and, once established, always wanted to play more comic roles. It can be glimpsed briefly in movies such as The Big Lift. His gift for tragedy, however, overshadowed all else. Those who had only seen him on film were often surprised by his jokiness. Sometimes his humour could be black, even desperate, but it was always there.

* Montgomery Clift: A Biography by Robert LaGuardia, W.H. Allen, 1977

Fly Away Home transferred to Broadway, opening at the 48th Street Playhouse Theatre on 15 January 1935. Monty went too, at a salary of $50 a week. He was playing Broadway at the age of fifteen on his first professional booking – something virtually unheard of. He was doubly blessed in that the play was a success and ran for seven months, which in those days was substantial. Sunny was there all the time, eating lunch with him and taking him to and from the theatre.

Monty learnt all he could from the cast, particularly Mitchell, watching when he ran through a scene and learning how he rounded his character. He was much keener than the other youngsters in the cast. They fooled around, playing jokes on each other, but Monty would not join in. He could be found before curtain up in his dressing room studying drama, and was never one of the crowd. He felt isolated at times but was not a natural mixer, and had little in common with most people.

But he was not unpopular. Some of the adult cast members found him positively endearing. A talented and serious boy, he would talk for hours about the theatre and absorb whatever they told him.

Fly Away Home closed in June 1935, and by now Monty had unbent enough to join in a few pranks. After all, even the most earnest professional enjoyed the odd jape. He managed, with the other youngsters, to pelt the rest of the cast with grapes and on one occasion dropped an ice-cube down someone's back.

By now the Clifts had moved yet again, this time to an apartment at 116 East 53rd Street. Bill was back from Chile and had openly resumed seeing Marie. The children all knew her. Sunny accepted the situation on the surface but it rankled underneath. Robert LaGuardia interviewed Marie for his book, and she told him that sometimes the fire brigade would arrive while she and Bill were together. No one knew who had phoned but they made an educated guess. With two of her three children away, and the third starting a career, Sunny had more time to reflect on her situation. Clearly it did not please her.

She was still in contact with Aunt Sophie, who continued to make fitful promises of family reconciliation, but nothing happened. But Sunny had made her mark on Broadway. Every agent and every producer knew her. Her ambition for Monty made her a 'character'.

Even before the show had closed Monty was booked for another Broadway run. This was the Cole Porter/Moss Hart Ruritania musical *Jubilee*. Although the show itself is now seldom performed, part of it will live forever through its hit song 'Begin the Beguine'. It was set in a fictitious English court, with a large cast of eighty. Monty played Prince Peter, looking dapper in gold-embossed uniforms. The cast were directed in dialogue by the great actor and former Yale professor Monty Woolley.

The stars were Mary Boland and Melville Cooper, two veterans who played his parents, the King and Queen. Tragedienne Miss Boland had made several films, including a few silents, but her excellent diction made her a natural when talkies arrived and she quickly made several more. She eventually settled in Hollywood, specializing in comedies with Charles Ruggles. The British-born Melville Cooper was also to have a long Hollywood career. With his exaggerated accent he played upper-class twits, which made him perfect for the King. There was little about comedy that Cooper did not know.

Jubilee was to preview at the Colonial Theater, Boston. As Sunny was about to board the train from Grand Central Station to get there, with Monty on her arm, she was paged to take a telephone call. A female voice warned her that if Monty opened in Boston he would be kidnapped. There had been a spate of kidnappings reported in the press and Sunny took the warning to heart, but it did not stop her from going. They were staying with the influential Footes, whom they had met in Switzerland, and when the police had been informed of the threat guards were posted outside the theatre.

Although they were of a similar age, there was not much love lost between Ed Foote and Monty. According to Patricia Bosworth, the morning after *Jubilee* had opened he found Monty in the bathroom admiring himself in the mirror. Foote was covered with acne at the time. 'My God, you're ugly,' Monty told him as he walked out. Monty got his come-uppance, though. He too was to develop acne, and at a time when it was crucial to his career that he looked his best.

The threatening calls persisted both at the theatre and the Footes', and the caller was eventually traced. It was, as had been suspected, another stage mother who had put her son up for Monty's part. Had Monty backed down, her son would have got it. Hell hath no fury like a stage mother scorned.

There were two princes in the show and Monty had to share a dressing room with the other, a street-wise fifteen-year-old called Jackie Kelk. They detested each other. As they were minors, their mothers acted as chaperones, but Sunny and Mrs Kelk loathed each other too. Sometimes the atmosphere in the dressing room was icy. Jackie Kelk was not the sort of companion whom Sunny would have chosen for her son, and Mrs Kelk felt the same way about the precious Monty. The show transferred to New York's Imperial Theater on 12 October 1935, where it ran for a respectable five months. Not, however, a major hit.

While Monty was treading the boards, learning his chosen trade, Sunny had her final showdown with Aunt Sophie. She was summoned to Washington to see her and arrived full of expectation that she would finally be introduced to her relatives, half expecting them to be lined up waiting for her to curtsey to them.

The old lady had no such thing in mind. She had decided that she needed a companion and that Sunny was right for the job. She told her she must move into the Hotel Wyoming and abandon her family. She could at a push bring Ethel, but certainly not the boys. Aunt Sophie flew into one of her insane rages when Sunny protested, accusing her of ingratitude and screaming that she never wanted to set eyes on her again.

Sunny returned to New York in a state of shock. But she recovered, and her determination to be recognized remained undimmed. She set about searching for Andersons and Blairs and urged Bill to do the same, travelling widely to see those who were prepared to see her. Aunt Sophie, however, must have felt troubled by her shameful behaviour, for when she died some years later she left Sunny a legacy of $25,000.

When *Jubilee* closed Monty went to Dalton experimental school with Ethel for a while, but was unsettled there. So Sunny brought him back to New York and continued his private education, adding ballet to the curriculum. How Jackie Kelk would have loved that.

The following year, 1937, Sunny remained in New York but arranged for Monty to spend summer at Newport, Rhode Island, with the Benton family. Brooks had met Ned Smith, the younger brother of Mrs Benton, at school in Pennsylvania and it was hoped that the boys would be company for each other. Bill drove him down in his aging green Buick, a car he was later to give to Monty who loved it with a passion, driving it hard for years until it virtually fell to pieces.

Ned was waiting when Monty arrived and did not take to him at first. Monty was travelling in white summer clothes, chosen by Sunny. Ned, a sportsman, was not impressed. It was not the best of beginnings, but their friendship was to last ten years. As they went on camping, fishing and hiking trips together, Ned discovered that Monty was remarkably athletic beneath the city clothes, that he would work out each day, could hike for miles and liked fishing. Monty, for his part, discovered that Ned liked reading. They had a lot in common.

But Ned never took to certain things about Monty. Ned was a Quaker and, young as he was, held certain views on personal conduct. He felt that Monty, also from a Quaker family, should have similar standards. Ned noticed a certain theatrical looseness in his companion's speech, which he mistrusted. Occasionally Monty would introduce him to theatrical acquaintances and Ned was not taken with them. He did not think the theatre was the best influence on him.

The theatre, though, much to Monty's regret, was not having any influence on him at all at the time. After such a spectacular start to his career – two Broadway plays, back to back – nothing followed. A sixteen-year-old is, after all, not that easy to cast.

But he enjoyed himself with Ned who, in addition to much else, taught him to sail. Sunny rang him every day and sent him parcels of new clothes; he was embarrassed when they arrived. One day he was visited by a young man who was in the area and who hoped to become an actor. Four years older than Monty, he had not yet broken into the profession but had heard of Monty's success and asked for advice. This was Van Johnson.

Monty himself had to wait until the autumn of 1937 before he worked again. But then it was Broadway once more, when actor/manager Frederic March hired him for a period piece by Horace Jackson entitled *Yr Obedient Husband*. March had already made over a dozen movies, including the acclaimed Barrymore lampoon *The Royal Family of Broadway*, and won an Oscar for *Dr Jekyll and Mr Hyde*. His leading lady on stage, however, was invariably his wife Florence Eldridge. They were a popular twosome. Miss Eldridge herself made occasional forays into films. The cast also included Dame May Whitty who, on stage since 1881, knew a trick or two about stealing a scene. They made a formidable trio of stars.

There was a tour before the Broadway opening and Sunny accompanied Monty. Although seventeen, he was still technically a juvenile and obliged to travel with a chaperone. He had begun to open up and lose some of his inhibitions during the summer with Ned, but Sunny's presence clamped him up again. He felt happiest on stage performing. A teenager who needed to rebel, he was beginning to dislike his mother with her dampening authority over his life.

In Cincinnati he made the papers – not for his performance, but for the lack of it. He caught flu and, a few hours before curtain up, Sunny sent for the doctor. Monty was ordered to bed, which left the Marches in dire straits as he had no understudy. Eldridge insisted the director's wife play Monty's part; the alternative was to cancel until Monty recovered. An announcement was made before curtain up and the press were informed. The papers were full of the story; however Monty was mentioned only because of his illness, and it was Kay Johnson, the director's wife, who was the heroine.

Yr Obedient Husband opened at the Broadhurst Theater, New York, in January 1938 and closed within eight days. March, who had sunk much of his own capital into the production, spent a little more by taking out an entire page in *Variety* which contained solely the two words: 'Oops! Sorry!' The New York *Journal* said: 'The best performance is Montgomery Clift's. His single scene captures some of the ingratiating humour that is sadly lacking in the rest of the production.' Again it was comedy that brought him praise.

He was not long out of work. *Eye on the Sparrow*, a comedy by Maxwell Selser, opened at the Vanderbilt Theater, Broadway, on 3 May 1938. It was barely more successful than *Yr Obedient Husband*. Monty came in for a certain amount of mockery from the cast by arriving and departing in a chauffeured limousine courtesy of Sunny.

Another comedy, *The Wind and the Rain*, followed, and opened for a week at the Millbrook Theater, New York. Among the cast was Celeste Holm, now best remembered for her wise-cracking roles in movies such as *All About Eve* and *High Society*. A year older than the seventeen-year-old Monty, she too, had yet to break into movies. When she did so she won an Oscar within a year for *Gentleman's Agreement*, directed by Elia Kazan, who was to become an important part of Monty's life.

Although his last three shows had had short runs, his looks and talent had already brought him a reputation. Monty was now a known Broadway figure, so much so that he came to the attention of the vigilant Hollywood talent scouts. Producer David O. Selznick came to see him. Selznick was planning a Technicolor blockbuster called *The Adventures of Tom Sawyer* and was searching for the ideal Tom. He invited Monty to test for the part. The fourteen-year-old Anne Baxter was already cast.

When the day for the test came, however, Monty did not look as good as usual. As though in retribution for his cruelty to Ed Foote, he had broken out in spots. In *Starring Roles* Ron Base quotes the late Anne Baxter: 'He [Monty] was suffering such a bad case of acne at the time, the test had to be cancelled.'* Perhaps Selznick himself was not in the best of moods at the time. His wife Irene, Louis B. Mayer's daughter, writes in her autobiography that he had trouble with his testicles, which hung rather low and had caught in a drawer. Selznick eventually cast ten-year-old Tommy Kelly as Sawyer and Ann Gillis in Anne Baxter's part. The film, alas, lost over $300,000 at the box office and little was heard of Kelly afterwards.

* *Starring Roles* by Ron Base, Little Brown & Co (UK) Ltd, 1994

Selznick now concentrated on his next epic, *Gone with the Wind*, while Monty broke into the big time with his next play. This was yet another comedy, albeit a controversial one. His name blazed outside the theatre like a star. *Dame Nature*, by Patricia Collinge, was based on a French play by André Birabeau. Monty played a fifteen-year-old schoolboy who has impregnated a schoolgirl of the same age. To emphasize his youth he wore short trousers, much as Sunny had made him wear when they returned from Europe. Then, the trousers had caused him to run from a beating; now, they brought in the crowds.

Before opening on Broadway there was the customary out-of-town try-out, this time in Westport, Connecticut. Sunny came one weekend and surprised the cast by sharing a bedroom with her son. People thought that unorthodox, to say the least.

Dame Nature opened at Broadway's Booth Theater in September 1938. The cast was nervous, aware that such an inflamatory theme could backfire. Monty's character had to confront the problem of awakening sexuality whilst living with an overbearing mother: exactly his problem in reality. In the play his mother was thirty-four-year-old Jessie Royce Landis, soon to become a leading Hollywood character actress. His brother was Morgan James, fresh from drama school and in awe of Monty at rehearsals. But Monty was chummy and supportive and they became friends. Morgan was to play a leading part in awakening Monty's sexuality.

Sunny was now Monty's manager. Whatever he did, she had the final say. She drove producers, and her son, mad. He felt that if she did not relinquish her grip he would explode. But as always, the play took him out of himself. Patricia Collinge was clearly thrilled by his performance in rehearsals and told him so. Her trust was well placed. According to Richard Watts, writing in *Tribune*: 'Young Mr Clift has an enormously difficult characterization to manage, and on the whole handles it excellently, although there are times when he makes the youthful father too neurotic for comfort.'

In reality, Monty was even more innocent than the schoolboy he played in *Dame Nature*. He was frustrated and curious about sex. Brooks, just over a year older, and already experienced, urged him to start bedding women and instructed him on chat-up lines, what women liked and the various techniques of masturbation. At first Monty had been disgusted by Brooks, but now masturbation was his only solace. The truth was that at nearly eighteen, handsome, appearing in a sophisticated sex comedy on Broadway and with a fierce if unharnessed sex drive, Monty was a virgin.

He had received no sexual education from his parents. Sunny would not face up to his manhood, still claiming him as her baby, and Bill was not close enough to him for such things to be discussed. According to Duane McKinney, an actor colleague of Monty's at that time and quoted by Barney Hoskyns in *Beautiful Loser*: 'He acts about sex as if he were looking up an escalator and saw other people riding up and down but did not know how to get on'.* Eighteen-year-old virgins were not uncommon in the 1930s and Monty was one of many. Birth control, when it was taught at all, was taught only to the married. The unmarried, and teenagers in particular, were expected to abstain. To participate was wicked, and pregnancy while unmarried a stigma.

Sunny did not accept that Monty might have sexual feelings. All he needed were friends, she believed, until the right girl came along, and she would decide who she was. She encouraged Monty's friendship with Morgan James, who came from a wealthy family. He was invited to dinner but could not take Sunny seriously. Her elaborate place settings amused him, as did the way she spoke, with her consciously British vowels.

A conscientious actor, Morgan would tell Monty how he prepared for a play. Once, when he had to play a sailor, he had spent a night wandering the docks, picking up girls, to get the feel of the thing. This was 'Method' long before it arrived. Monty developed a crush on him.

Monty had a regular stream of visitors at the theatre, among them Orson Welles, Katharine Cornell, Elia Kazan and Libby Holman. Holman was to become a friend for life, and stuck by him later when many turned their backs.

They were fascinated by each other from the start. Monty knew exactly who she was because Libby was profoundly notorious. She was a gifted torch singer with a rich voice of exceptional range, described by one critic as 'a dark, purple menace'. Having become famous on Broadway she became infamous in the law courts after having been accused of murdering her multi-millionaire husband and inheriting 6 million dollars. Zachary Smith Reynolds, of uncertain sexual preferences and impotent, had been found dying from a bullet wound in the head in the small hours of the morning of 6 July 1932. He and Libby had been fighting drunkenly immediately before the shooting, after he had caught her kissing another man.

The charges were dropped but the murder had never been cleared

---

* *Beautiful Loser: Montgomery Clift* by Barney Hoskyns, Bloomsbury, 1991

to public satisfaction, and Libby was, in the minds of many, an unconvicted murderess and unscrupulous fortune hunter. Unlucky fates had subsequently been met by several of her friends, and some viewed her as a harbinger of doom. When she had returned to the stage after the death of her husband there had been shouts of 'Murderess!' and 'Whore!' from the audience. Movies based on Zach's death were later made, including *Reckless* with Jean Harlow.

By the time she met Monty she was thirty-four years old and striking, not beautiful but exotic, her lipstick and nails a matching scarlet and her hair raven, like something drawn by Aubrey Beardsley. She had had a stream of young male lovers, but flaunted her lesbian affairs with Jeanne Eagles and Tallulah Bankhead. She was a devoted mother of three boys and the papers had carried stories of the lavish celebrations she had staged for her son Topper's eighth birthday. She had hired a band whose members included Benny Goodman, Teddy Wilson, Gene Krupa, Lionel Hampton and the queen of jazz singers, Billie Holiday – just about the finest line-up that could be had.

Monty was flattered that Libby had come to see him. For her part she told her friend George Lloyd, as quoted by Jon Bradshaw in *Dreams That Money Can Buy*. 'I've just seen the most divine young actor in the world . . . He's 17 [sic], much too old for me, but I'll get him if it takes the rest of my life.'* Libby was talented, sophisticated, wilful and scandal-ridden, but never a bore, and Monty was smitten with her. They spoke together in French for, like him, she knew the language perfectly. She is reputed to have had a malign influence over Monty; in fact it was he who tried her patience.

Libby had numbered Noël Coward and Clifton Webb among her friends, but was estranged from the latter. Webb, who was to become a star in 1944 by playing the gossip columnist in *Laura*, had started his career as a dancer and had danced with her on stage many times. They had been inseparable. But Webb loved his mother, Mabelle, and took her nearly everywhere with him. She accepted his boyfriends without question. If possible, she was even camper than her son. One evening, when Webb and Libby were both drunk, Libby had clearly had her fill of Mabelle and slurred, 'Mabelle's *ruined* your life. Why don't you chloroform the old cunt?'†

That did it for their friendship. He had burst into tears. 'Libby Holman died tonight,' he spat at her. He told his friends she was

---

* *Dreams That Money Can Buy* by Jon Bradshaw, Jonathan Cape Ltd, 1985
† *Dreams That Money Can Buy*

'a black angel of death'.* Libby, who affectionately referred to him as 'that old faggot', was dismayed. She had meant no harm – it was just her way of expressing herself.

Libby had come to see *Dame Nature* at the invitation of the Theater Guild, who had mounted the play and were hoping she might invest in a tour. She did not, but earmarked Monty for further attention.

When he was not with his admirers he was with Morgan James, who introduced him to burlesque, or what was left of it. New York had had many of these fun shows in the 1920s but, after a cleansing campaign inaugurated by the mayor, there were precious few left. Shows had been closed, artists imprisoned and hefty fines imposed. New York was cleaner but drearier, the remnants of burlesque being banished to the outskirts of town. Morgan knew where they were and took Monty by train to Newark, New Jersey, to see them.

Monty, the most dedicated of actors, adored burlesque, revelling in its sleaziness, fascinated by the way men ogled the scantily dressed girls bouncing about in their feathers and sequins. He and Morgan were much younger than the average punter, and in any case Monty cut a conspicuous figure in his expensive suits. There was something honest about burlesque to which he responded. As the drums pounded, the trumpets blared and the spotlights hit the girls, he felt at home. He even took photographs, but had to be careful as there could be objections.

As he so clearly enjoyed the seamy side of life, Morgan also took him to some of the less respectable bars off Broadway. Monty liked these, too, chatting to drunks and layabouts and seeming to seek them out. The rougher they were, the greater the attraction. It was the danger that drew him.

At home, Sunny decided he needed more music lessons and hired a Steinway.

* *Dreams That Money Can Buy*

4

Throughout his adolescence, Monty had crushes on various people, sometimes women like Diana Barrymore, John Barrymore's daughter, but more often men. He was never to grow out of crushes, but Lehman Engel was one of the strongest. Monty had deliberately sought him out. He was an orchestral conductor, and when Monty learned he was giving a lecture in Connecticut, several hundred miles from New York, he made a point of attending – a source of surprise to Engel. They made the train journey back to New York together, and by the time they reached the city were friends – which was exactly what Monty had planned. They would spend hours discussing music.

Monty was a reasonable pianist himself by now and specialized in Chopin – hence the Steinway – but he was shy of playing in front of anyone. It was an invasion of his privacy. To Monty, music was an intensely personal thing, never just background noise.

Sunny, hoping to impress the conductor, told him she was writing the biography of an industrialist, which was the first anyone had heard of it. He did not believe her and, like Morgan James, could not take her seriously. However, according to Barney Hoskyns in *Beautiful Loser*, he later speculated that Sunny might have been the mistress of this wealthy man. It would explain how she was able to continue to spend so extravagantly when Bill was out of work. This seems doubtful. Sunny was too moral and independent to have been anyone's mistress – by now Monty was her life, she had little interest in extra-marital affairs. Any money she spent was earnt through her own endeavours.

Monty was back on Broadway, at the Lyceum Theater, on 25 April 1939 in Karel Capek's *The Mother*, staged by Miles Malleson. This superb British character actor had immortalized the role of Canon Chasuble in the film of Oscar Wilde's *The Importance of Being Earnest*, with Margaret Rutherford as Miss Prism.

Russian-born Alla Nazimova, playing the title role in *The Mother*, was one of the most remarkable characters in a remarkable industry. She had been, without doubt, the silent screen's most glamorously erotic star, billed as 'The Woman of 1000 Moods'. For a time only Valentino had rivalled her at the box office. It was said that no man was safe in her presence; certainly she detested them. She was a rampant lesbian with her own personal harem, and there was wild gossip about her all-female orgies. In 1923 she over-reached herself financially with her production of *Salome* in which she employed only homosexual actors. It lost a fortune.

She had a riveting stage presence. But talkies had largely done for her career, and, together with the *Salome* debacle, this had left her professional stature unstable. She had picked up the pieces and got on with the process of living. Gone were the days of lotuses and champagne. Now, in 1939, she was sixty and playing a mother. But what a mother! She gave it everything she had and went through an entire range of over-hyped emotions.

On opening night the Lyceum was full of her fans – largely effete young men. There was uproar when the curtain came down. But she was wily and knew that her fans alone, now fewer than they had been, could not sustain the run of the play. 'I do not like this,' she muttered through gritted teeth as the fans stomped the floor.

Neither did the critics. It closed after four days.

No offers followed. Monty consoled himself by going on holiday with Lehman Engel on the SS *Orizaba* to Mexico. Lehman had originally booked a single passage for himself but had readily agreed that Monty could go with him. When Sunny found out she immediately phoned Lehman telling him to forward his ticket to her so that she could upgrade it for a double cabin. When the two young men arrived on board they were staggered to find that Sunny had booked them not a double cabin but a suite, filled with flowers and chocolates as though they were a honeymoon couple.

They stayed at the Hotel Marik in Cuernavaca where they met movie star John Garfield and his wife, who were friends of Lehman's. The previous year Garfield had had a hit with *They Made Me a Criminal*, and he was in Mexico to promote his latest film, *Juarez*. He was crippled with dysentery and hating every minute – all he wanted was to get back to hygienic America. The quartet moved on to the fishing village of Acapulco, which agreed with Garfield's bowels no better than Cuernavaca.

From Acapulco the Garfields returned to America, while Monty and Engel went back to Cuernavaca. Then Monty went down with amoebic dysentery. Once the germ takes hold it never leaves. It can be controlled, but remains for life. He was to be a martyr to amoebic dysentery from then on. He returned to America earlier than planned. Gravely ill, he went to the Tulane Medical Center's Ochsnee Clinic in New Orleans, which specialized in treating such ailments.

When he had recovered sufficiently to leave he was cast in *Life with Father*. Rehearsals started and he dyed his hair red, as the part required. But before the opening he was replaced: the promoters had decided he was too sophisticated. Forgetting all the successes he had had in the past, and bearing in mind the short run of the Nazimova play, he took his dismissal to heart, convinced he was a failure.

Then he met the Lunts. Alfred Lunt and his British wife Lynn Fontanne were the toast of Broadway. As Mason Wiley and Damien Bona write in *Inside Oscar*, 'The team of Alfred Lunt and Lynn Fontanne was as about as illustrious as any the American theatre had to offer.'* Although Sunny was still his manager, Monty had by now also acquired an agent, Leland Hayward, then a fast-rising talent scout and stage producer, who in the 1950s was to transfer his talents to films, producing among others *The Spirit of St Louis* and *The Old Man and the Sea*. Hayward sent him to audition for the Lunts, whom Monty had seen on stage several times, for a new play by Robert Sherwood called *There Shall Be No Night*. He read for them in their rehearsal room at the Theater Guild and they took him on at once. From then on Sunny's hold was to weaken.

He worked with them for nearly two years and much of his early style was derived from Alfred Lunt. Monty, who was to become acclaimed as the first of a new breed of 'Method' stars, was actually schooled by one of the most traditional of stage performers. Declamation was an important part of Lunt's method and, although at times he bordered on the regal, there was a fundamental honesty about what he did that made his characters

* *Inside Oscar* by Mason Liley and Damien Bona, Columbus Books, 1986

strike home. He had a habit of seeming to ponder over his phrases as he spoke them.

A friend of the Lunts, American actor Dick Van Patten, recalled in Robert Guenette's TV documentary *His Place in the Sun* how strongly they felt about Monty: 'All they did was rave about Montgomery Clift,' he said. 'He was their favourite actor, and you know how fussy they were. They loved him . . . they thought he was going to become a great, great star because of his acting ability.'

The Second World War had broken out in September that year, and Sherwood's play was about the war. His motivation was Russia's invasion of Finland, and his play was a plea for strength to enforce justice: Sherwood had had an earlier theatrical triumph with *The Petrified Forest*, which had been turned into a film in 1936 and given Humphrey Bogart his first break. It was a trend-setter in that Bogart played an anti-hero, eclipsing the one-dimensional heroes prevalent until then. Sherwood's 1939 film *Idiot's Delight*, with Clark Gable and Norma Shearer, was another success. In this movie, set in neutral Switzerland, a variety performer encounters an old flame. Sparkling comedy soon leads to an impassioned outcry against war.

Lunt was directing and starring in *There Shall Be No Night* for the Theater Guild. After out-of-town try-outs it opened at the Alvin Theater in New York on 29 April 1940. Lynn Fontanne was playing his wife and Monty their son. The cast included Sydney Greenstreet, a young actor called Billy Le Massena who was to become one of Monty's most durable friends, and Phyllis Thaxter.

Monty worshipped Lunt and admitted openly to copying his mannerisms. He really could not do otherwise, because so many people accused him of it. Many thought they could trace Lunt's influence in his subsequent performances. In time he developed his own, much imitated, style but he never severed his artistic connection with Lunt. The conscious, tapering pauses between words were one of Lunt's hallmarks. Those pauses later became synonymous with 'The Method'.

Lunt scooped the reviews, and after a six-month Broadway run *There Shall Be No Night* toured for a further eighteen months. An experienced actor/manager and strict disciplinarian, Lunt stood no nonsense. The Gestapo was currently terrorizing Europe and Lunt, with bleak humour, likened himself to it. There was no more disciplined, nor happier, performer than Monty when he was under the control of Alfred Lunt, who became what Bill Clift never had the opportunity of being – a father figure. Lunt's love for his wife awed Monty. It was quite different from the only other example of married love he had experienced, the autocracy of Sunny and the ducking out of Bill. Monty became Lunt's obedient son.

Nevertheless he still accepted financial support from Bill. It was at about this time that Bill passed on to him his old Buick, which Monty loved and refused to change for a newer model. During the run Monty became friendly with literary agent Janet Cohn. A lady with her finger on the theatrical pulse, she was usually present at important events. She had a house in Westchester and Billy Le Massena and Monty would spend weekends with her, careering there in the Buick which Monty always drove like a maniac. They spent so much time in Westchester that they eventually rented a house for themselves at Pound Ridge, dubbing it the Red Barn.

Sunny did not like this at all. Brooks was at Harvard by now, Ethel at Bryn Mawr and Bill often with his mistress. So Sunny was left alone for days on end. She took to arriving at the Red Barn to surprise her son. It surprised and infuriated him. He would be rude to her, ignore her, then fly off to Janet Cohn's, leaving her alone. But she followed. Everyone was embarrassed by Monty's nastiness to his mother. But she put up with it, wearing an indulgent smile. He doesn't mean it, she seemed to say. He did mean it. He now had a life and a vocation. She had no part in it. But she would not let go. His mood changed whenever she was with him. On one of her surprise visits she planted some bulbs in his garden. He uprooted every one. She came back with a further supply. This time, however, she got Billy Le Massena to plant them while Monty stood resentfully by.

Phyllis Thaxter also visited, and they would go for trips in the Buick. In a telephone conversation with the author Phyllis recalled 'I adored him. We had a great deal in common in that we both lived in the same environment and were both in love with the theatre. I respected his talent and loved his humour – he had such a sense of humour. He was nineteen then but it was already apparent he was quite brilliant – the Lunts thought the world of him, and he loved them, too. Being with the Lunts was a remarkable thing for a young talent. We did think of marrying and I remember thinking, "Wouldn't that be lovely?" But eventually we both realized it wasn't to be. He was very inhibited then. As he matured he became less inhibited.' Occasionally they might cuddle up together like best friends, but that was all. Nothing further took place.

Phyllis did not find Sunny monstrous. During their relationship Monty went down with colitis, as frequently happened. While he was in hospital Phyllis stayed with Sunny, and remained there when Monty came home: 'I didn't see any friction,' she said. 'They seemed very happy to me. I didn't see them coming into a room and actually kissing each other – I didn't see that – but they seemed happy enough to me. Mrs Clift could be very persuasive but she was not domineering. She was a positive lady, a determined person, and there's no doubt she helped Monty a great deal.' Phyllis remained friends with the Clift family and is still in touch with Ethel.

Some of the cast suspected that Monty was homosexual. In fact he had had a boyfriend since 1940, a lad of his own age whom he had met in a gym. It was a casual affair, although fairly lively from the sexual viewpoint. He had started experimenting sexually in a furtive way, and it was only a matter of time before he fell into a regular partnership. This did not, however, inhibit his affair with Phyllis. At that time he considered sex with men a diversion, something thrillingly illegal to be enjoyed on the quiet. It amused him to envisage Sunny's shock should she ever find out.

Those in the cast who did not think he was gay assumed he was sleeping with Phyllis. He encouraged this. There is no stigma attached to homosexuality in the theatre, but Monty put up a conventional front: he could not bear to become an object of ridicule. He had been brought up in an environment that despised homosexuality and could not shake it off. He had the opportunity to experiment further when *There Shall Be No Night* hit the road. Regular performances in different cities presented plenty of opportunities, and there was no shortage of callers.

The movie studios again took an interest and MGM actually offered a seven-year contract, starting at $750 a week, with an appearance in the war morale-booster *Mrs Miniver*, starring Greer Garson.

Sunny and Bill urged him to accept but, arrogant enough to believe he could pick up a movie contract whenever he wanted, he would not hear of it. As Le Massena verified, he was conceited in those days. The money was no inducement: Sunny already provided him with whatever he wanted, and he had been brought up to believe that money would always be available whenever he needed it. It never meant much to him.

It was the Lunts who put him off the movies. Alfred Lunt was an old-timer, the movies were upstarts and a threat to live theatre. The screen was no place for a serious actor. 'They were a little upset,' recalled Dick Van Patten in *His Place in the Sun*. 'They didn't like the idea that he was running off to the movies . . . they weren't too happy about that.'

Eight months into the tour, in December 1941, an unforeseen incident occurred which shocked the world. The Japanese bombed the US naval base at Pearl Harbor in Hawaii. The USA declared war on Japan, which meant that Russia, previously a villain, was now an ally. *There Shall Be No Night*, with its anti-Russian theme, had to close. The company gave its last performance in Rochester, Minnesota, followed by a farewell party given by the Lunts at their home in Wisconsin.

Monty was desolate: his days with them had been the happiest of his life. They presented him with a framed photograph, inscribed 'From Your Real Parents'. There was an element of fun in this, as Monty had played their son in the play, but it was also a bald statement of their feelings for him. He felt the same way towards them. The inscription must have been hurtful to Sunny.

Patriotism was rampant and Monty tried to enlist in the army. Being a skier, something he had mastered on one of Sunny's European excursions, he tried to become an officer in an elite mountain regiment. He was rejected on medical grounds, due to his recurring colitis, and persuaded that the best war work he could do was to return to the theatre and maintain public morale.

He began taking drama classes from Bobby Lewis, known behind his back as 'The Buddha' because of his rotund figure. Lewis had been a founder-member of New York's Group Theater and now taught in a West Side studio. Among his other pupils, although not in Monty's class, were Libby Holman and her new husband, handsome young actor Ralph Holmes.

Libby bumped into Monty one day as she was leaving class. He apologised and gave a courtly little bow. Memories of him in *Dame Nature* flooded back, and she confessed, as quoted in *Dreams That Money Can Buy*, 'Just looking at him made me feel like I'd caught an incurable fever.' It was a fever from which she was never to recover. It was her infatuation that spurred her to back an 'experimental' play which developed through Lewis's classes.

Mexican Mural by Ramon Naya was a sequence of scenes providing the framework for a plea for an understanding of the problems of the Mexicans. The setting was Veracruz the day after a carnival. Monty played a Mexican appalled by the squalor in which he is forced to live. Libby was his co-star. The experimental nature of the piece appealed to both of them. Its social message was also important. Libby was a sincere worker for minority causes and had spent thousands of dollars championing racial equality. She supported black crusades and later donated funds to Martin Luther King. She had stuck by her beliefs and been threatened several times for appearing with black performers, particularly in the South where lynchings were not unknown.

Libby was a left-wing idealist but a practical one. Her son Topper, listening to his mother spouting off one day, had piped up, 'Wouldn't it be nice if we gave all our money away?'

'No, dear,' she had replied, 'It wouldn't.' She had a house in Manhattan and a country mansion called Treetops, where her late husband had met his death.

Another cast member who was to become a lifelong friend was Mira Rosovskaya, later shortened to Rostova. In 1933, when Mira had been eighteen, her family had left their native Russia and fled to Germany. Mira became an actress with a Hamburg repertory company. When war broke out in 1939 the family fled again, this time to New York. She continued to act, but her thick accent barred her from many roles. A serious actress, she studied with Bobby Lewis and absorbed his progressive ideas.

Monty admired her dedication while she admired his talent. An introspective woman, isolated by her foreignness, she understood what it was like to be outside respectable society. She took to Monty, calling him 'my comrade'. To all appearances Mira was a complete contrast to Libby. Libby was flash and could be aggressive, whereas Mira seemed drab and shy. But under the skin they had more in common. Both were strong, determined women, and both had an enormous crush on Monty.

Libby joined the cast later than the others, and no one ever forgot their first sight of her. Everyone had been warned by Bobby Lewis to treat her as just another cast member, but she had no intention of becoming just another cast member. Her first appearance at rehearsals set the seal. She entered the theatre and stood motionless until every eye was on her. She was tanned and taut with hair cascading down her back, her mouth a scarlet gash and her perfume, Jungle Gardenia, wafting about her. Mira looked like a sparrow confronted by a vulture. Libby's reputation leaped to mind and the unsaid word 'murderess' reverberated around the auditorium. Monty wanted to laugh because she was so theatrical.

He made two other lifelong friends among the cast of *Mexican Mural*, Kevin McCarthy and Augusta Dabney. They had recently married and were deeply in love. According to Patricia Bosworth, Augusta endeared herself to Monty from the start by sidling up to him and telling him that the newly arrived Libby made her think of a 'black widow spider'. He laughed out loud.

The cast rehearsed for a month. Improvisation was the keynote and aspects of the Stanislavsky method, which Lewis had adapted to suit his teachings, were applied. Billy Le Massena was the stage manager and also had a small role.

The actors developed an intimacy between themselves which became, as Lewis put it, quoted by Milt Machlin in Libby, 'sensual as hell. I'd organized all sorts of improvisation to free the actors physically . . . I had everybody hugging and clutching each other, during the breaks there was much gliding into dark corners.'*

'As opening night approached,' writes Jon Bradshaw in his biography of Libby Holman, 'a predictable tension and excitement welled up among the players . . . although in the end the play would serve to enhance only Montgomery Clift's career. Indeed, most of the excitement revolved around him. As an actor, he was mesmerizing; and offstage, he was even more beguiling. His colleagues tended to cluster around him and Monty accepted their admiration easily and without arrogance.' He added, 'everybody was in love with him. He was absolutely mesmerizing in the show, and offstage he was like Pan, an enchanter.'

The public, however, were not enchanted. Mexican Mural opened on 26 April 1942 at the tiny Chanin Auditorium on the fiftieth floor of a huge building at 122 42nd Street. Closing after just three performances, it was a box-office disaster but a critical hit: 'Some of the acting is excellent, especially Montgomery Clift's superlative portrait of a brooding beaten youth who cannot endure the coarseness of his environment,' wrote Brooks Atkinson, in the New York Times. Tennessee Williams, a friend of Libby's, saw the show and wrote, also in the New York Times, that it was among the ten best plays he'd ever seen.

There was talk of a tour, but nothing came of it. Due to the lack of public support and the fact that the critics had barely mentioned her performance, Libby was disinclined to finance the play further. In any event she had other plans, which included a coast-to-coast recital tour with black musician Josh White. She had studied negro music and had become an expert on black composers, the first white woman to sing many of their songs. Some had not been sung in public at all but were folk items she had dug up from obscurity. On tour she continued with her pioneering ways, bravely refusing to stay in segregated hotels and speaking out for black rights. Monty did not see her for nine years. When they met again he was a changed man.

* Libby by Milt Machlin, Tower Books, 1980

It was a troublesome summer for Monty. His colitis flared up, painfully and dangerously, and he returned for treatment to New Orleans where he remained in hospital for two months. Although he was ill he made a point of writing to Bobby Lewis to thank him for his help on *Mexican Mural*.

When he was discharged he returned to New York and regularly saw Mira, who was convinced she could help him as an artist. Her own career was an uphill battle but he had shining possibilities. She was a natural, perceptive teacher and found satisfaction in coaching.

He also spent time with the McCarthys, who were in Cape Cod where Augusta was in repertory. Kevin had been called up into the army but was stationed nearby and seemed to have plenty of leave, which enabled him to visit his wife. Monty drove down to stay with them. Bobby Lewis came too some weekends and they would go out for lobster lunches. He saw Augusta in her play and surprised her one night by blacking up and coming on stage as an extra. They laughed a lot on that holiday.

Monty was back in comedy in the autumn of 1942, as a fourteen-year-old in Thornton Wilder's *The Skin of Our Teeth*. This play had the background of the grand theme of man's survival against insuperable odds. Monty loved it: he found cosmic themes spellbinding. As time went on he came to the conclusion that there was not much point to anything, but in his youth he was an idealist.

Monty met Wilder through Janet Cohn. Wilder, then in the army, thought he would be ideal for the part and certainly he had no difficulties playing a fourteen-year-old. The large cast also included the notorious Tallulah Bankhead, now forty and trying desperately to cling on to her youth, and reunited him with Frederic March and Florence Eldridge, with whom he had worked in *Yr. Obedient Husband*.

The director was Elia Kazan. Born in Turkey, the son of a Greek carpet merchant, he had been raised in New York. After studying at Yale Drama School he had made a name for himself during the 1930s with the Group Theater until it closed in 1941. This was his first venture for the commercial theatre.

The Group Theater, which had members of the Communist Party among its ranks, had consisted of a group of razor-keen youngsters who believed theatre needed revitalising and that they were the ones to do it. Among its members were actors John Garfield and Franchot Tone, drama teacher Lee Strasberg and playwright Clifford Odets. Odets' credits included *Golden Boy*, a successful play filmed in 1939 with William Holden, whose big break it had been. Odets was to follow this with other screenplays, including *The Country Girl*, *The Sweet Smell of Success* and *The Big Knife*, one of the keenest exposés of Hollywood corruption.

In the 1950s Lee Strasberg was to popularize the ideas of the Russian Constantin Stanislavsky in the West with his Actors' Studio, a continuation of the work of the Group Theater. The Actors' Studio became a workshop celebrated for teaching the Method, a school of acting with which Monty and Marlon Brando, among others, were to become identified.

Stanislavsky, director of the Moscow Arts Theatre, had had great success and he and his company had toured the world. His system has had many interpretations, but a consistent thread demands that an actor base his character's emotions on incidents that have taken place in his own life. A series of exercises, including improvisation, had been evolved to foster this technique. It was to produce a whole new breed of naturalistic performers including, in addition to Monty and Brando, Shelley Winters, James Dean, Marilyn Monroe, Julie Harris, Karl Malden, Eli Wallach and Paul Newman. Much ridicule has been poured on Method actors and their laborious preparation exercises, but their success rate speaks for itself.

Kazan was an advocate of certain aspects of Stanislavsky and created a strong personal rapport with his actors. An actor himself, he could demonstrate what he wanted. Referring to the Method, Louis Giannetti and Scott Eyman wrote: 'It was popularly associated with Elia Kazan, who was often said to have "invented" it, but he repeatedly pointed out that Method acting was neither new nor his. It was an offshoot of Stanislavsky's system of training actors . . .'* Through Stanislavsky Kazan brought a European realism to his work which had not been prominent before among American actors.

Monty was by no means a Stanislavsky purist (indeed, Mira Rostova insists he was not a Method actor†) but was influenced by his theories, or by what remained of them under Western teachers. He took what suited him from the system. Bobby Lewis and now Kazan were the first to introduce him to it. Together with Alfred Lunt, whom Monty had introduced to Mira, Kazan was his most potent shaping force.

Kazan had an earnest approach. In rehearsals, actors crawled about in dungarees long before they were fashionable. Abstract ideas were given physical form. Analysis was endless. After each session the actors would

---

* *Flashback: A Brief History of Film* by Louis Giannetti and Scott Eyman, Prentice-Hall, 1986
† Telephone conversation with the author

sit in a circle and comment on each others performances. Hollywood movies were despised. Monty thrived on the atmosphere. It was how acting should be: hard work, introspective, dedicated and devoid of glamour. An actor was a man with a mission.

None of this went down well with Tallulah Bankhead. A Broadway star of the old school, she was no fan of Kazan or his ideas.

'From the instant Tallulah Bankhead strode on stage,' wrote Kazan in his autobiography *A Life**,

> followed by her black maid who was loaded down with more paraphernalia than was necessary for a first rehearsal, I guessed what she had in mind: to get me fired . . .
>
> Four stars, and Monty Clift, who was to become a star, were lined up before me. I introduced them to each other. The traditional show-business embraces were not forthcoming; they nodded, smiled, waved hands, kept their distance. Monty was visibly impressed with the select company he was part of . . . Florence Eldridge March chattered, straining to be believed the cordial one . . . Tallulah responded with her horse's laugh and nicotine cough . . . When rehearsals started . . . the tensions between the Marches and Bankhead, which I'd anticipated, were really there; and it was my daily job to prevent fights between them . . .
>
> The first dress rehearsal was a nightmare of hysteria. Bankhead was never quiet offstage, never on time for her entrances, never anything but hateful to the other actors. Florence March was wretched and, it seemed to me, frightened; Freddie furious . . . and Monty Clift awed by the minefields of temperament exploding around him. We were all relieved when . . . we were able to slink away from each other . . .

Monty resented Bankhead's disruptive presence, but was comforted by Molly Kazan, Elia's wife. As Kazan puts it, he 'valued' her 'motherliness'.

Eventually, and in front of a cowering, but secretly delighted, Monty, Kazan brought matters to a head. He shouted at Tallulah, swore at her and continued to do so until she walked off-stage, followed by her maid, with as much dignity as she could muster. The cast gave him a round of applause. 'I'd made the grade,' he wrote. 'They considered

* *Elia Kazan: A Life*, André Deutsch, 1988

me a director. That occasion was the first time I'd permitted myself the anger that can save your life.'

Kazan describes Monty as 'another sexual borderline case' and 'remembered him . . . as an insecure boy who'd curl up on the floor at the foot of the chair where Molly was sitting and confide his problems to her. Molly was, for a time, his surrogate mother.'

The Skin of Our Teeth opened on 18 November 1942 at Broadway's Plymouth Theater to full houses and excellent reviews. Bankhead scooped the lot and was given the Critics' Circle Award.

'There's nothing as reassuring to an actor as laughter from an audience,' writes Kazan.

> Bankhead got more than her share; the audience adored her. She looked at me as she came out of her dressing room to leave the theatre, but she didn't say a word. If I'd expected a concession from her, I wasn't to get it; the expression on her face offered this contrary message: 'Despite the obstacles you . . . put my way' – so I read her – 'I came through, didn't I? You no-good Turk bastard!'

The play itself won a Pulitzer Prize. Monty was mentioned in *Theater Arts* as 'a young man of . . . great seriousness of purpose'.

After this Kazan accepted an offer from Hollywood, despite his expressed contempt for the movie capital, to direct *A Tree Grows in Brooklyn*. It was highly acclaimed, with two of his actors receiving Oscars and the script a nomination.

Monty, alas, was unable to complete the run of *The Skin of Our Teeth* as he went down with colitis again and had to return to New Orleans. When he got back to New York he continued seeing Phyllis Thaxter but was nervous of going to Janet Cohn's. Since she was friendly with Tallulah he had no wish to bump into her. She was everything he hated about the theatre.

He spent much time at the Red Barn, however, and, when Mira was away, used her apartment on East 55th Street, a poky, rather shabby place above a launderette which he eventually took over from her. Sunny and Bill lived within walking distance. He could not bring himself to cut the umbilical cord, despite his arguments with Sunny. He stayed with his mother and father for days on end and still accepted an allowance from Bill, which paid his rent when he was not working.

Monty did not become less of a loner, and could disappear for days not telling anyone where he was going. Sometimes he was with boyfriends; if he was, and bumped into anyone he knew, he was clearly embarrassed and only introduced the boyfriend as a last resort. At one party he attended he ran out of the room when he heard that a troupe of dancers was expected. He dreaded the thought that some of them might be gay, and would have been at a loss as to how to treat them in front of his friends – most of whom could not have cared less. At the few gatherings he attended he would huddle with other actors discussing work.

His practical jokes became outlandish: his favourite was to hang from windows, by his hands, outside the high-rise apartments of his friends. He would dangle for minutes at a time, which presented no physical problem because training had put him in fine condition, but had he fallen he would have been killed. The point of the joke was to shock those inside. Both Kevin and Mira were the butt of these hangings. Both had on occasion left a room where they had been with him, and returned to find it empty. Then his head would appear from outside, grimacing through the window. He once did it upside down for Mira, bat-style.

On 10 January 1944 he opened at the City Center, New York, in another Wilder play, *Our Town*, a revival of an earlier production. Wilder was becoming infatuated with him. This was another experimental piece without scenery, just the sort of thing he liked.

This was followed by Lillian Hellman's *The Searching Wind*, a melodrama about the affairs of an American diplomat based in Europe while war was brewing. It was filmed two years later, starring Robert Young and Sylvia Sidney, with a screenplay by Hellman herself. The timing was wrong as the war was over and the theme less crucial. It did not do well. Monty played the diplomat's grandson, a soldier who returns badly wounded, with his spirit broken as well as his body.

He prepared for the part with Mira, as was to happen regularly. Many of his interpretations owe a debt to her. Tireless researchers, they dissected dialogue, improvised scenes not in the play and delved into character.

'It was this preliminary probing that Monty really loved,' Mira is quoted as saying in Robert LaGuardia's biography. 'Performing on a stage frightened him. He was always so afraid that something would go wrong while he was up there . . .' The play opened at the Fulton Theater, New York, on 12 April 1944. The *Herald Tribune* critic wrote: 'Clift brings a fierce intensity to the part of the disabled grandson which is the very stuff of fine acting . . . Clift offers the year's best acting job.'

Monty's brother Brooks, by now a soldier himself, came to see the play. In 1943, after graduating from Harvard, he became an army counter-intelligence agent and remained so until 1946. Then, inspired by Monty's success, he studied with the American Theater Wing and, after an abortive attempt at acting, became a TV producer and director. Monty had been photographed by *Vogue* magazine and Brooks cut out the picture and carried it in his wallet. He told everyone his brother was 'magnificent' in the play.

Another admirer of Monty's was Marlon Brando, then little known as an actor. He was in a play in New York called *Truckline Café*, by Maxwell Anderson. It was directed by Harold Clurman, who co-produced it with Elia Kazan.

Brando was twenty, with a stocky, stunning physique and the face of a bruised angel. His trademark was the jeans and T-shirts he wore, and he was shortly to inspire the youth of the entire world to dress the same way. He was studying drama with Stella Adler, a gifted teacher whose parents had been dominant forces in the flourishing Yiddish theatre of New York during the early years of the century. She had worked with Stanislavsky in Germany and taught her version of his system, which was not necessarily in accord with what was being taught at the Group Theater.

Since Brando and Monty were to be linked in the future, both dubbed Method actors, it is as well to note Miss Adler's conception of Stanislavsky. Charles Higham writes in his biography of Brando:*

> From Stanislavsky she had learnt that an actor must take his inspiration from a scene's intrinsic truth. Instead of relying on effective memory – the recollection of events in his own experience, as Strasberg wanted – Adler insisted the actor become the instrument of the playwright's vision, not imposing his ego on the play. Such a thesis was the opposite of Strasberg's, who believed in drawing everything from the actor's own entrails . . .

Brando went to see Monty in *The Searching Wind*. In *Songs My Mother Taught Me*† he writes:

> He *was* good, and after the play I introduced myself and we went out for dinner. Since we shared a lot of similar experiences there

---

* *Brando* by Charles Higham, Grafton Books 1989
† *Songs My Mother Taught me* by Marlon Brando and Robert Lindsey, Century, 1994

was a lot to talk about and we became friends, though not close
ones. There was a quality about Monty that was very endearing;
besides a great deal of charm he had a powerful emotional intensity,
and, like me, he was troubled, something I empathised with. But
what troubled him wasn't evident. Later on, I went out with a girl
he had dated, and she said she thought he might be a bisexual or
a homosexual, but I found it hard to believe. I never asked him
and never suspected it, but if he was a homosexual, I imagine he
was torn asunder by it. Whatever the reason, he was a tortured
man . . .

Later Brando expands on Monty's sexuality: 'I do not know for a
fact that Monty was a homosexual. Afterward, some people told me
he was, but I have heard so many lies told about myself that I no
longer believe what people say about others. I do know he carried
around a heavy emotional burden and never learned how to bear it.'
So much for those who claim Monty and Brando had sex together.

There were times when Monty's attitude to his work could rile Brando
and he once, memorably, disparagingly described Monty as walking 'as
though he had a Mixmaster up his arse'. But by and large he was a
caring friend and whenever they were together, which was not often,
he showed he cared.

During 1945 Monty became interested in Theater Inc., founded
by director Norris Houghton. Houghton was dazzled by Monty and
wanted to mount a play for him. Monty was too committed to other
projects for it to happen then, but they did work together, later, in
the spring of 1953. But this was not the glorious reunion for which
they had hoped.

5

The Searching Wind ran for a year on tour, which was not necessarily a good thing for Monty. Long runs frustrated him. Once he'd put his character on the boards the challenge was over. He seems, however, to have enjoyed this run. Cast members recall him doing impressions of Chaplin and Cornelia Otis Skinner.

By now he was represented by Leland Hayward, who was married to movie star Margaret Sullavan who had had a success with *The Mortal Storm* in 1940. He had not met Sullavan but, when Hayward introduced them in a hotel lobby, he courteously bowed and exaggeratedly kissed her hand. It was a comic, but gallant, gesture and she was charmed.

A member of the cast, Dudley Digges, intrigued him. He was an older actor of vast experience and Monty was in awe of his technique. He enthused about him, likening him to Alfred Lunt in an interview he gave to the *Herald Tribune* on 16 July 1944. Digges worshipped Chekhov and they would read scenes together before curtain up.

The Searching Wind was never Lillian Hellman's favourite play. But she retained affectionate memories of Monty and Dudley Digges, writing in her book *Pentimento*:*

* *Pentimento* by Lillian Hellman, Macmillan London Ltd., 1973

Of *The Searching Wind* I have very little now except the memory
of a wonderful old actor, Dudley Digges, arriving at 7.30 each
night during the run of the play to meet Montgomery Clift, a gifted
inexperienced young actor in his first large part [sic]. Together they
would sit on the stage until the second curtain call and go through a
scene from Shakespeare or Ibsen or Chekhov, or a series of poems,
anything that Digges had chosen to teach Monty. It was mighty
nice, the two of them, and I took to going to the theatre several
times a week just to stand in the wings and watch the delicate
relationship between the dedicated old and the dedicated young. I
was never to see much of Clift after the closing of the play, but in
the years that followed, mostly unhappy ones for him, I am told, I
would often get a long-distance call from him, we would arrange to
meet, never manage it, but always we would talk of Dudley Digges,
who died a few years after *The Searching Wind*.

Monty respected Lillian Hellman's uncompromising attitude, which
had already been seen in plays such as *The Children's Hour* (1934) and
The Little Foxes (1939). One of her much-quoted sayings could have
been a maxim for him; 'I cannot and will not cut my conscience to fit
this year's fashions.'

Mira, in Monty's eyes, was the authority on Chekhov and any point
in the text which was unclear would be gone through with her. She,
after all, knew the Russian originals. She had built up quite a following
in Greenwich Village where she taught. Her technique was spoken of
with reverence although few, if any, had actually seen her act, apart
from classroom demonstrations.

Her voice was measured, her conversation pared of frippery, and
she could have an electrifying effect on students. Her reputation seems
to be based on exercises she had performed while at Bobby Lewis's
classes – the same classes which had spawned *Mexican Mural*. While
there she had enacted a single scene from *The Seagull*, portraying the
sixteen-year-old Nina. Although she was more than twice that age
herself by now, many were convinced she was perfect for the part –
the definitive Nina. She must, indeed, have been exceptional to have
generated such feelings.

Mira, to Sunny's chagrin, was now an intrinsic part of Monty's life.
He discussed every offer with her. She coached him again in his
next role, as did Bobby Lewis. The play was Elsa Shelley's *Foxhole
in the Parlour*, which opened at the Booth Theater on 23 May 1945.
Monty was a soldier who suffers a nervous breakdown. Here, from the

Journal-American, is just one of the many glowing reviews he received: 'Montgomery Clift, recently of *The Searching Wind*, is as touching as he is terrifying in the role of the returned soldier with a Messianic complex gleaming with abnormal brightness in his war-weary eyes.'

Again the movie studios made offers and, again, encouraged by Lunt, he rejected them. The theatre management tried to cash in on his popularity and arranged for a group of girls to besiege him after the performance. The press were alerted to stand by. Monty found out and refused to play ball, leaving the theatre by another entrance. He was not interested in having his picture in the papers via such a route.

Performance was everything to him. He was not after mass acclaim and would sooner have played to a small appreciative audience in a good play than a large one in a bad play. He was a perfectionist. During the run of *Foxhole in the Parlour* the noise of the air conditioner distracted him so he ordered it to be turned off. The fact that the audience then had to swelter did not concern him. It was a small price to pay for excellence.

Another cast member was actress Ann Lincoln, who fell in love with him. They spent weekends together but, like Phyllis Thaxter, she came to realize that things would not work out. In an attempt to make him jealous she went out with Brooks. Monty was mildly offended that she should choose Brooks over him, but in the long run did not care. He was kind to her, however, for the rest of his life. She became an alcoholic, unable to work, and he regularly sent her money. Then, when he became a movie star, he tried to put her way what work she could do. He left her a bequest in his will.

One night Billy Le Massena came backstage with Thornton Wilder. Monty wrote to Kevin McCarthy that he could listen to Wilder talk all night. Wilder did not speak just of the theatre and its allied arts – he had a bitchy streak and no one was safe from his malice. Monty would fall about as Wilder crucified his compatriots. He would pepper his anecdotes with references to Gertrude Stein and Sigmund Freud, both of whom he had known.

They became close. Wilder, like Mira, would advise him on which plays to accept and encouraged him to continue to reject Hollywood. There was mutual hero-worship. Wilder promised he would write a play for him and Monty pressed him to do so. Wilder, too, was one of twins and Monty told him how close he was to Ethel. He had kept in touch with her throughout her college days and, after she had married and moved to Texas, saw her as often as he could.

That summer he flew to Hollywood at the invitation of Warner

Brothers. Despite his reservations, eventually, and mostly from curiosity, he succumbed to a screen test. This was due to the insistence of Leland Hayward combined with, perhaps, a pandering to vanity. No matter how dedicated he was, and how fervently he dismissed the idea, the blandishments of Hollywood were hard to resist.

But Monty was not a success, and came over on screen as callow. The film for which he tested, *Pursued*, was eventually made and released in 1947. It starred a sleepy-eyed thirty-year-old who disguised his considerable talent behind a facade of carelessness. His name was Robert Mitchum.

Monty was glad to get away from Hollywood. He hated the premise that the studios called the shots and that actors were at their command. The actors he met seemed bitter about the studios that had made them, yet were helpless without them.

For all his success in the theatre he did not get every part he wanted. He learned that Guthrie McClintic, husband of Broadway's Katharine Cornell, was producing Shaw's *Candida* and was desperate to play Marchbanks. McClintic chose Brando instead.

But he directed him in his next play, a collaboration between Donald Windham and Tennessee Williams entitled *You Touched Me!* It opened at the Booth Theater, New York, on 25 September 1945, having been produced in Pasadena in 1943 without success. Monty thought McClintic a 'prick', according to Patricia Bosworth, and, as that comment might indicate, it was not the smoothest of productions.

Williams attended rehearsals but was not too encouraging, as he was suffering from one of his periodic bouts of depression; it was difficult to see why, as *The Glass Menagerie* had just opened to great success. Monty had seen it and raved about both the play and Laurette Taylor's performance. It was due to the success of *The Glass Menagerie* that *You Touched Me!* was being staged – before that, few people had been interested in the works of Tennessee Williams.

Monty was at first thrilled to be working with the exciting new playwright, but his enthusiasm wore off. He did not take to Williams, particularly when the man was drunk, which was often. But the main problem was William's bawdy openness about his homosexuality. Monty shied away from any open declaration of homosexuality, which inflamed his feelings of guilt. People laughed about Williams behind his back, and Monty dreaded that the same might happen to him.

Monty's dislike of Williams was reciprocated by the playwright. Williams preferred his men rougher, and he was repelled by Monty's closet attitude to his sexuality. When they had first met Williams could see that Monty was impressed; he accepted that, but wanted no more. He got no more, for as soon as he opened his mouth to utter some homosexual lewdery Monty fled. Even so, Williams was fair enough to admit that Monty was excellent in the play.

Again Mira had coached him and was with him right until curtain up. People might snigger at their co-dependency, but it paid dividends.

While Monty was playing *You Touched Me!* he learned that Libby Holman was involved in another scandal. The war had recently ended and her husband, Ralph Holmes, who had been a pilot in the air force, had been found dead from barbiturate poisoning in his New York apartment. They were separated and she had only discovered his corpse, in a state of putrefaction, after it had lain there for several days warmed by the central heating.

The papers had had a field day and Libby had hidden herself away with friends. Her loyal staff informed all callers that she was unavailable, and no forwarding address or telephone number were forthcoming. Monty rang constantly but was unable to reach her. In the end, according to Milt Machlin, he gave up and sent a telegram: 'Libby you know where to find me if you need me.'

Towards the end of the run of *You Touched Me!* he was visited backstage by film director Howard Hawks. Hawks was a tough and talented Hollywood veteran of over thirty movies and had been in the business since the silent days. His hits included *Bringing Up Baby* and *The Big Sleep*. Carole Lombard and Lauren Bacall were among his discoveries.

Despite his failure at Warner's Monty was still being pursued by other studios; MGM was especially enticing, particularly because he was in debt to the tune of over $1000 and had no future work lined up. He now began to think differently about Hollywood. If there was a particular film that he fancied, then perhaps he could be persuaded – for a price. He told Leland Hayward to investigate.

He saw in the New Year of 1946 skiing in Utah, oblivious of his overdraft. He had driven there in his Buick, now nicknamed Beulah. Meanwhile Hayward was negotiating with MGM, and as a result Monty drove on to Hollywood to see Louis B. Mayer, who was sufficiently interested to offer a six-month trial contract.

His attitude to the movie mogul was rather superior. But that dexterous magnate was charm itself, although it took patience when Monty referred to him as 'dear boy', a phrase he had picked up from Alfred Lunt. It sounded all right coming from an old ham, but a touch pretentious from a juvenile lead.

Monty was tested at MGM and Mr Mayer discovered, as the world was to discover, that Monty was photogenic. Mayer was keen to take him into his film family and offered to extend the six months into a generous seven-year contract. This was unacceptable to Monty, who needed to be free for stage work. As heartily as Monty despised films, so Mayer despised the stage. 'What has acting to do with being a star?' he had once asked. To Mayer's staggering amazement, Monty turned down his offer.

While in Hollywood Monty visited Phyllis Thaxter and Sidney Greenstreet. Both had gone into the movies and both lived in considerable style. He respected both actors, and Elia Kazan, whatever his scruples, had also accepted the crock of gold.

Hollywood showed courage in hiring Kazan, as his left-wing policies were well known. The days of the Communist witch-hunt were about to dawn, culminating in the notorious hearings of the House Committee on Un-American Activities, during which colleagues were encouraged to inform on each other and report their Communist, or alleged Communist, activities. Many were black-listed and never worked again.

At the end of his contract, with nothing further signed, Monty drove back to New York with Jeanne and Fred Green, friends he had met through the McCarthys. They spent fourteen days driving in a leisurely way across the country. When he spoke of Hollywood he referred to it as Vomit. Back in New York the Greens stayed with him and Jeanne helped him decorate. The place was in need of it – Mira, the previous tenant, had not been particularly house-proud. He painted the apartment a dull maroon.

Monty thanked Leland Hayward for his help but informed him he had no wish to work in Hollywood after all. But he shifted through dozens of scripts with Mira.

One evening about this time, Patricia Bosworth records, he was coming through Grand Central Station when he saw a young man sitting on his suitcase crying. It was not entirely the Good Samaritan in him that inspired him to ask if he could help. The young man was seventeen and good-looking and, to Monty's surprise, spoke only French. He was a novice monk on his way from France to a monastery in Quebec. He'd missed his train and did not know what to do. He could not understand the indicator board. The man's name was Brother Thomas.

The next train to Quebec was not for a couple of hours, so Monty took him home. They remained friends for the rest of their lives, and although they did not see much of each other they regularly corresponded. Monty was a collector of heroes, and when Brother Thomas sent him a photograph he kept it on his mantelpiece for a while. The young monk had sorted out his life and come to terms with his spiritual conflict. In his way, Brother Thomas was quite an inspiration.

Then Howard Hawks offered Monty *Red River*. Leland Hayward had learnt that Hawks was casting the film, with John Wayne in the lead, and had put up Monty as second lead. Hawks, recalling how impressive Monty had been in *You Touched Me!*, sent him a script.

Monty agreed to meet Hawks for discussions, and this time he was filled with enthusiasm. He had thought long and hard about Hollywood, and the longer he thought about it the more it appealed. He could make a lot of money quickly. That was important. It also appealed to his ego: to be world-famous did not seem so unappealing now. Once again Monty flew to Hollywood. This time he came back with an agreed deal for a single picture worth $65,000 which would certainly take care of his money problems for a while.

Not Mira, nor Dudley Digges nor the Lunts were thrilled with the news; indeed, Alfred Lunt was scathing. Bobby Lewis was particularly disappointed, as he had earmarked Monty to play Trepilov in his production of Chekhov's *The Seagull*.

Red River is a sprawling Western based around the development of the cattle drive known as the Chisholm Trail. Set in the nineteenth century, it features the friction between two cowboys – Wayne, the hot-blooded stubborn pioneer Thomas Dunson, and Monty, his adopted son Matthew whom Dunson discovered as a child wandering across the desert with a cow after his parents had been murdered. Dunson has a bull, and from this humble beginning a mighty herd is founded and driven across America from Texas to Minnesota. In addition to Comanche attacks, Dunson has to deal with insurrection from his men and the inevitable tussle for power with Matthew. It was unorthodox casting – the macho veteran versus the sensitive newcomer.

Most of the film was shot in Rain Valley, Arizona, and it lived up to its name. The rain bucketed down to such an extent that storm sequences had to be written into the film.

Wayne and Monty did not particularly take to each other. That was a foregone conclusion – they had little in common. Wayne, a genial man with no axe to grind, had no time for effete Broadway actors who spent their off-camera hours in broody silences or, worse, reading. He was a man's man who liked some spirit of camaraderie.

He found precious little with Monty, whom he later described to *Life* magazine as 'an arrogant little bastard'. It was an off-the-record remark but found its way into print.

At 40, Wayne had spent twenty years making movies. He was the leading Western star, as comfortable on a horse as on foot. He took one look at Monty and shrugged his shoulders, unimpressed.

Monty's reputation as a homosexual had, of course, preceded him. Wayne was not bothered, for he had worked with actors most of his life. A consummate professional, he had seen many handsome would-be stars come and, mostly, go. He trusted Hawks, and if Hawks had hired Monty then he had his reasons. Monty was no threat to him.

A major obstacle stood in the way of Monty playing a cowboy. He could ride well but he could not punch, and he was required to have a screen brawl with Wayne at the end of the film. Wayne was the master of cowboy punch-ups. It is widely quoted that Wayne fell about laughing when Monty first attempted to spar with him. If he did, he underestimated his man. Monty put this to rights by taking boxing lessons. He psyched himself up for the fight as he psyched himself up for any role.

The brawl is the long-anticipated climax of the film, symbolizing the clash between two monumental forces. 'Those two are gonna tangle for certain. When they do it ain't going to be pretty,' someone in the film remarks early on. The fight is choreographed with Wayne delivering the first few punches. Monty takes his punishment. When he retaliates, the effect is devastating as he throws a mammoth punch from the shoulder at Wayne. It would not have disgraced Muhammad Ali in his heyday. Monty follows it up by another straight right to the jaw. Wayne was delighted.

Hawks convinced him not to try to outplay Wayne but to underplay him. Monty's character is understated throughout. Hawks spent time and patience nursing him along in the new medium, helping him overcome his awe of the great Wayne. Monty's voice is attractively light and husky, with an unmistakable New York intonation. For all his European education he spoke like a well-heeled New Yorker. Whatever character he played, the accent never varied.

In black and white, full of sweeping location shots, with moody lighting and 'day for night' effects, the action is complemented by a lush score by Oscar-winning Dmitri Tiomkin. A glorious chorale washes over the opening credits, welling up at times throughout the film. The cut usually shown today is 133 minutes long. This was exceptionally long for the time – as, indeed, it is for today.

Slim and svelte, there was never a more elegant cowboy than Monty. Clearly he was made to be a matinee idol. Except that he despised it, and himself for playing it.

He said as much to Jeanne Green. Whenever there was a delay in filming he visited the Greens at their house in Palm Springs where he would help them to redecorate, happily perched up a ladder, spattered with paint. He and Jeanne also took flying lessons. But whenever they were alone he would pour scorn on the film industry and himself for becoming part of it.

He did not see the rushes until location filming ended in November 1946. The script had been altered, as scripts invariably are, and he felt his part had been watered down. Nevertheless, he was objective enough to realize he came over well.

Among others who thought the same was Billy Wilder. The writer and director had just completed *Foreign Affair* with Jean Arthur and Marlene Dietrich, had seen Monty on Broadway and was keen to cast him in a film. Monty had seen *Double Indemnity*, an earlier Wilder film with Barbara Stanwyck and Fred MacMurray, and was happy to listen to him. He had, in fact, done more than listen, and signed up with Wilder.

Wilder was already working on the script for their film, which had the working title of *A Can of Beans*. An exposé of Hollywood, it was eventually released as *Sunset Boulevard*. It involved two main characters, Norma Desmond, redundant silent movie queen, and Joe Gillis, a young writer who is kept, gigolo-style, by her and whom she eventually murders in a jealous rage.

Wilder had conceived the role of Norma for Mae West. He had been besotted by her ever since his arrival in Hollywood as an Austrian immigrant in 1934. As Wilder's biographer, Maurice Zolotow, writes, 'Billy had a mysterious affinity with Mae West. She represented a platonic idea of The Whore, whose mystery Wilder was forever trying to unravel. There was about her a certain supurb vulgarity and fleshiness that reminded him of Viennese and Berlin prostitutes.'*

Together with his partner, Charles Brackett, Wilder was working on *A Can of Beans* for Paramount. He was convinced that Monty would play opposite Mae West, whom Wilder hoped to persuade to be the star although she had not made a movie since the failure in 1943 of *The Heat's On* – about which a critic had disparagingly written 'The Heat's Off'. She had returned to the theatre and vaudeville, hating everything

* *Billy Wilder in Hollywood*, by Maurice Zolotow, Pavilion, 1988

about Hollywood. Like Monty, she had been brought up in the theatre and basically despised film people.

The coupling of Monty Clift and Mae West would certainly have been memorable but was doomed never to happen. Norma is supposed to be in her fifties and West was fifty-five at the time. She was, however, outraged that Wilder had the temerity to offer her the role of a fifty-year-old. She never played older than twenty-nine. As Zolotow writes, 'She recoiled in disgust . . . She did not consider herself a faded flower. She was in the prime of her life . . .' It was the most stupid mistake the usually astute Mae West ever made. She was perfect for Norma Desmond. She *was* Norma Desmond, and reacted to Wilder's offer in precisely the way Norma would have reacted.

So Billy Wilder had to find a new Norma, but was still confident he had his leading man. As Zolotov continues, 'Wilder had already got a commitment from one of the most exciting new actors in the Broadway theatre – Montgomery Clift. While they were completing the screenplay Clift was making his first two films, one of which was *Red River* with John Wayne. The plan was for him to make *Sunset Boulevard* as soon as Howard Hawks had wrapped up the cattle drive on the Chisholm Trail.' It was an exciting prospect.

Meanwhile, he had another month filming *Red River* on the sound stage at Hollywood. His dedication threw some people but, once they got used to him and his quiet periods when he went off alone to ponder his motivation, they realized he was friendly enough.

He got on particularly well with Noah Beery Jnr, another actor in the film. Films were second nature to him. Noah Beery, his father, had been one of the silent screen's most celebrated villains and half-brother of Wallace Beery, a leading screen tough-guy.

When on location, Monty and Beery Jr had shared a tent with Walter Brennan. Although only in his fifties, Brennan had settled for a career playing toothless old men. Chewing on a pipe and spitting into the fire, he would deliver homilies. He played the same role, with minor variations, in over five hundred films. He was famous for his anecdotes. Sometimes he would forget which ones he had told and repeat himself several times over. When he lurched into a story for the umpteenth time Beery and Monty would exchange glances above Brennan's head, struggling not to laugh.

With Hawks's help Monty scaled down his performances to suit the camera. Stage actors invariably give too much when in a studio for the first time. He watched other actors and was aware that he was the new boy, working with veterans.

The shoot finished in December 1946, after which he went to Texas to visit Ethel and her husband. From Texas he went to New Orleans. He liked the city and it was a useful base, as he could check on his colitis at the hospital and visit the jazz haunts and bars. He was arrested in New Orleans and spent a night in jail, which he seems to have rather enjoyed. The charge was vagrancy.

He had been drunk and shouting on the pavement when the police asked him to move on. He let loose a stream of oaths. He was taken to the police station and bundled into a cell with other drunks, most of whom had been there before. Some were singing and dancing, others quietly throwing up, and one loud-mouthed queen stripping off her clothes. The atmosphere was lively, the language foul, and the air heady with cigarette smoke and other fumes. It was not that different from some of the rougher gay bars he went out of his way to find. Monty wrote to the Greens enthusiastically, giving them full details. He was up before a judge the next morning and his case dismissed.

By now Monty knew his way around the dives of New York and probably New Orleans, too. When Morgan James had awakened his taste for burlesque, Monty had investigated all manner of bars and it did not take him long to tune into the homosexual network to which, naturally, he was specially attracted. Then, like today, New York housed many such venues, albeit of a furtive nature. In addition to bars, homosexuals had turned many cafes and restaurants into rendezvous.

The bars offered a variety of choice from full transvestism through drag cabaret and cruising joints. Mae West had discovered them a decade or so earlier and based two of her plays on them. 'Reds' was a popular bar on Third Avenue and Fiftieth Street that had started life as a speakeasy in the 1920s. It still flourished.

Monty had also discovered the delights of the YMCA on Sixty-third Street where many gay young man stayed on moving to New York.

He loved the recondite atmosphere of these places. The danger that lurked in the shadowy interiors. His homosexuality responded to kindred spirits. He did not have to pretend he was something else. It was not so much an awakening as a recognition of mutual interests.

Who knows if he physically responded to the advances that must have been made to such a handsome young man but his narcissism was given a boost. He loved being admired. If he did respond it was in the region of casual sex, probably mutual masturbation or oral sex. He certainly did not form a lasting attachment. The nearest he had got to that was with Phyllis Thaxter. For Monty at that time, love was an ideal emotion, preferably viewed from a safe distance. And he had not committed himself to a homosexual lifestyle yet. He was too young to know what he wanted. Shortly after Monty returned to New York he received a movie script, via Leland Hayward, from producer Lazar Wechsler. This was *The Search*, to be directed by Fred Zinnemann, who had contacted Monty about it while he had been making *Red River*.

Although Monty had given his word to Billy Wilder that he would do *Sunset Boulevard*, the director had not contacted him since. Wilder was experiencing horrendous casting problems with the female lead. Since Mae West had turned him down, he had futilely approached both Pola Negri and Mary Pickford. Negri's reaction had been similar to Mae's; she had been Valentino's leading lady and, as far as she was concerned, her palmy days were far from over. Mr Wilder knew what he could do with his script. Pickford had agreed to do the part but had made so many stipulations that Wilder himself had backed down, foreseeing a nightmare.

Zinnemann came to hear of Monty through Peter Viertel, writer of *The Search*, although he later left the project which was taken over jointly by Richard Schweizer, David Wechsler and Paul Jarrico. Viertel was the son of Salka Viertel, writer of many of Garbo's hits and, some suggested, her lover. Both he and Garbo were later to become friends of Monty's. Peter Viertel had seen Monty on stage on Broadway and recommended him to Zinnemann.

The Austrian-born director, now forty, had arrived in America in 1929 and appeared as an extra in *All Quiet on the Western Front*, a landmark in American cinema. Zinnemann had then graduated to director through the ranks of script secretary and maker of short documentaries. He had been acclaimed for *The Seventh Cross* in 1944, an MGM film about escapees from a Nazi concentration camp, starring Spencer Tracy.

The Search, although its story was fictitious, was to be shot in semi-documentary style on location in Switzerland and various German towns. It concerned the many displaced child casualties of war. As he himself puts it in *Fred Zinnemann: An Autobiography:**

In the midst of the flotsam and jetsam in the wake of World War Two in Europe were thousands of starving, orphaned children; most had come out of concentration camps, having lost track of their families. Some were living in the ruins of devastated cities,

* *Fred Zinnemann: An Autobiography* by Fred Zinnemann, Bloomsbury, 1992

The house on 33rd Street, Omaha, Nebraska, where Monty was born.

Ethel and Monty in Bermuda, 1926. (*The Brooks Clift Collection*)

Ethel, Brooks and Monty in St Moritz, 1929. (*The Brooks Clift Collection*)

Ethel, Monty and Brooks with a friend. (*The Brooks Clift Collection*)

Monty and Ethel at Fort Lauderdale, Florida, 1933. (*The Brooks Clift Collection*)

Monty at Edgar Allan Poe's grave, 1928. He always loved books. (*The Brooks Clift Collection*)

Monty at sixteen . . . and looking even younger. (*The Brooks Clift Collection*)

The author aged twenty.

Monty with child actor Ivan Jandl and
Aline McMahon in *The Search*, 1948,
the first of his films to be released. He
received an Academy nomination.
(*MGM, courtesy The Kobal Collection*)

Publicity still for *Red River*, the first film he made.

Marlon Brando. Publicity still for *The Wild One*. Brando had a great respect for Monty's talent.

Monty, Olivia de Havilland and Ralph Richardson in costume for *The Heiress*, 1949.

Publicity shots
circa 1950.

Monty and Elizabeth, 1951. Publicity still from *A Place in the Sun*. The world's two most beautiful people.

with no one to turn to and fending for themselves as best they could. Gradually they were gathered up by the United Nations Relief and Rehabilitation Administration.

Monty was to play the lead, Ralph, a GI who finds a homeless boy in a blitzed German town and takes him in, planning to bring him to America if he cannot locate his parents. The boy, resentful at first, refuses to speak, but gradually responds to his kindness. Meanwhile, his mother is desparately trying to find him. Eventually, accidentally, they are reunited.

Zinnemann had contacted Monty while he was in Hollywood finishing *Red River* and they had met at Armstrong-Schroder's café on Wilshire Boulevard: 'It was immediately clear he was the right choice,' writes Zinnemann.

> Exuberant and full of energy, he was an electrifying personality. Most important, there was no danger of our picture becoming the vehicle for a star, as he was quite unknown to the general public, having only just finished his first film. Clift asked if he could see the script. I told him there was nothing [yet] on paper but that a Swiss writer, Richard Schweizer, had started work on a screenplay. 'As soon as you have something, let me know and I'll come over,' said Monty. Three months later we sent him a 15 page synopsis and he came.

Monty accepted a small fee, but this was not entirely altruistic. *Red River* had not yet been released and there were no immediate plans to release it. Howard Hawks was in litigation with Howard Hughes over the rights. Although he believed he had done well, Monty had no way of assessing what the public reaction to him would be when it was released. Another movie up his sleeve could do no harm, particularly one with so poignant a theme.

Although Wechsler had got him cheaply there were stipulations attached, as there always would be with Monty. His contract was a forerunner of what was to become the norm. It was agreed that he would work no longer than six weeks and that he could alter his dialogue as he felt fit. Also Mira Rostova would accompany him as his personal drama coach.

Other cast members included Wendell Corey as Monty's GI pal, and Jarmila Novotna as the lost boy's mother. Novotna was audacious casting as she was not an actress but a prima donna, a member of the

Metropolitan Opera Company since war had broken out in 1939. Her imperious interpretations of the roles of Octavia and Donna Elvira have been eulogised in operatic history.

At forty she was at the height of her powers. But she was a Czech, and Czechoslovakia, like much of Europe, had suffered under the Nazis. She felt strongly about the film and accepted a fee that was only a small proportion of what she could command at the Metropolitan. 'The problem was,' wrote Zinneman in a letter to the author, 'I insisted on having a Czech actress in order to keep the authentic feeling the film required. Having interviewed a number of Czech actresses in Prague with negative results, the idea of using Ms Novotna proved to be a very happy solution. She turned out to be enormously cooperative, to the point of agreeing to play the part without using any makeup at all.'

Ralph was supposed to be an army engineer, so before shooting Monty stayed with a platoon of army engineers in a US zone of occupied Germany. As Zinnemann says, 'The script called for an army engineer, so nothing but that kind of unit would do.'

After he had absorbed sufficient material Mira joined him in Zurich in June 1947, and they put up at the Storchen Hotel. They took separate rooms and Mira, as was to become her practice, virtually disappeared from view as far as the other guests were concerned. She was seldom seen in the main rooms or out walking. Drama was her life and she was interested in little else.

Zinnemann was on location at the time of their arrival, but his wife was there and Monty took her to dinner. She described him, as quoted by Robert LaGuardia, as 'a knight in shining armour'.

The knight was less shining when he read his shooting script the next day. He felt Ralph did not ring true as a GI, and got down to work with Mira. Between them they developed Ralph's character, creating him as Frankenstein created his monster, taking a bit from one source and a bit from another. The end result, however, was no monster but a rounded human being. Ralph now had faults – he could be moody, abrupt, selfish, even arrogant in the way that an American, coming from an unbombed land of plenty, could be in a devastated country. There is a lack of interest in the boy's plight when he first finds him but, as the interest develops, so does Ralph's concern.

Mira gave him a focus. She understood precisely what he was trying to do. They would rehearse in his room every evening. It is difficult to say whether she was in love with him or not, but she was certainly dedicated.

Their alterations were sometimes a surprise to Zinnemann, who had

had no chance to see what was coming up. But it was not necessarily an unpleasant surprise, and he was pliable enough to appreciate the improvements. He was none too pleased to see Mira constantly on the set, however. Whatever Zinnemann felt about Monty's performance was irrelevant to her. If she thought Monty's take was below par she told him so; if she thought he was good she told him that, too:

'She did, in fact, appear on the set for the first couple of days,' wrote Zinnemann to the author, 'and inconvenienced me to such an extent that I had to ask her to stay away from then on. It is quite possible that she added to his performance. The only tangible thing I can tell you is that she contributed to changing his dialogue, which was originally very heavy-handed and not at all the way Americans talk.'

Monty rewrote much of his dialogue and, to some extent, that of the boy. The rewrites were undoubted improvements. Zinnemann stated later, in Robert Guenette's TV documentary about him called *His Place in the Sun*, that without them 'it would have been a total disaster'. Wechsler, of course, had employed his own writers and was furious that Monty chose to over-ride their work. But Monty would not relent, and sometimes the atmosphere was tense. Monty was contracted for six weeks but the film took longer. He agreed to stay on providing he could continue to rewrite his dialogue. Wechsler could not do other than agree.

The boy was played by Ivan Jandl, a ten year-old Czech radio actor whom Zinnemann had found in Prague. 'He did not speak English,' Zinnemann wrote, 'and, having spent his childhood in Czechoslovakia during the Nazi occupation, he refused to speak a single word of German. Monty had an amazing way of almost immediately getting into the child's confidence.'

The Zinnemanns had a son, Timmi, and sometimes, on a day off, Monty would accompany them for a day's boating on Lake Zurich. He usually got along with children. The Zinnemanns could not sail, but Monty was an experienced sailor. All went well until he dived into the lake. The repercussions of his dive shot the boat away and it was in danger of capsizing in the choppy water. Fortunately Timmi flung himself overboard and grabbed the dangling tow-rope, steadying the boat until Monty swam back and took charge again.

The crew and cast liked him very much. As Zinnemann says in his autobiography:

Monty fitted in very well. His preparation was typical of the Actors' Studio 'Method', helping actors to achieve an unusually deep insight into character and teaching them the means of expressing it . . .

As a person, Monty was super-sensitive and therefore enormously vulnerable. It was as if he had no skin to protect him. Beyond a certain point he kept his own counsel, and he could be very devious if necessary in trying to accomplish what he thought was right for his performance. It seemed wise, sometimes, to let a man of such enormous talent find his own solutions in his own way.

In *His Place in the Sun* Zinnemann recorded how delighted he was, after the film was released, when a viewer asked him, 'Where did you find a soldier who could act so well?'

6

At the end of 1947 something came along that shook Monty up – it indeed shook up the whole theatrical Western world. Marlon Brando opened in Tennessee Williams's *A Streetcar Named Desire* on 3 December 1947 at the Ethel Barrymore Theater New York. The play was directed by Elia Kazan and produced by Irene Selznick, wife of David O. Selznick and daughter of Louis B. Mayer.

Brando played Stanley Kowalski, the epitome of rough trade, every woman's, and some men's, dream of rape come true. Jessica Tandy was the fragile Blanche Dubois, a faded beauty whose unrelenting nymphomania coupled with her delicate mental state was precipitating her into insanity. Williams had poured a lot of himself into the make-up of Blanche – his insecurities, his obsession with sex and his fear of growing old. There were rave reviews for the play, and especially for Brando. John Chapman of the *New York Daily News* wrote simply, 'Mr Brando is magnificent.'

Streetcar became the hottest ticket in town and Brando the brightest star. The famous flocked to see him.

Brando introduced a new type of hero: a type not previously acknowledged by a playwright but a type with which Williams was acquainted. A raw, working-class, uneducated hoodlum who instinctively knew that the only route to true happiness was through fulfilled sex.

When casting, both Burt Lancaster and John Garfield had been considered. Williams had only seen Brando on the stage and never met him. But the producers thought they should meet and arranged for Brando to travel to New England where Williams had a house.

Brando arrived in his jeans and T-shirt, all biceps and stocky legs. As Charles Higham writes in *Brando*, 'Once he [Tennessee] saw Marlon's physique in jeans and T-shirt and his sullen, sexy, stubborn face, Williams was ecstatic. He knew he had his Stanley Kowalski . . . Brando met every requirement for the part.' To put the seal on his spell, Brando freed Williams's bunged up lavatory and fixed his faulty electric wiring for him.

Brando, in fact, was far from a hoodlum. He was a sensitive, idealistic man and a dedicated actor with his own radical ideas on the subject. As Peter Manso writes in his biography *Brando**, 'If Clift had introduced a kind of passion that was on the immature side, primarily adolescent, filled with wonder and longing, then, as Billy Redfield observed, Marlon was delivering something that was "uncomfortable and dangerous".'

Although he didn't get much chance to show it in "Streetcar", even Brando's understudy was brilliant. This was Ralph Meeker, who in 1951 was to make his film debut in Fred Zinnemann's *Teresa*, which starred Pier Angeli and another newcomer, John Ericson. One of the great mysteries of Hollywood is why Ericson did not become a bigger star. Meeker went on to have successful film career himself, although always in the shadow of Brando.

Brando was not helped in his portrayal of Stanley by Jessica Tandy. Experienced actress through she was, her Blanche could not equal his Stanley. Williams, thrilled by Brando's grasp of the part, did not worry too much. He thought Miss Tandy would find the right level as the run progressed.

If Tandy was intimidated by Brando's runaway success, she had more to bear, recorded Charles Higham in *Brando*. Brando teamed up with a crowd of drunken sailors on the way to the theatre one night and told them she was an easy lay. They presented themselves at the stage door, demanding to be let in.

Tandy was never the perfect Blanche – that distinction fell to Vivien Leigh, who opened the play in London in 1949. She, fortunately, made the film of *Streetcar* with Brando, and the record is there for all to see. As Brando says 'She *was* Blanche Dubois.' He was, however, also impressed

---

* *Brando* by Peter Manso, Weidenfeld and Nicolson, 1994

by the French Blanche – Arletty, the star of the French film *Les Enfants du Paradis*.

Always keen to keep his finger on the acting pulse, Monty now took classes at the fashionable Actors' Studio, which emphasized the teachings of Stanislavsky. By the mid-1950s Stanislavsky ideas would also become part of the London theatrical scene and be rekindled in Paris and Berlin, where they had never entirely disappeared. They even spread to the Communist bloc and in Poland it was to be taught at the Lodz National Film School, where it was eagerly absorbed by a young Jewish actor called Roman Polanski. Polanski was inspired to attend the Lodz school after seeing Monty's films and hearing that he was an exponent of the Method.

But in 1948 the Actors' Studio was based at the Malin Studios, in a shabby corner off Broadway. Its very shabbiness seemed to synchronize with the post-war spirit of earnestness. The war had cleared away much phoniness, and now it was time to present the truth on stage and film. A new spirit of enthusiasm was abroad.

Monty had joined the Actors' Studio in the first year of its existence, and met Stella Adler, the teacher who profoundly influenced the young Brando. Brando and Monty spent hours together discussing the motivation of various roles and even appeared in an amateur film, a fun sequence in which they burlesqued silent film actors, something Monty often did for friends. Earnest as Method actors were, there was clearly also time for fun.

They laughed, too, over memories of Talullah Bankhead, with whom Monty had played in *The Skin of Our Teeth*. Brando had just finished a tour with Tallulah in Cocteau's *The Eagle Has Two Heads*. His agent. Edie Van Cleve, had put him up for the part after he had had a success playing Marchbanks in *Candida*, the role Monty had wanted.

Tallulah had never bothered with Monty sexually as she knew he was gay. Brando, however, was different. According to Charles Higham's biography of him she had tried to seduce him on a couple of occasions. She once let her hand wander up the inside of his leg, making for the crutch. Brando let her carry on, knowing she would not have the guts to seize her objective.

Tallulah was of an earlier generation when her bisexuality had shocked, her language appalled and her drinking outraged. All of this had added to her charisma. By 1948, however, it didn't mean much at all. Marlon, as the younger generation, could, and did, sometimes shock her. According to Charles Higham he once saw her in an expensive restaurant and shouted out, 'Tallulah, how the fuck are you?' She was mortified.

Brando did not finish the run of *The Eagle Has Two Heads* and Monty
was asked to take over. He refused – he had no ambition to work with
Tallulah again. But he had gone to Washington to see the play and
travelled back on the train to New York with Brando. They attended
a party given by Jerome Robbins, then a dancer also studying Method
but now remembered as the choreographer of such films as *The King
and I* and *West Side Story*.

After the party, Marlon and Monty left together on Marlon's
motorbike, Monty in his cashmeres and loafers clinging on to the
pillion, his hair streaming out behind, Marlon in his leathers. They
proved too much for Robbins, who, in LaGuardia's account, sighed,
'If anything happens to them, we've just lost the shining lights of the
American theatre.'

Due to legal difficulties with Howard Hughes, Howard Hawks was
unable to release *Red River* for over a year. In the meantime, Fred
Zinnemann surged ahead with *The Search*. He thought, from Monty's
unsentimental performance, that he had something special. Monty was
as content as he ever would be with anything he did, and bucked
up even more when he heard from Hawks that a preview version
of *Red River* had been screened and audience reaction to him had
been enthusiastic. Monty himself had seen a rough cut and not been
over-impressed.

At the Actors' Studio he studied dramatic versions of Dostoevsky and
worked on *Crime and Punishment* with Mira and Maureen Stapleton,
a fellow student to whom he became close. Bobby Lewis again asked
him to appear in *The Seagull*, which had not yet got off the ground,
but Monty would not commit himself. He was inundated with offers
for film and stage work but seemed happy to take his time idling about
and going on book-buying sprees; his apartment was full of modern
novels and the classics, which overflowed from his couch on to the
floor. He was a great reader of wide taste.

Returning to Europe for *The Search* had been a culture shock. He
had known pre-war Europe, before the cities had been ruined and left
people starving. None of this seemed to have affected America much,
and the contrast was staggering. He felt guilty.

The Search, backed by MGM, was released in March 1948. It was
an instant success in both the USA and Britain, which surprised Louis
B. Mayer who had forecast that Monty had made a terrible mistake
by appearing in cheap European-made merchandise, even though his
studio was backing it. Mayer now tearfully pleaded with Monty to
join MGM.

Monty was taken aback by the success of the film. He had been expecting an artistic coup, not a blockbuster. He got both.

'*The Search* is absorbing, gratifying, an emotional drama of the highest order,' wrote the *New York Times* reviewer, while *Tribune* contented itself with 'Montgomery Clift is superb.'

Alfred Hitchcock wanted him for *Rope*, a Grand Guignol story in which a pair of male lovers murder a colleague for kicks; Monty would have been partnered by Farley Granger. In *The Life of Alfred Hitchcock: The Dark Side of Genius**, Donald Spoto writes 'the clearly sociopathic, dominant partner, which Hitchcock had hoped Montgomery Clift would play, was eventually given to John Dall. Clift, whose film career was just under way, dreaded a role that could perhaps raise eyebrows.'

Rope raised more than just eyebrows, particularly in its original stage incarnation when the homosexuality of the lovers was more pronounced. But it was still there in the film, albeit subtly, and Monty, who lived in fear of his sexuality being exposed, did not favour drawing attention to it by playing a homosexual on film. Although he would have liked to work with Hitchcock he was relieved he had turned it down.

He was precipitated even further into the spotlight, if that were possible, by being nominated for an Oscar for *The Search*, as were Zinnemann, Ivan Jandl and, ironically, the writers. He took Sunny and Brooks to see the film, forgivably bragging that he had written most of his lines himself, despite the writers being Oscar nominees.

He was regularly stopped nowadays and asked for autographs, and when fans discovered his telephone number it rang so much he had to change it. Girls followed him down the road, calling out after him and banging on his door irrespective of whether it was day or night. He was human enough to be swayed by his success, but felt decidedly vulnerable.

Had he signed the contract Mayer had offered, and moved to Hollywood, he would have been better protected. He would have been assigned a suitable place to live, either in Beverly Hills or in the better part of Hollywood, where many of the staffed apartments were on long lease to studios. Hollywood was geared for stars – it created and nurtured them. If they played ball with the studio then it played ball with them, doing its best to ensure a trouble-free and, by and large, pleasant life.

New York was for actors whom only theatre-goers revered, not

* *The Life of Alfred Hitchcock: The Dark Side of Genius* by Donald Spoto, Wm Collins & Co., 1983

Hollywood stars. He was a famous face in a rapacious city. He did not feel safe. Even so he would not move to Hollywood – the idea repelled him. He felt a traitor by even being in films, particularly with Lunt breathing disapproval at him every time they met, so he was certainly not going to throw his lot in with the movie moguls. Its very incestuousness oppressed him, for the colony members socialized exclusively with each other.

He loved the anonymity of New York – even though he was less anonymous now than he had been. Los Angeles had a large gay community but it was too near Hollywood. Everyone had an eye open for transgressing stars and the possibility of blackmail. Few of them ventured forth.

He had met a new lover, a young Italian New Yorker called Dino with whom he was to remain for five years. He was not in love – it's doubtful that he ever fell in love – but he was fond of him and did not feel he could take him to Hollywood.

He was, however, prepared to travel to Hollywood for the Oscar ceremony, even though there was no guarantee he would win. He was facing stiff competition. Laurence Olivier was heavily tipped for *Hamlet*, and Libby Holman's old sparring partner, Clifton Webb, was up for *Sitting Pretty*. All the sparkle Webb had given his dancing routines now came out in his playing of what were, in effect, acid-mouthed old queens thinly disguised as heterosexual wits.

Among the nominated actresses, Jane Wyman was up for *Johnny Belinda* and Olivia de Havilland for *The Snake Pit*. Of the two, Miss Wyman was in the greatest need of a fillip: she had just lost a baby and was about to divorce Ronald Reagan. Miss Wyman never uttered a word about her marriage to Reagan, although thousands of dollars were awaiting her if she had decided to do so.

The Oscars Ceremony was held shortly after *The Search* had opened, on a cold and snowy night untypical of Los Angeles. Robert Montgomery was the MC and most of the awards were presented by starlets, among them Ava Gardner and a stunning seventeen-year-old raven-haired, azure-eyed beauty called Elizabeth Taylor, who according to *Inside Oscar*, made her entrance to the tune of 'Did You Ever See a Dream Walking'.* People literally gasped at her loveliness.

Among the winners that night was writer-director John Huston for *The Treasure of the Sierra Madre*. His award was presented by MGM's new British hope Deborah Kerr, soon to star with Monty in Fred Zinnemann's

* *Inside Oscar* by Mason Wiley and Damien Bona, Columbus Books, 1986

From Here to Eternity. Also, not so many years in the future, Huston was to work with Monty and be accused of contributing fatally to his eventual non-recoverable nervous breakdown.

Ivan Jandl won his special juvenile Oscar and, since he could speak no English, it was collected by Zinnemann. Alas, it did him no good. 'Ivan, now in his late 40s [sic], lives in Prague and is going bald,' wrote Zinnemann in his autobiography in 1992. 'Or so I thought, until I heard that he had died, alone and forgotten, a year ago. It seems that the Oscar he had received had brought him nothing but bad luck. The regime punished him for getting a splendid award from the "capitalist" West; they did not allow him to work in films and forbade him to accept foreign contracts or travel abroad.'

The Best Actor award went to Olivier, as everyone predicted. He was not at the ceremony, being on stage elsewhere at the time, so Douglas Fairbanks Jr accepted it on his behalf. Olivier serenely announced he would be celebrating his success, which had driven some of his competitors to near suicide with envy, simply by having an extra drink after his show. His laid-back attitude made many want to murder him.

Hamlet received a Best Picture award. It was a British film, made by Rank, and Hollywood was not best pleased. The *Hollywood Reporter* summed up the feeling of many by stating: 'Hamlet was NOT the best picture of the year . . . Have we a bunch of goofs among our Academy voters . . .?'

The Search did wonderfully well, though. In addition to Jandl's Oscar it received an award for Original Story. Although both Zinnemann and Monty were nominees, as was the script itself, neither won. But Monty was realistic enough to realize that it was too much of a long-shot to expect to win an Oscar for his first film – especially when Olivier was in the line-up. He was among the minority who did not begrudge him his award; he considered Olivier a fine actor and continued to admire him. They later became friends, and Monty made trips to London just to see him in Shakespeare.

Back in New York it was decision time, and he accepted a three-picture deal from Paramount at $150,000 a picture plus script approval and choice of director. One of the films was to be *Sunset Boulevard*, for which he had already pledged himself to Billy Wilder. Wilder had sent Monty a draft script and Monty told him he loved it but, as it was still not ready to shoot, his contract was to start with *The Heiress*, principally a vehicle for Paramount's top female star and fellow Oscar nominee Olivia de Havilland.

The Heiress was an adaptation of the play *Washington Square*, based on Henry James's novel of the same name. He was to play the unscrupulous fortune hunter Morris Townsend on whom, at the end of the film, Oliva was to wreak a withering revenge. The cast included Miriam Hopkins and Ralph Richardson and the director was William Wyler, who had already notched up triumphs with Bette Davis's *Jezebel*, Olivier's *Wuthering Heights* and Greer Garson's *Mrs Miniver*, for which he had received an Oscar.

This was Wyler's first film since his other Oscar winner *The Best Years of Our Lives*, three years earlier. Charlton Heston was to remark, 'Doing a picture with Willie is like getting the works at a Turkish bath. You damn near drown, but you come out smelling like a rose.'

Monty was working on *The Heiress* when *Red River* was released in July 1948, just four months after *The Search* had come out. *Time* profiled him, *Look* magazine made him the recipient of its prestigious Achievement Award as 'The Most Promising Star on the Hollywood Horizon', *Cosmopolitan* lauded him, and *Life* devoted its entire front cover to him. He won the *Motion Picture Herald* Star of Tomorrow vote, and *Photoplay* received more fanmail for him than for any other star. It was a lot for a young man to take in.

As recently as 1992, film critic Barry Norman listed *Red River* among his *100 Best Films of the Century* and added,

> in a broad sense *Red River* is a kind of *Mutiny on the Bounty* set on the prairie. Think of the autocratic Wayne as Captain Bligh and Clift as Fletcher Christian and the parallels become clear . . . The frontier spirit and the sheer awfulness of a prolonged cattle drive, with its effect on the nerves and temper of the participants, are splendidly evoked as, too, are the machismo and masculine rivalry (the old bull versus the young) of Wayne and the tensely brooding Clift.*

Analysing Monty's first two films, critic Jack Babuscio wrote in *Gay News* No. 104:

> His choice of films reveals a great deal about the inner man. In his first two films, both made in 1948, Clift pioneered a new style in screen heroes – one which was to exert a profound influence on his

---

* *100 Best Films of the Century* by Barry Norman, Chapman's, 1992

fellow actors: the disillusioned innocent who ultimately is forced to rebel against the hypocritical morality of an oppressive society.

In *Red River* ... this attitude was manifested in an attack on arbitrary authority in the form of the domineering Dunson (Wayne) ... while in *The Search* ... it can be seen in the abstract concept of war and its awful dehumanisation of the individual spirit.

1948 was, in fact, Clift's annus mirabilis. *Red River* established him as a major new talent.

Brando, too, was being offered films. According to Peter Manso's biography, he was unsure if he had screen potential and asked a friend, David Diamond, 'Do you think I'm what one would call handsome? Do you think I'm as good looking as Monty?' 'What you've got is balls, which Monty doesn't have,' Diamond told him. 'Marlon looked at me,' Diamond added, then he said, "Tell me more."

Also, Peter Manso writes, 'Clift was on everyone's tongue since *The Skin of Our Teeth* three and a half years earlier ... setting in motion a contest that would last for years until they played opposite each other in *The Young Lions* in 1957 ...' He quotes Kevin McCarthy as adding,

Marlon was aware that he [Monty] was a big star. Monty was aware that Marlon was somebody to be watchful of. At the heart of it was that Marlon didn't understand the meticulous way Monty worked, which was sort of colder. Monty knew what he was doing at all times – he was much more analytic. Not that he wasn't full of emotion, but it was approached intellectually. Marlon, I think, acted out of some innate understanding. It wasn't studied, it just HAPPENED – and so he thought Monty was uptight.

Manso continues,

'Whenever the two of them appeared at parties, it really was something,' said a girl who was on the scene at the time. 'You didn't know whom to look at first. Marlon had such basic animal magnetism that he stopped conversation when he entered a group. Monty, meanwhile, was elegance personified.'

Even Ellen Adler agreed, 'I was around sixteen,' she said, 'and I think we went to somebody's apartment after theatre for drinks. Monty was there with some people, and we got talking. He was so polite and charming, always with the match for the cigarette. Marlon

stood it for as long as he could, and then he came barging over and
pulled me away. "She's my Jew, Monty!" he roared. Monty just
grinned and shrugged.'

While Brando was contemplating a film career, according to Manso,
he asked his agent Edie Van Cleve, 'How much is Clift getting in the
movies?' and added, 'I want a dollar more.'

Monty agreed to be interviewed by the press for *Red River*. He had few possessions, still lived in his walk-up apartment over the launderette and made no attempt to pretty things up for the reporters. They were charmed by him and wrote of an unspoilt young man, dazed by his success.

Meanwhile work continued on *The Heiress*. Mira was with him and, as she had done on *The Search*, coached him in the privacy of his room. Gossip was rampant as to what exactly they got up to together – the truth was very little, apart from working on his script.

He and Olivia de Havilland retained a mutual respect and were scrupulously polite to each other. Robert LaGuardia reports her as having later said, 'I had a sense that Monty was thinking almost entirely of himself and leaving me out of the scene. It was difficult for me to adapt to playing that way. But my having to adapt to him, and not his adapting to me, was really part of my character, so in the end it worked.'*

Monty was in awe of Ralph Richardson and impressed at the way the British actor could retain the same nuances and inflections

* At the time of going to press Miss de Havilland is working on her memoirs, in which she intends to expand on this statement. As is her prerogative, she prefers to keep her recollections for the publication of her own book. The author thanks her for her courtesy.

throughout several takes. He worked well with William Wyler, although the director's approach was too clinical for his absolute comfort. In order to get the right period feel for the piece, Wyler encouraged him to grow a moustache. It did not suit him. 'Please don't bawl me out in front of the crew,' Wyler remembered Monty asking him as they started to film. 'I don't bawl out actors, I might correct something,' Wyler replied.*

Monty was no more impressed by Hollywood this time than he had been previously, yet he did his best to fit in. He dined with columnist Louella Parsons and lunched with the Wylers at their mansion, where he played tennis with Charlie Chaplin.

It was there that he met Salka Viertel. Then approaching sixty, she possessed an intellectual world-weariness that fascinated him. Hollywood was seething with unrest at the time and she was reputed to be a Communist – consequently dangerous company. This did not deter him. Shelley Winters writes in her memoirs, *Best of Times, Worst of Times*† that she was leaving a party one evening and, 'I noticed in a dark convertible two people necking in a rather sexual manner. When I peeked in again, I realized it was Montgomery Clift and Salka Viertel, Garbo's writer and a very important person in the Hollywood firmament. She was about sixty years old. As I write this, I wonder wistfully if Aiden Quinn perhaps likes to neck with 60 year old ladies.'

With notable exceptions he was not drinking a great deal at that time. In his biography of Monty, Robert LaGuardia quotes Kevin McCarthy as saying, 'Monty's version of being "drunk" was a few glasses of wine and a bit of bravura.' But other guests of Salka's report him being drunk, crawling across the floor on his hands and knees and kissing her feet. This was acceptable behaviour at Salka's and although it might seem an extravagant gesture she regarded it as her right and took it with the proffered pinch of salt. If he was drunk it did not take much to get him so, for he had a low tolerance of alcohol. Others could drink more and stay sober.

Salka introduced him to Garbo, who did not take to many people but took to Monty. They had a rapport and both despised Hollywood, even though they both made a bundle out of it. The two became friends and would huddle together, ignoring other people, locked in introspective conversation. One of the things they did not discuss was MGM. The powerful studio had sent Monty several scripts and he rejected them all. He was not

---

* *Montgomery Clift* by Robert LaGuardia, W.H. Allen, 1977
† *Best of Times, Worst of Times* by Shelley Winters, Simon & Schuster, 1989

interested in cashing in on his stardom, although many advised him to do so.

According to Patricia Bosworth he wrote to a friend, Ned Smith, that 'I am embarrassed by myself in *Red River* and proud of *The Search*.' He did not think he would be proud of *The Heiress*. He could see from the rushes that it was very much Olivia's film and that Wyler clearly saw it that way. As the plain but feisty Catherine she was going to walk away with the movie.

Filming ended in November 1948. He immediately took off on a European holiday, starting with a few days in London where he saw Olivier in *Richard III* at the Old Vic and dined with him. While in England he was contacted by his agent. A 'technical fault' had been discovered on one of the scenes in *The Heiress*, and it would have to be redone. Monty had to fly the 6000 miles back to Los Angeles. He accepted it, without any show of temperament, as part of the job.

He did one day's filming with de Havilland, then returned to London and checked in at the Savoy. Elizabeth Taylor and Robert Taylor were also in London, making *The Conspirator* and staying at the Dorchester. So was Patricia Neal, making *The Hasty Heart* with Richard Todd. In her autobiography, *Patricia Neal: As I Am**, she writes:

> I also met Montgomery Clift for the first time. He had been at the 'Actor's Studio' but our paths had never crossed there. One night he asked me to go to the theatre. I was dressing when he rang me up. 'Patricia,' he wailed. 'I have the most terrible news for you. I'm so sorry, but I could get only one ticket for the play.' I assured him that was alright, that we could do something else. 'Oh, no, that's not what I meant,' he stammered. 'I can't take *you* with me tonight.' So I stayed at home and that was the last I ever saw of the gorgeous Mr Clift.

Red River had recently opened in London. An interviewer from the *Star* managed to grab an interview with him, and the following piece appeared in the edition for 26 January 1949:

> Catching up with London today was a lean young American with chiselled good looks whom Hollywood regards as a combination of Humphrey Bogart and Gary Cooper and Tyrone Power – Montgomery Clift, seen by filmgoers here in *Red River*. Little

* *Patricia Neal: As I Am* by Patricia Neal, Century Hutchinson Ltd, 1988

of Mr Bogart, Mr Cooper or Mr Power was visible when I called at the Savoy today but there was a good deal of Mr Clift and it was easy to see why Hollywood is so excited . . .

'I flashed through London on my way through,' he told me. 'Now I'm going to catch up with all the things there wasn't time to see.'

Mr Clift . . . is a bachelor – 'I'm still waiting to meet the girl I'd like to marry' – and is regarded as something of a puzzle in Hollywood. He won't sign a long-term contract – 'I value my freedom too much' – and turned down so many screen offers before *Red River* that film makers decided he must be a millionaire: 'Actually I was flat broke,' he told me. 'but I just didn't like the scripts.'

The following day the *Daily Express* added:

Montgomery Clift, who made star grade with one picture – *Red River* – and is now swiftly rising to the top ranks of heart throbs, arrived in London . . . and revealed himself as one young man who is not after the big money – at least, the not-so-enormous money. He wants to take less money than is customary in Hollywood for the ascendant star, so that he can have the right to turn down parts he doesn't like. For this he is prepared to take only £12,500 a year.

Clift – twenty-eight, tall and dark . . . turned down picture contract after picture contract. 'What would have been the use of taking them?' he says. 'I might have made a hit earlier but I would have had no acting experience behind me.' Now he is a surprised star. 'I can't see what's so special about my performance in *Red River*, he said. 'When I saw it I felt that I had done any number of things the wrong way. Now there is enough money to pay my bills. Amazing.'

Apart from detours about his love-life he was usually honest with the press. This was not often the case during the late 1940s, when stories were invariably manufactured by press officers to fit the required image. He could never see the point of that.

From London Monty went to Paris for the theatre and ballet. Thornton Wilder, who was also there, took him to tea with Alice B. Toklas. The three then went to an exhibition of Impressionist paintings owned by Gertrude Stein.

Then he went on to Greece and to Rome, where he had arranged to meet Fred Zinnemann. They flew to Israel together, with writer Stewart

Stern, and explored the possibility of making another semi-documentary film along the lines of *The Search*.

As Zinnemann writes in his autobiography,

> In May 1948 the British mandate for Palestine came to an end. Survivors of the Holocaust were streaming into the country ... There was now a new hope for them which, at the same time, was a cause of enormous alarm to the Arabs ... No sooner had the United Nations recognized the State of Israel than the first Arab-Israeli war began. Enormous events were impending; after the experience of the UN Displaced Persons' camps in Germany I felt a strong need to witness what was going to happen next, and perhaps make a film continuing the style of *The Search*. Monty Clift seemed to feel the same way and wanted to come along ... Joined by a talented young writer, Stewart Stern, we flew from Rome in an old DC-3 of Trans-Caribbean Airways, which was the only airline available to civilians wishing to enter the country. We saw history before our eyes ...

They also heard musical history: Leonard Bernstein was conducting a concert in Jerusalem, then under siege by the Jordanians. On another occasion they watched as a kibbutz was scoured for land mines. Violence erupted intermittently between Arabs and Jews as the border was disputed. The three of them stayed in a kibbutz where the primitive food caused Monty's dysentery to flare up again. He had constant stomach cramps, but that was something with which he had now learnt to live.

The zeal of the Israeli soldiers for their new homeland inspired him and he felt part of a family. It was a sexual thrill just to be there alongside these virile young men. At night he would return to Zinnemann and reel off ideas for the movie. For a while he was happy: he seemed to be involved in something useful. The soldiers, in turn, were flattered that a movie star was interested in them. This was no precious actor but a man as brave as any, even reckless at times, who frequently strayed within range of Arab guns.

The idealism rubbed off on to him and, although not a political animal, he became pro-Israel – it was a period when all Jews were special to him. He even spoke warmly (and he was about the only one who did) about some of the hard-faced Jewish studio bosses, men who, it almost seemed, would cut a throat without a qualm and who had considerably less in common with the Israeli soldiers than he did.

From Israel he travelled to Cyprus and Greece and from there to Switzerland, where he wrote a long letter to Sunny telling her of his adventures. He travelled back through Rome, Paris and London before returning to New York before Christmas. He checked into a hospital straightaway for treatment for his dysentery.

Not long afterwards he was arrested for soliciting – his nightmare come true. All he did was pick up a young man on 42nd Street, but the police saw him and arrested him: homosexuality was against the law. Fortunately the matter was settled by his lawyers and kept out of the press, although the news spread in the industry. The papers were, however, full of his other activities. His popularity had increased while he had been abroad. *Red River* was nominated one of the top five box office attractions of 1948. Another poll had elected him the world's most eligible bachelor. Paramount were building him into an all-American heterosexual sex symbol. The police charge had shaken him and the mad film publicity, albeit of a positive nature, unnerved him even more. He felt he was sitting on a time bomb. Although his bank balance was thriving he hated the deception he was forced to live and began to regret ever going into the movie business.

But he was in films up to his neck and, to underline the point, he had to have lunch with the movie world's gossip columnist and famous party-giver Elsa Maxwell. To express his reluctance he arrived looking deliberately scruffy. She thought this charming, as she did that he still lived in his $10-a-week apartment, and wrote so in her column. The fans liked him even more for being different.

Actor Karl Malden, who lived near Monty, wished he was more ordinary. When Monty felt like being sociable he would climb up his fire escape on to the roof of the Maldens' building, scamper over it like a squirrel, then jump down on to their fire escape. Malden and his family had shocks on several occasions.

Kevin McCarthy was about to play Romeo and asked Monty to coach him. He did so willingly, working through the night. Monty loved Shakespeare and longed to make a movie version of *Hamlet*, but there was no chance of that. Olivier had already done it and collected an Oscar.

But there was a chance to make *Sunset Boulevard*. He heard from Paramount that Billy Wilder had now found his leading lady and was ready to start shooting in April. However, in the meantime Monty had thought deeply about it and no longer wanted the part. He had played an opportunist in *The Heiress*, and Joe Gillis, the character in *Sunset*, was from the same stable. He did not want to be thought of as a gigolo, and kept hoping the project would fall through. Now, to his horror, he was summoned to fulfil the Paramount contract he had signed.

Wilder had finally settled for Gloria Swanson. She was superb as Norma Desmond, and now it is impossible to envisage anyone else playing the role as perfectly. Director George Cukor had suggested her. She had not made a film for years and had become a talk show hostess on New York television. Someone made the grave error of inviting her to Hollywood for a screen test. Billy Wilder's biographer, Maurice Zolotow, records her reaction: 'I suddenly got a call from somebody at Paramount – my old studio, you know, the one you might say I built – and some nauseating little creep said they wanted to fly me out to the coast at once – at once, mind you – and take a screen test for the role in this movie. Test for a part in a picture? Me? Test? I was revolted.'

Finally Cukor persuaded her to test for Wilder's partner, Charles Brackett, telling her it was for the benefit of the young man who was to play opposite her. Swanson recalls the incident in her own memoirs, *Swanson on Swanson**.

> 'Who is that?' I asked.
>
> 'Montgomery Clift,' Mr Brackett said. 'A promising new star. Excellent. Have you seen him?'
>
> 'No,' I said . . .'

Monty was told to attend. He was assured that this was because Brackett wanted to test Swanson – exactly the reverse of what Swanson had been told. Shooting, Monty was told, would commence on 11 April. He flew into a panic and left town.

Zolotow continues:

> 'Two weeks before the first day of shooting . . . Wilder faced disaster. Montgomery Clift broke his contract! Suddenly he would not play Joe Gillis. No. He would not listen to Wilder's pleas and he would give no explanation except that his agent told Billy he suddenly felt unable technically to give a convincing performance as a young man in love with a woman twice as old as he! He was incommunicado. The truth – as we all knew back in New York . . . was the opposite. Not only could Clift, an actor of great subtlety and power, portray a young man in love with an old woman, but he was – and had been for some years – in the grip of a romantic

* *Swanson on Swanson* by Gloria Swanson, Michael Joseph Ltd, 1981

obsession with a woman about thirty years older than he was –
Libby Holman . . .

Libby was in fact sixteen years older, they were never in the grip of a
romantic obsession, and they had not met since since *Mexican Mural*.
When Wilder heard of Monty's reasons for breaking his contract,
according to Ron Base in *Starring Roles* he spat out: 'If he was any
kind of actor, he would be convincing making love to any woman.'*

In the end William Holden took over, but not before Wilder had
had almost as much difficulty replacing Monty as he had had with
Mae West. Brando, who had not yet made a film, was considered too
threatening. Fred MacMurray, who had had a success with Wilder in
Double Indemnity, was asked but was, to his regret, unavailable. Gene
Kelly was considered, but was under contract to Louis B. Mayer who
would not release him.

As it stands, *Sunset Boulevard* is a masterpiece. With Mae West and
Monty it would have been a completely different movie. It is intriguing
to imagine what they would have been like together. How would Monty
have got on with the teetotal, anti-smoking Mae West, whose idea of
shooting a scene was do her part one day, ensuring the angles and
lighting were to her satisfaction, then let her co-star do his part the
next day? This was how *My Little Chickadee* had been shot with W.C.
Fields, but was not quite the style to which Monty (and Mira) were
accustomed.

He still kept in regular touch with Sunny – he was unable to
distance himself from her – but his attitude towards her became
pricklier. Sometimes, if he had drunk too much, he could get nasty.
He blamed her for over-protecting him, which, he felt, accounted for
his insecurity. He loved her but also resented her, and wanted her to feel
his resentment. Above all he blamed her because he was homosexual.
That, he felt, was totally her fault, and he may have been right.

Sometimes, in these dark moods, he would swear at her in a way
he knew she would hate. But she never registered shock. She took
it all indulgently, knowing the incandescent effect it would have on
him. She refused to be riled. It was a contest of wills which she
invariably won.

Now that Monty was doing well, Bill asserted himself. To Monty's
and Sunny's amazement he presented his son with an account, itemizing
how much he had spent on his European education. It cut Monty to the

* *Starring Roles* by Ron Base, Little Brown & Co., 1994

quick – he did not have a mean streak in his body, but did not expect his father to charge him for his education. Nevertheless he insisted on repaying every penny, although it took him several years to do so.

8

In August 1949 Monty returned yet again to Europe – he had been there several times already that year – to film *The Big Lift*. Mira went with him, as was statutory in his contract.

Up until then he had spent the year in a fever of creativity. He had seen everything on stage that had remotely interested him, being particularly impressed by Arthur Miller's *Death of a Salesman*, which he had seen several times. On a visit to Paris he had encouraged Thornton Wilder to write the play for him that he had promised. It never came to fruition but Wilder, then in the throes of depression because his career was going nowhere while Monty's was taking off fast, spoke to him of his idea to write something based on Kafka themes. Monty read all Kafka's work to ensure he would be conversant with it when Wilder produced the goods.

He had told his agent – now Lew Wasserman – to look for further film possibilities. Monty ploughed through hundreds of scripts but turned them all down, and hired a part-time secretary just to handle his mail. He planned to form his own film company with Kevin McCarthy, for which he would produce, direct and star. In preparation he bought an option on *You Touched Me!*, the Tennessee Williams and Donald Windham play which was the last thing he had done on Broadway.

The Big Lift was being filmed in Berlin, and before going there he stopped off for two weeks in London, staying at Claridge's. Stacks of fan letters were delivered to him daily. He met up with the McCarthys – Kevin was having a success with *Death of a Salesman*, and the two of them went to the theatre several times. He also saw two W.C. Fields films – he was a fan of Fields.

The Big Lift was a cheap budget movie but, as with *The Search*, Monty believed in the subject matter. It was set just after the Second World War, during the time of the Berlin Airlift, when the Russians blockaded Berlin and British and American planes ferried supplies to the city. Monty's character and his co-flier, played by the doughty Paul Douglas, held opposing views on how to deal with the desperate Germans.

Directed and written by George Seaton, it was to be shot in the pseudo-documentary style he liked on locations in the Russian, French, American and British sectors of Berlin. All the military personnel used were actual members of the armed forces. Newsreel of the time was incorporated, and there are sequences of dated airport routine – the last word in sophistication at the time – that try the patience today.

Monty plays Danny MacCullough, a naive idealist prepared to believe good of everybody, including the Germans. The Douglas character, Hank, is more straightforward, an endorsement of the American way of life which he preaches with the subtlety of a sledgehammer.

Both men fall for German girls. Hank bullies his into adopting American standards as opposed to those of the recently defeated Third Reich. When she eventually rounds on him in temper he applauds – at last she is thinking like an American, as opposed to spouting party propaganda. Danny has a quieter, more intense affair, planning to marry his girl and take her to America. He listens to her viewpoint when she speaks in favour of the Germans and is almost taken in, but she is not all she seems. Her family had SS connections, which she had concealed and of which she is proud, and she only wants to snare him to get to America and back into the arms of her German lover who has fled there. His idealism is shattered by her duplicity.

Victor McLaglen must have loved the film. In New York he had warned Monty about associating with suspected Communists like Salka Viertel and the left-wingers of the Group Theater. There could be no accusations of Communist sympathies against anyone associated with *The Big Lift*.

For all its earnestness there is humour in the film. There is even slapstick at one point, when Monty is in a night club raided by the military police. A male trio is singing on stage, and to escape detection he joins them, miming to the song. It's one of his rare examples of comedy. Cary Grant could not have done it better. When his career got underway, his penchant for tragedy swamped everything else. It is a pity there is not more of his comedy on film; he loved doing it and it might have assuaged the persistent legend that he was a one-dimensional depressive.

There was not much comedy on the studio floor from Mira, at least not intentionally, although sometimes there may have been some smirking behind her back when crew members could see the hold she had over Monty, a hold which over-rode that of his director. It was whispered that Seaton was not in control of his film and Mira was taking over Monty's performance. No director likes to hear talk of that sort, particularly if there's a grain of truth in it.

Monty was adamant that she stay and threatened to leave himself if she were banned from the floor. Seaton had no choice other than to concede. Mira felt she had been insulted, as she probably had been – after all, she was there at the star's request – and was all for catching the next plane back to America. She told Robert LaGuardia she felt she had been treated with 'hostility'. 'Everyone thought that I had some sort of hold on Monty,' she said. 'The truth was that he did follow almost all of my suggestions but only because we were of one mind on what mattered in acting.' She stayed: in the cause of good acting Mira would put up with a great deal.

Douglas, a tough man on and off screen, felt that Monty was hogging their two-shots, almost pushing him out of frame. Patricia Bosworth says he responded by threatening to 'break your fucking foot' if Monty did it again. They did not speak much after that.

By the end of filming both Seaton and Monty were more or less happy with their performances. The cost was heavy. Seaton had a bruised ego, Paul Douglas and Monty detested each other, Mira's feathers were ruffled, and the crew had enough gossip to ensure them dinner invitations for the rest of the year. The film was over budget and Seaton blamed this on Monty's constant demand for retakes. This was not entirely fair, as there had also been time-consuming technical problems.

Shortly after Monty's return to America *The Heiress* was released. As he had anticipated, Olivia de Havilland stole the reviews and went on to pick up her second Oscar. Contrary to his expectations, though, the film was much praised.

Motion picture exhibitor Harry Brandt quoted in *Inside Oscar*, said, 'I've seen every picture made in 1949 and this should not only win the Academy Award but get second and third place too.' Hermione Isaacs wrote in *Films in Review*, 'Wyler is that rarest of craftsmen who can take such a drama, already completely fulfilled in theatre terms, and convert it to film without ever permitting the play-form to dominate the screen.' *Variety*, the trade magazine, was, however, not bowled over and predicted that audiences would find it too long. It was right: *The Heiress* never took as much money as *Red River*.

Embarassingly for Monty, Gloria Swanson was asked to go on a publicity tour to promote *The Heiress*. Since she was now a Paramount artist, making *Sunset Boulevard*, the studio wanted to put her back in the limelight. He was nervous he might bump into her, as he had agreed to promote the film by personal appearances himself. He felt he had to do that to appease Paramount, who were still smarting over his withdrawal from *Sunset Boulevard*. Understandably, Swanson had been affronted by his absence at her test. She was not appeased when told that his objection was that he did not want to be seen making love to an elderly lady.

He was about to start one of the most important films in his career. *A Place in the Sun* was an adaptation of *An American Tragedy*, Theodore Dreiser's block-busting novel of social conscience. Monty's co-star was to be seventeen-year-old Elizabeth Taylor. Elizabeth, under contract to MGM, had been loaned to Paramount for the film. Paramount, eager to promote the forthcoming Clift/Taylor partnership, had arranged for them to accompany each other to the premiere of *The Heiress* at Grauman's Chinese Theater in Hollywood.

Monty tried to duck out at the last minute. He did not want to go to the premiere at all, least of all with some young actress whom he did not know. He had not been at his best in *The Heiress* and knew that Richardson and de Havilland had outshone him. He would be embarrassed in a cinema full of people, with the glare of the spotlight on him.

Elizabeth herself was not over-keen to accompany him, either. In David Heymann's *Liz* she admitted she was 'absolutely terrified . . . Because Monty, first of all, was a New York Method trained actor and I felt very much the inadequate teenage Hollywood sort of puppet that had just worn pretty clothes and hadn't really acted except with horses and dogs.'* They had never met but she had once caught a glimpse of him when he had been in director George Stevens's office in Hollywood, discussing *A Place in the Sun*.

Monty took Mira with him to Hollywood and she, together with a

* *Liz* by David Heymann, Heinemann, 1995

Paramount press officer, went with him to pick up Elizabeth. He left them in the car while he went to collect her. Elizabeth was living with her mother Sara, who answered the door. Mrs Taylor had planned much of Elizabeth's career as a child star and was accustomed to handsome men, but even she was smitten by Monty in his tuxedo. She proudly introduced Elizabeth to him.

When Elizabeth got into the car, according to Kitty Kelley's *Elizabeth Taylor, The Last Star* she said, 'Sorry about mother, she can be a real pain in the arse.'* He laughed out loud. It was the beginning of a rapport between them that never waned.

Mira and the press officer got out round the corner from Grauman's, leaving the two young people to make their glamorous entrance alone. Elizabeth was wearing a white and green evening dress created by MGM's Helen Rose, and as she clung to Monty's arm they seemed the perfect couple. She straightened his bow tie, and the crowd gasped. It was enchanting. Flashbulbs popped. In the news footage of the time he looks perfectly relaxed. The papers later dubbed them the most beautiful couple in movies.

He was embarrassed by his performance in the film, as he knew he would be, but she bolstered him, telling him how good he was. The audience approved as well, giving him a round of applause when the lights came on. He made a greater impression than he had anticipated. In *His Place in the Sun* someone was reported to have remarked, at the point in the film where Catherine shuts him out of the house, 'How could she have locked the door on such an extraordinary man?'

For some reason Monty nicknamed Elizabeth Bessie Mae. Later her other close friend, Rock Hudson, was to call her that too. Afterwards they went to a party at William Wyler's and were among the last to leave. This imminent co-star's irreverent attitude to Hollywood delighted him, and he felt optimistic about *A Place in the Sun*.

It was a pity there was not more optimism about in general in Hollywood at that time, but for some it was a precarious place to be. Senator Joseph McCarthy had stated from Washington that he had names of American Communists whose sole purpose was subversion. Many on his list were film-makers, who, McCarthy stated, were bent on spreading destruction through the socialist messages of their films. He was about to start a witch-hunt which still reverberates today. Hollywood trembled from Louis B. Mayer downwards.

Some, in an attempt to save themselves, gave names of suspected

* *Elizabeth Taylor, The Last Star* by Kitty Kelley, Coronet, 1982

Communists to the House Un-American Activities Committee. Those who refused to testify became unemployable. Some were forced to leave Hollywood. Elia Kazan was one who was questioned for his left-wing sympathies. Monty was warned, again, about the danger of his alliance with such men.

Harassment extended through the ranks, and its victims included even the mighty Chaplin. As Kenneth Anger writes in *Hollywood Babylon** 'the "Red Tide" cast a pall over Hollywood as insidious as the newly pervasive Los Angeles smog. With the House Un-American Activities Committee granting them open season, movieland's fanatical right wingers emerged from the woodwork, wrapped themselves in the flag and came out punching – generally below the belt.'

Monty was not political but he had principles and would not be brow-beaten by the Committee. He did not do much more than continue to stick by his friends, but that was more than many did. In *A Place in the Sun* he achieved the high point of his stardom. He was twenty-nine. Part of the film's originality was the way in which it was shot: director George Stevens specialized in an extended series of close-ups, each one dizzyingly cascading on to the next. Such a technique had not been applied before in a major film. At first Monty had reservations about Stevens – he had seen his 1935 film *Alice Adams* and was not impressed. He did not think Stevens had the stature to tackle *A Place in the Sun*, but later he revised that judgement.

It had been Stevens' idea to make *A Place in the Sun*. The book had already been filmed in 1931 by Josef von Sternberg, under its original title of *An American Tragedy*. Von Sternberg was the man who in Germany in 1930 had made *The Blue Angel*, the film which had brought Marlene Dietrich to fame. *An American Tragedy* had failed at the box office and no one was keen to film it again, but Stevens was obsessed by the project. Since 1923 he had been working in Hollywood on light-weight films. *A Place in the Sun* was weightier than anything he had ever done. He had persuaded Paramount it would be ideal for Elizabeth and Monty.

It is a strong story. An ambitious but poor young man makes headway with a rich, spoilt girl and they plan to marry. Meanwhile, he murders his plain and pregnant girlfriend, who had demanded he marry her. He is condemned to the electric chair. As critic Pare Lorentz wrote of the von Sternberg film, 'It is the first time, I believe, that the subjects of sex, birth control and murder have been put into a picture with sense,

---

* *Hollywood Babylon* by Kenneth Anger, Delta Publishing, 1975

taste and reality.' In the novel the death of the pregnant girlfriend is accidental; in Stevens's film it was strengthened to murder.

Filming was due to start in autumn 1949 and continue for six months. The budget was $2½ million, a lot of money then. When the principal casting was settled, with Monty as George Eastman, the anti-hero, and Elizabeth as Angela Vickers, the rich girl (featured in a white Cadillac convertible every bit as beautiful as herself), it was decided that Shelley Winters would play Alice, the plain girl.

This was going against type. Winters, a room-mate of Marilyn Monroe's, usually played sex-bombs. Blonde, wise-cracking and cigarette-smoking, she was the archetypal good-time girl. But she had gone out of her way to persuade Stevens she was right for this particular part.

After much badgering he agreed to meet her, but not before he had turned down nearly every other available actress in Hollywood. Winters clinched the deal by arriving for their meeting dressed in character, in drab old clothes and wearing no make-up. He agreed to test her providing she looked as she did then.

Monty partnered her for her test. 'Monty was such a joy to work with that I felt as if I already knew him very well,' she wrote in her memoirs.* After she had got the part and filming had finished she said, 'The whole experience was a joy.'

Not for Mira, who, as usual, got the cold shoulder from the director. She was also a source of wonder to Winters, who wrote, 'Can you imagine having a coach when you were being directed by George Stevens? But I guess that Monty was insecure at that stage in his career and needed someone with him. She was his coach, nutritionist, friend and, perhaps, lover. And although she was on the film for the whole six months, Stevens never acknowledged her existence.'

According to Winters, Mira would sometimes get her hand into shot while gesticulating to Monty. Stevens never lost his cool but merely asked his assistant to move her to one side. She writes, 'I guess Monty was entitled to his coach, although she did some strange things . . . She might have been an invisible cockroach, the way George treated her.'

As always, there were two schools of thought about Mira's value to Monty. Winters had her doubts but admitted she could be wrong. In one particular scene with Winters Monty decided, via Mira, to do the take differently from the way they had rehearsed it. Stevens did not argue, but merely set things up. Winters was sure it was wrong. But

* *Shelley* by Shelley Winters, Granada Publishing, 1980

when she saw the rushes, she changed her mind, '. . . all we saw on the screen were Monty's eyes lit up (with the rest of his face in shadow), my face lit up and his hands lit up . . . I was stunned when I saw those rushes.' Some, however, thought the scene worked so well because of Stevens's expertise rather than Mira's.

'George Stevens clearly didn't necessarily like having me around,' Mira noted in David Heymann's Liz,

> but he didn't say too much . . . It turned out Monty coached Elizabeth more than the director did. They rehearsed their scenes for hours; Monty would take copious notes on Liz's performance and then review them with her. Their camaraderie not only helped her acting; it forged a lasting tie between them.
>
> On the other hand, perhaps too much has been made of their friendship. It was primarily Elizabeth who wanted a romantic involvement. Monty would go to bed at night, and she would invariably find some excuse to visit him. She would make him a cup of tea and then maintain she needed to rehearse the following day's scene. Elizabeth always used an aggressive approach concerning men.

There could have been a spot of jealousy there.

In the same book Heymann recalls Luigi Luraschi, vice-president of Paramount International, saying of Elizabeth: '. . . she couldn't stop talking about Montgomery Clift. I had the distinct and unmistakable impression that she had fallen in love.' Billy Le Massena, also quoted by Heymann, was another who believed this of Elizabeth.

> Monty had the facility of making anybody – male or female – fall in love with him. I thought Elizabeth Taylor, like Marilyn Monroe during a later period, truly adored him. He encouraged Elizabeth, mainly, I imagine, because he was a bit ashamed of being homosexual. I'm not suggesting he didn't care for Elizabeth – he did. But, from his viewpoint, he saw the relationship as purely platonic.

They behaved like close friends rather than lovers. In one particularly grand scene, when Elizabeth was in full evening dress, he whispered in her ear, lewdly but unerotically, 'Your tits are fantastic.'

The weather was freezing and Lake Tahoe, where they were to film Winters' murder, was deep. Both Winters and Monty were nervous that if anything went wrong one of them might get drowned. They agreed to ask Stevens for stuntpeople. When face to face with him, though, Winters went ahead but Monty held back. 'I gave the silent Monty a dirty look,' she writes. To get them to do it, Stevens jumped into the freezing lake himself. Without further ado Monty and Winters played the scene.

Stevens also wanted shots of Elizabeth and Monty in bathing suits. Monty refused, which was strange. He was no Arnold Schwarzenegger but had no reason to be ashamed.

In order to prepare himself for his death cell scene, which takes place in the final moments of the film, he spent a night in a murder cell at St Quentin. He then got into a huddle with Mira to work out how it should be played. Stevens wanted a big reaction, but Monty did not see it that way. He felt he should be numb – devoid of feeling and expression. Stevens relented, and Monty walks to his death like an automaton.

At the wrap he was heartily glad to be finished. He felt disappointed in Stevens, who, he was convinced, had let everyone down. Later Stevens won an Oscar and Monty conceded he had been wrong.

Elizabeth found the film fulfilling. *A Place in the Sun* was her debut as a real actress. She acknowledged that for the first time she had been playing a woman as opposed to a caricature. In no small measure it was Monty's influence which brought this about.

Hedda Hopper saw the rushes and, as reported in Kitty Kelley's biography of Elizabeth, wrote a piece for her syndication. 'Where on earth did you ever learn how to make love like that?' she gushed to Elizabeth. Hedda had known Elizabeth since her arrival in Hollywood as a child. From what she had seen, Elizabeth had just kissed childhood goodbye.

Hedda upset Monty. She was charm itself in her huge floppy hat, but her mere presence irked him. He was not a topic for gossip. He called her 'the old gobbler' and asked Elizabeth why she bothered to cooperate with her. The question had never occurred to Elizabeth. She was a child of Hollywood and it was the way things were done. It sold seats. Why fight it?

He himself later gave an interview to *Picturegoer* in which he said, 'I like acting; and I can only act to my own satisfaction when I have a part in which I believe – a story that means something to me . . . I look for the character that will stir me up and force me to do my best.' It was as much as anyone ever got from him on the gossip front.

Shortly after this, the headlines of the world's press screamed out that 'Clift and Taylor' were to wed. He was furious and embarrassed, blaming it on Hedda. Certainly she had fuelled the fire, but the story was actually leaked by George Stevens to stimulate interest in the film.

Elizabeth was as surprised by it as Monty, although not as appalled – she was used to reading accounts in the papers of events in her life that had never taken place. She was, in fact, dying to get married and had told Monty so. His reply, according to Kitty Kelley was 'Marry a monkey, if it will make you happy.' He was not so glib when she told him she was engaged to Nicky Hilton, son of Conrad Hilton who owned the hotel chain of the same name. In *Liz* David Heymann recounts how Monty had met the young Hilton when he had visited Elizabeth on the set. He was a gambler and, it seemed to Monty, a womanizer. Monty did not approve: he could be very prim at times. 'Will you come and visit me after I'm married?' she asked him. His reply disappointed her; 'I don't think dear Nicky is my kind of guy.'

Long before its release, word spread that he was superb in *A Place in the Sun* and he was flooded with offers. Among these was a Broadway *Hamlet*, with Katharine Hepburn as Gertrude. Surprisingly, he turned this down. Much as he wanted to play Hamlet, he was too nervous of possible adverse reaction to his movie. He would have felt exposed playing Hamlet in a theatre. George Stevens then asked him to play the lead in *Shane*, the tale of a mystic maverick in the pioneering days of the Old West. He turned this down, too, and Alan Ladd took the part. Stevens was eventually nominated for another Oscar. Setting aside these and other work prospects, Monty chose to go to Europe for a holiday with Kevin and Augusta, visiting first Paris and then Rome.

In Paris he attended an Yves Montand concert as well as seeing *Hamlet* and the French version of *A Streetcar Named Desire*, translated by Jean Cocteau. He shared Brando's enthusiasm for Arletty, the French Blanche Dubois. Sometimes he would disappear for a day or so, and Kevin and Augusta left him to his own devices. But his days of anonymity were clearly over. Nowadays anyone with whom he had an encounter knew exactly who they were getting. He was as big a star in Paris as he was in London or New York, and autograph hunters frequently stopped him. He did not mind and even seemed flattered, providing they did not talk to him for too long or ask personal questions.

Augusta noticed he was taking pills. He told her, according to Patricia Bosworth that they 'increased his energy, and stopped his pain'. He was joking, but he did have pain from his colitis and he felt better for taking pep pills. He travelled with an extensive range of medication: whatever the medical problem, Monty would have a remedy for it.

In Rome they visited Tennessee Williams and Luchino Visconti, who were involved in an Italian production of *Streetcar*. In 1948 Visconti had had a success with *La Terra Trema*, a three-hour film about Sicilian fishermen with a cast consisting entirely of peasants – not an actor among them. Now he was enthused by Tennessee Williams and American Method actors, particularly Monty and Brando. He welcomed Monty with open arms, and told him he'd seen his films.

Visconti wanted to make a film with Brando of Proust's *A La Recherche du Temps Perdu*. He was enthralled by *Streetcar* and, in fact his pet name for Williams was Blanche.* The first Italian version of *Streetcar* had opened in 1949, with Vittorio Gassman as Stanley. Visconti had spurred him on to an excess of violence, which excited him. Now he eagerly questioned Monty about the Actors' Studio.

Monty and the McCarthys were guests at a fancy dress ball which Visconti gave. Monty went as a wizard, his face and costume prepared for him by the young Franco Zeffirelli, then a stage director yet to turn to films. Monty took numerous photographs.

In Milan they visited the set of *Umberto*, directed by Vittorio De Sica. Monty had seen De Sica's *Shoeshine* and told him how much he admired it. They vowed they would work together one day.

The three Americans travelled home on the *Queen Mary*, which ran into a storm. Monty scurried about on deck, even though he was advised by the crew to remain below. But the raging elements attracted him, and when he did return to his cabin he hung out of the porthole, rather as he had once suspended himself outside high-rise apartments. He seemed to court death at times, though it was the danger that attracted him rather than a wish to kill himself.

Back in America he and Kevin McCarthy laboured over *You Touched Me!* for six months. He was never satisfied with what they had done. Every line was rewritten dozens of times, and the finished script was the size of a telephone directory. Lew Wasserman was asked to find a suitable film company to make it. Monty suggested John Huston as a possible director – that is if he did not direct it himself, as he thought he might. He had liked Huston's *Key Largo*.

Monty and Kevin rented a house on Cape Cod in order to recce the film. The prospect of personally producing a film seemed to frighten him and, as always when frightened, he started drinking heavily. Alcohol never had a good effect on him. Time meant little to him and he worked on a twenty-four-hour clock, eating and sleeping when he felt like it.

* *Luchino Visconti: The Flames of Passion* by Laurence Schifano, Harper Collins, 1990

Kevin came in one evening and found him eating off the kitchen floor. Once, in the dead of night, Monty started cleaning up the house, driving to and from a rubbish dump. He was careless where he put his cigarettes and the furniture became covered with burns. Kevin was frightened he might cause a fire. That was always an occupational hazard for anyone who lived with Monty.

He suffered alcohol-induced bouts of depression, intense while they lasted. Kevin and Augusta thought a pschyiatrist might help. Prepared for an outburst, they were surprised when he agreed to see one. The psychiatrist in question was fifty-three-year-old William V. Silverberg, who had himself studied under Franz Alexander, a pupil of Sigmund Freud. If Monty was seeking a cure for his homosexuality he chose an unlikely physician, as Silverberg himself was a homosexual. Much has been said of Silverberg's sinister influence over Monty, but whatever his overall effect he brought Monty comfort for years to come. It was comfort for which he paid a great deal of money, but he felt secure with Silverberg and saw him regularly.

Monty did not consult Silverberg until he had tried a cure for alcoholism. He had drunk comparatively little before going into films, but now there was no doubt that he was daily consuming far too much alcohol. He was admitted to the Columbia Presbyterian Hospital. When he was discharged he was prescribed Antabuse, a drug which provoked a physical revulsion when alcohol was taken. But it did not work. Within weeks he had to return to the hospital as he was still drinking. As soon as he was discharged he started drinking again.

Silverberg was progressive, even by psychiatric standards. He did not consider alcohol a threat and considered the time to stop drinking was when a patient felt he wanted to do so. This might seem to negate the reason for visiting him in the first place.

Monty moved from his flat above the launderette to a smart duplex at 209 East 61st Street; more appropriate to his status. He bought a few items of furniture, but his suitcases remained spread over the floor for months. He hired a part-time cook who cooked job lots, then froze them, so that he could thaw them when he wanted.

Elizabeth Taylor married Nicky Hilton in May 1950. The wedding coincided with the opening of her film *Father of the Bride*, and the publicists went mad. Monty was scared he had lost her.

The Big Lift, which he had filmed in Berlin, opened the following month to lacklustre reviews. 'There are some acute touches,' wrote Gavin Lambert, 'just enough to make the slick evasions of the rest all the more regrettable.' That August *The Heiress* opened in Britain and he agreed to fly to London to publicize it – any excuse to get to Europe. He stayed at the Connaught, an exclusive hotel favoured by royalty. Another American visiting Britain was Irene Dunne, who was playing Queen Victoria in Nunnally Johnson's film *The Mudlark*. He promised he would see it while he was in Britain, and kept his word; they were photographed together at the airport.

He also attended a Command Performance at the London Palladium and willingly posed for photographs with cast members including Glynis Johns, Margaret Lockwood, Claudette Colbert, Michael Wilding and Gloria Swanson. He attended a party given by Tyrone Power, among whose guests were Noël Coward, Clifton Webb, Michael Wilding and Marlene Dietrich, whom Wilding was vainly trying to persuade to divorce her husband and marry him.

Gloria Swanson was there too. They had met briefly at the Command Performance photocall, which somewhat allayed the embarrassment. His last association with her had been when he had failed to turn up for her *Sunset Boulevard* screen test and it had been reported that he was unhappy at having to make love to an older woman. He had affronted one of the greatest stars in the history of cinema. On this occasion both were frigidly polite.

After London he flew to Italy, where *The Heiress* was about to open. Italian reporters asked him how he felt about Elizabeth's marriage. The interviews were conducted through interpreters and he took it good-naturedly, even having dinner with one of the journalists. While in Italy he learned that Libby Holman's fifteen-year-old son Topper had been killed in a mountaineering accident. He sent a message of condolence and offered to go to her if she needed him.

While in Italy he was hideously embarrassed when a nubile young blonde woman tried to get into his room. He discovered it was a publicity stunt devised to spice up his image as a red-blooded heterosexual. He did not see the funny side. Monty's sense of humour was somewhat different, as he was to show back in America.

In the 1950s Laurence Olivier and his then wife Vivien Leigh had moved to Hollywood, where Leigh was to make *Streetcar* with Brando, and Olivier *Carrie* with Jennifer Jones and Miriam Hopkins. They had rented a house on San Ysidro Drive, next door to Danny Kaye and his manager wife Sylvia. Kaye threw a party, to welcome the Oliviers to Hollywood. 'Welcome' was perhaps hardly appropriate as both were Oscar winners, Olivier for *Hamlet* and Vivien for her performance in *Gone with the Wind* as Scarlett O'Hara, the most sought after role in Hollywood.

In *Vivien Leigh* Hugo Vickers gives a detailed account of events that evening*. Kaye had invited 170 Grade A names to the Crystal Room of the Beverly Hills Hotel. The list included Louis B. Mayer, Bogart and Bacall, Spencer Tracy, Groucho Marx, Ginger Rogers, Cyd Charisse, Lana Turner, Errol Flynn and Marilyn Monroe, who had just made a hit with a smallish part in *The Asphalt Jungle*. Vivien Leigh was on an unnatural high that night. She danced wildly till dawn, creating a fracas around her. It was a decade since she had played Scarlett and now she was playing Blanche, but she still looked lovely in her organdie gown as she shrilly called to friends from the dance floor. Vivien was to be directed in *Streetcar* by Elia Kazan, another guest at the party. Her behaviour alarmed him: he recognized a hysteric when he saw one. She had already played Blanche in London and was tired from the run. Kazan thought she might be better employed resting before the shoot rather than dancing the night away.

Vivien, however, was not the entire focus of attention that evening. Monty shared the limelight. He had not been invited but, clearly drunk, gatecrashed the Crystal Room in the small hours. He was loud and oafish, and those who witnessed the spectacle despised him. Such things did not happen in Hollywood, where protocol, in its way, was as strict as that of Buckingham Palace. Mr Mayer nearly had apoplexy and the incident was never forgotten. Monty thought it a great laugh. Others – important people – did not laugh but remembered.

Monty, like Vivien was gaining a reputation for erratic behaviour. His acting, however, was revered. Marilyn Monroe told people at the party that she adored him. Gary Cooper was another of his admirers. According to Larry Swindell in *The Last Hero*† he had formed his own company and bought the rights to Alfred Hayes' novel *The Girl on the Via Flaminia*, in which he wanted Monty to co-star with him. But he had difficulty with the financing and eventually sold it to Leland Hayward and Anatole Litvak; one of his stipulations was that Monty should still be in it. Unfortunately the movie was never made.

* *Vivien Leigh* by Hugo Vickers, Pan Books, 1989
† *The Last Hero: A Biography of Gary Cooper* by Larry Swindell, Robson Books, 1981

9

A *Place in the Sun* opened in August 1951. The film grossed $3½ million, a great deal for the time, and was listed by *Variety* as the eighth-highest grossing film of 1951. Charlie Chaplin eulogized it as 'the greatest movie ever made about America'. By now *Streetcar* was also on release and, after initially dumbfounding some sections of the public, was generally hailed as a masterpiece.

Raymond Chandler, the detective novelist and creator of Philip Marlowe, saw both films. Marlon impressed him, but Monty did not. He admired *Streetcar* but 'despised' *A Place in the Sun*, describing it as 'as slick a piece of bogus self-importance as you'll ever see'. In a letter written to his friend Dale Warren on 11 January 1952 he wrote dyspeptically:*

> to mention it [*A Place in the Sun*] in the same breath as *A Streetcar Named Desire* seems to me an insult. *Streetcar* is by no means a perfect picture, but it does have a lot of drive, a tremendous performance by Marlon Brando, and a skillful if occasionally rather wearisome one by Miss Vivien Leigh. It does get under your skin, whereas *A Place in the Sun* never touches your emotions once.

* *Selected Letters of Raymond Chandler* edited by Frank MacShane, Jonathan Cape, 1981

Everything is held too long; every scene is milked ruthlessly. I got
so sick of starry-eyed close-ups of Elizabeth Taylor that I could
have gagged. The chi-chi was laid-on not with a trowel, not even
with a shovel, but with a dragline. And the portrayal of how the
lower classes think the upper classes live is about as ridiculous as
could be imagined. They ought to have called it *Speedboats for
Breakfast*. And my God, that scene at the end where the girl
visits him in the condemned cell a few hours before he gets the
hot squat! My God, my God! The whole thing is beautifully done
technically, and it reeks of calculation and contrivance emotionally.
Mr Montgomery Clift gives the performance of his career, which is
not saying a great deal, since he has already demonstrated in *The
Heiress* that he didn't belong on the same screen with first class
actors. The picture was made by a guy who has seen everything and
has never had a creative idea of his own. Not once, but twice in
the picture he uses that great trick which Chaplin used in *Monsieur
Verdoux*, where instead of a fadeout to close an act he shoots out of
a window and watches the darkness turn into daylight. But this slab
of unreal hokum makes $3\frac{1}{2}$ million dollars and *Monsieur Verdoux*
was a flop. My God, My God! And let me say it just once more.
'My God!'

Chandler must have seen the film on a bad day, for his sentiments,
about both *Place* and Monty, were in the minority. But neither was film
critic Pauline Kael over-impressed: 'An almost incredibly painstaking
work . . . mannered enough for a very fancy Gothic murder mystery
. . . the town is an arrangement of symbols of wealth, glamour and
power versus symbols of poor, drab helplessness – an arrangement
far more suitable to the thirties than to the fifties.'

But despite some of the acid comments, Elizabeth created a sensation.
'The real surprise of *A Place in the Sun* is the lyrical performance of
Elizabeth Taylor', *Look* magazine had written: 'Miss Taylor here reveals
an understanding of passion and suffering that is electrifying.'

Elizabeth herself later wrote, in a magazine article entitled 'Elizabeth
Taylor Takes Off':

As far as I'm concerned, he [Monty] introduced a new dimension
into screen acting. Marlon Brando and Jimmy Dean are often
credited with bringing the Method technique to the movies, but
Monty was actually the first. During the film we developed a loving
and lasting friendship. Though we were linked romantically by the

media, I sensed from the beginning that Monty was torn between what he thought he should be and what he actually was. All in all, I think *A Place in the Sun* was the best movie I did as a young adult.

Elizabeth was in England at the time and had been there since June, making *Ivanhoe* with Robert Taylor and George Sanders. Before that she had been staying with Monty. She had separated from Nicky Hilton in December 1950, although both sets of parents hoped for a reconciliation, and moved back with her own parents. While there, she read in the papers of her husband's evenings out with the likes of Mamie Van Doren, Terry Moore (a former child model who became a leading lady and escorted Monty to various functions at Paramount's request) and Joan Collins. The disappointment of her broken marriage made her ill, and she was admitted into the Cedars-Sinai Hospital in Los Angeles.

When she was discharged she returned to New York and stayed with Monty for a while at East 61st Street. Meanwhile, Howard Hughes offered Elizabeth $1 million to marry him. She didn't take him seriously.

While she had been in England she had resumed her friendship with Michael Wilding, the British actor when she had met some three years earlier. Within a short time she had fallen in love with him, and they planned to marry when his divorce came through.

Wilding had achieved fame in a series of Mayfair romances with British actress Anna Neagle, produced by her husband Herbert Wilcox. Wilding, now approaching forty and losing his hair, was playing romantic leads with the aid of a hairpiece.

He had enormous charm and a self-deprecating sense of humour, and was under no delusions about his talent: 'I was the worst actor I ever came across,' he later told the author. Years later, when it was put to him that his fans would love to see him in a new show, he chortled through his gin, bald pate gleaming, 'My fans? Who're they? Three old ladies in Budleigh Salterton?' Elizabeth had competition for his love in the shape of Marlene Dietrich, with whom Wilding had been having a torrid affair. At fifty she was thirty-one years older than Elizabeth and ten years older than Wilding, but still a formidable opponent. Only a fool would underestimate her.

Elizabeth returned to New York in October 1951 and told Monty about her new love. Wilding, with his old-fashioned, stiff upper lip style, was not Monty's idea of an actor, but he had met him and liked him and so was as supportive as he could be. Monty and

Elizabeth sometimes had a drink together in Gregory's, a small bar popular with Monty until he got punched in the face by a drunk, after which he stopped going. Sometimes they ate together in cosy Continental restaurants, laughing a lot. They seemed perfectly happy, cocooned in their own little world, needing no one else.

On her return to New York Elizabeth checked into the Plaza Hotel as a guest of the management. She was under the impression that she could remain a complimentary guest as long as she wanted since she brought much publicity to the hotel; but it was not so. She discovered this when she received a summons to fly to Hollywood for retakes of *Ivanhoe*. She checked out of the Plaza and was given a bill for $2600. Monty and Roddy McDowall, a mutual friend, were in her suite at the time and all three had been drinking. While Elizabeth packed, in a temper, the men threw flowers around the apartment and rehung the pictures upside down. Later, as Alexander Walker relates in his biography *Elizabeth** she found that Monty had been busy while her back was turned: 'When she unpacked . . . out fell every moveable fixture from the Plaza bathroom that the inebriated Monty Clift had managed to detach or unscrew – tap tops, bath towels, cabinet handles – and even the empty martini pitcher. Elizabeth got down to writing one of those sorry notes . . . this time to the management.'

One of the most exciting things that happened to him during this period was a meeting at a party with James Jones, author of the best-selling novel *From Here to Eternity*. The burly thirty-one-year-old ex-soldier, cigar-smoking and heavy-drinking, cast a spell over Monty. He thought this was what manhood should be about, and knew he fell short of the mark.

He read the book and was bowled over. At another meeting Jones told him that *Eternity* had been bought by Columbia Pictures and that he would like him to play Prewitt, the soldier who refuses to box for his regiment despite sadistic bullying. Prewitt, the plucky underdog, captured Monty's imagination. He knew the part was ideal for him and told Jones so. He often told people he wanted to play parts they offered, so as not to offend them (as Billy Wilder could endorse), but in this case he meant it.

He was not so enthusiastic about appearing in the gimmicky medium of 3-D, in which audiences view the screen with the aid of a pair of plastic spectacles containing one red and one green lens. One entrepreneur thought that if he could get Monty Clift to appear in 3-D he would

---

* *Elizabeth* by Alexander Walker, Fontana, 1991

be made. He had no luck: the techniques of film exhibition did not interest Monty, who regarded the newly developed CinemaScope with the same scorn he was later to view Cinerama. He had not yet appeared in colour and had no desire to do so. All he cared about was the role, the writing and the director.

He was in Hollywood in March 1952 for the Oscars. *A Streetcar Named Desire* had caused great excitement, but then so had *A Place in the Sun*. He, Shelley Winters and George Stevens were all nominees, and *A Place in the Sun* had received no fewer than nine Academy nominations. This time his hopes were high, and he knew he stood a good chance. However, he was pitching against Marlon Brando, who had also been nominated. As Graham McCann writes*: 'Montgomery Clift and Marlon Brando were the two figures who set the tone for the representation of male sexuality in the 1950s cinema. They were the two rebel males: Clift the aristocrat, Brando the proletarian.'

A Streetcar Named Desire had even more nominations than *A Place in the Sun*. In addition to Brando, Vivien Leigh, Kim Hunter, Karl Malden, Tennessee Williams and Elia Kazan were all in the running for Oscars. And while *A Place in the Sun* had been hailed as a masterly literary adaptation, much of its success was ascribed to the acclaim of teenagers who turned up in droves to swoon at Monty and Elizabeth. This was the era of teen power: Monty's wounded bafflement when faced with life struck a chord.

The ceremony was held at the RKO Pantages Theatre on 20 March. Fans had been queuing since 11.30 in the morning, jockeying for position, and by the time things started happening had blocked the road. Leslie Caron had been the first celebrity to arrive. *An American in Paris*, in which she had starred with Gene Kelly, had been a huge hit, both critically and financially, but strangely she was not an Oscar nominee. Spotlights stabbed the air as more stars arrived in their finery, stepping from their limousines. Commentators announced them and tried to grab a few words.

Monty was sitting with the Greens, with whom he was staying, and the McCarthys – Kevin had made a film of *Death of a Salesman* and he was also a nominee. Whether through nerves or alcohol, Monty did not behave well. His antics were noted by Sheilah Graham, the American-based British columnist who had once been the mistress of F. Scott Fitzgerald; 'Montgomery Clift, sitting with pal Kevin McCarthy, found everything too, too funny – rolling in

---

* *Rebel Males* by Graham McCann, Hamish Hamilton, 1991

the aisle at simple things like an usherette showing Brod Crawford to his seat.'*

Neither Marlon nor Monty won Best Actor – that honour went to Humphrey Bogart for his role in John Huston's *The African Queen*. From *Streetcar*, Vivien Leigh, Karl Malden and Kim Hunter were the ones who received Oscars. George Stevens won Best Director for *A Place in the Sun*, and there were awards for its editing and script. Although *An American in Paris* won the Best Picture award, *A Place in the Sun* was nominated Outstanding Picture of the Year by the National Board of Review of Motion Pictures. Shelley Winters won nothing apart from the hand of her escort Vittorio Gassman, the Italian Stanley Kowalski, whom she married the next year and who went on to star with Elizabeth Taylor and John Ericson in *Rhapsody*.

In May 1951 Monty flew to Reno at the request of Fred Zinnemann. That director's movie *High Noon*, starring Gary Cooper and Grace Kelly, had just been released. Oscars were to be awarded the following year to Cooper and its musical director, Dmitri Tiomkin, whose hit song, the eponymous 'High Noon', with lyrics by Ned Washington, was sung in the movie by Tex Ritter and became a hit for Frankie Laine. Nominations had gone to Zinnemann and writer Carl Foreman.

Meanwhile the city of Reno had made *High Noon* Western of the Year, awarding it a Silver Spurs trophy. Cooper couldn't make the ceremony, so Monty stood in for him. The Master of Ceremonies was Ronald Reagan, then a Warner Brothers contract player. It was a measure of Monty's popularity that he was able to take Coop's place: only another idol could have stood in for him. It was also a measure of his affection for Zinnemann that he went at all. Normally he avoided such things like the plague.

When he came back to New York he had the duplex renovated; Fred Green did much of the work. While this was being done Monty took trips out of town, including a stint in Las Vegas, a city he enjoyed, to see Marlene Dietrich in cabaret at the Sahara Hotel; he had met her several times already. She appeared in a Jean Louis gown which made her seem as though the top half of her body was covered by nothing bar a few sequins. Her stage technique amazed him and he called to see her afterwards. She once brought Ernest Hemmingway to see him in New York, but Monty found him a bore.

Still keen to play Prewitt in the projected *From Here to Eternity*, he visited James Jones in Tucson, Arizona. He and Jones drank heavily but

---

* quoted in *Inside Oscar* by Mason Wiley and Damien Bona, Columbus Books, 1986

he frightened Jones when he fell out of his car into the main road in a stupor. To Monty it was a step in the right direction – it was manly.

Not that falling about drunk was a novelty; he did a great deal of it. His friends were amazed that Silverberg found nothing wrong with this and did not urge him to stop. But his psychiatrist did not consider coercion to be part of his treatment and reiterated that Monty would stop drinking when he thought it right to do so. Monty would not listen when anyone suggested that Silverberg might not be the right doctor for him. By now he was convinced that the man was his salvation. Mira was among those who spoke out against Silverberg, and Monty icily snubbed her. Her comments cut him to the quick, and after that they were never quite as close.

Some people thought Monty and Silverberg were having an affair. There was no doubt that Silverberg was dazzled by him: he penned inscriptions to him in medical books he had written, describing him as 'my hero', while to Monty Silverberg provided a security that never came from his family. But there was no sexual dependency. Their relationship lasted fifteen years, until Monty's death – no affair of Monty's lasted that long. Colleagues of Silverberg's have vouched that he would never let a patient/doctor relationship go that far. More pertinently, Silverberg was in his fifties – far too old for Monty, for whom thirty was about the limit.

Monty was becoming increasingly addicted to prescription drugs, mostly Seconal and Nembutal, which he managed to get hold of with or without a prescription. Compared to the drugs in common use today these seem mild, but they had a dramatic effect on him and promoted wild mood swings. Whatever uppers he took, there was a compensatory proportion of downers. He took anything that might enable him to sleep at night, but remained an inveterate insomniac who would jerk awake after just a few hours.

It was two years since he had last acted and he had spent the interval planning things, getting his apartment in order and working on his screenplay for *You Touched Me!* The time had slipped away. He was still feted wherever he went and it brought enormous privileges, but he resented the restrictions that went with it. He was getting a reputation in the gay demi-monde but there was nothing he could do about that. He was not going to give up sex, even at the risk of his career, but he was careful. By and large he stuck to a few men for regular sex, but he had an active libido and often felt frustrated.

He was frustrated, when Kenneth Anger's notorious book *Hollywood Babylon* came out, to see himself referred to as Princess Tiny Meat, a reference to the alleged smallness of his penis. In the gay world penis size is everything and he was affronted, particularly as it was untrue. He was totally average in that department.

He was frustrated, too, about his career, which was why, in the summer of 1952, he took a role in Alfred Hitchcock's *I Confess*. Monty still considered himself principally a stage actor but, although he had had every opportunity to return to the stage, even in *Hamlet*, he did not do so. He worried, at times, that he had lost his nerve. Making films was easier and, with one notable exception, he never returned to the stage again. Hitchcock very much wanted Monty for this film: he had had his eye on him ever since he had first seen him in *The Search*, and had wanted him for *Rope*.

In *I Confess* he was to play a priest who faces the age-old dilemma of priests who hear criminal confessions and cannot divulge them. In this case the confession was from a murderer, and he would not reveal the identity of the killer even though he himself became suspected of the crime.

Hitchcock signed up Monty before settling on his leading lady. Olivia de Havilland, his first choice, met Hitchcock and Monty for lunch, as recorded in Robert LaGuardia's book. He was jumpy, and she felt he had changed since they had worked together on *The Heiress*. He now spoke more rapidly, even frantically at times. She suspected he might be spiking his drinks with drugs. Monty offered to drive her home after the meeting, but she refused as she had her own car. She added, 'and if I hadn't had my own car, I would still have said "no".'

She did not accept the part and it went to Anne Baxter, with whom Monty might have starred years earlier in *The Adventures of Tom Sawyer* had he not had acne. Miss Baxter was, in fact, Hitchcock's third choice. After de Havilland turned him down he favoured Swedish actress Anita Bjork, greatly admired for her portrayal of Strindberg's *Miss Julie* both on screen and on stage. But she had blown her chances when she had arrived at Warner Brothers, who were were producing the film, unmarried and with an illegitimate baby. In 1950 Ingrid Bergman had had director Roberto Rossellini's son out of wedlock. Her blatant behaviour had outraged audiences, to whom she was a scarlet woman. The Bergman scandal was still in people's minds and no one wanted a repeat. So Jack Warner cancelled Bjork's contract, and Miss Baxter had been hired just two weeks before shooting was to start.

I Confess was shot on location in Quebec and in studio in Hollywood. To prepare himself for the part Monty stayed at his friend Brother Thomas's monastery on the outskirts of Quebec. The monk was now in his twenties, but he and Monty still corresponded. Brother Thomas coached him on how to conduct himself as a priest. The normally heavy-drinking Monty remained teetotal for the week he was there, which showed his respect for Brother Thomas and his calling.

Mira joined him in Quebec for the shoot and they worked diligently, although he still felt some coldness towards her. Some evenings he would go out on the town, and sometimes he came back drunk.

Hitchcock and Monty did not get along, although Monty had been keen enough to work with him at first. The director found Monty's Method-style preparation for a role irritating. Hitchcock saw his film as a canvas and the actors as details, subservient to the whole. Monty felt he had to imbue every frame he shot with meaning, and, unless he was clear about his motivation, would not and could not act.

In one shot, for which Hitchcock had merely wanted Monty to look out of a window, the actor had driven him to distraction by searching for his motivation. There was none – Hitchcock simply wanted a linking shot.

Six years later, in 1958, when Hitchcock was making *North by Northwest*, James Mason pulled Hitchcock's leg by pretending to be excessively concerned about his motivation for a scene. Hitchcock responded, 'Sometimes that sort of thing really happens and, I can tell you, it's no joke.'* He went on to recall working with Monty and the trouble he had had when he had asked him to look out of a window for the linking shot. Mason adds, 'But . . . Clift was a magnificent actor, method in his madness or not.'

Other actors had found Hitchcock unhelpful, too. Doris Day was one. She had been thrilled when first told she would be working with him on *The Man Who Knew Too Much*, but the thrill wore off and she wrote of the experience in *Doris Day: Her Own Story*†.

He didn't direct. He didn't say a word. He just sat next to the camera, with an interpreter on either side of him [they were filming in Morocco], and all he did was start and stop the camera. Jimmy [Stewart] and I were left to our own devices. Hitch never spoke to me before a scene to tell me how he wanted it played, and he never spoke to me afterwards. On those evenings when we all had dinner, he was chatty and entertaining but we never spoke a word about the picture . . .

* *James Mason: Before I Forget* Hamish Hamilton, 1981
† *Doris Day: Her Own Story* by A.E. Hotchner, W.H. Allen, 1985

She said she felt like a 'lost soul' working with him. Monty felt like a lost soul even without working with Hitchcock, and he did not have such a hearty personality as Doris Day.

'There are some actors I've felt uncomfortable with,' Hitchcock recalled, 'and working with Montgomery Clift was difficult because he was a Method actor and neurotic as well.'*

For all his dedication, Monty was not always supportive to other actors. Anne Baxter found him difficult, but in her case – extraordinarily – because she felt he lacked motivation. Donald Spoto quoted her as saying she had to 'look longingly at him while baring my soul. To do that, I needed something, some response from him. But there was nothing, just a blank and distant gaze . . . he was so disturbed and unhappy, but Hitchcock never talked to him. He had the assistant director, Don Page, handle everything.' Anne Baxter realized that Monty was not being deliberately unpleasant, but was just allowing his personal problems to overtake his work. She ended up becoming very fond of him.

The cast stayed at the pleasant Chateau Elysee, but the atmosphere on the set was rarely pleasant. Mira's presence was disruptive, but Hitchcock was one of the few directors who did not ban her from the floor. Rather than reason with her himself, though, Hitchcock asked Karl Malden, who was playing a detective in the movie, to intervene. This was not easy, as Malden was an admirer of Mira's. He had many scenes with Monty and would work on these during the evenings with the two of them. He thought Mira contributed a great deal to character development.

Unfortunately, however, she did not seem interested in Malden's performance. Once a scene had been shot, all that Monty and Mira were concerned with was Monty's performance. Both would ignore Karl, as they did Hitchcock, and he felt he needn't have been in the scene. It soured his affection for them.

Monty distanced himself from the rest of the cast, huddling with Mira. Karl Malden told Donald Spoto, 'Monty depended on her, kept a distance from Hitchcock and from the rest of us to go over his lines with her, insisted on her approval before a scene could be shot. Naturally this created a deep division and tension.' The normally imperturbable Hitchcock was incensed, but kept his rage bottled up.

For his part Monty telephoned Silverberg, who had now replaced Mira as confessor. Monty was spiritually troubled. The faith of the

* The Life of Alfred Hitchcock: The Dark Side of Genius, by Donald Spoto, Harper Collins, 1983

monks, including Brother Thomas, had profoundly impressed him. He envied them and wished he had a faith of his own. When calling Silverberg Monty was reticent about giving the operator the number – terrified that reporters would discover he was consulting a psychiatrist. In those pre-Woody Allen days such a thing was considered shameful. In her dedicated, but now relegated, way Mira tried to help him too.

Although Hitchock had little patience with Monty as an actor he was intrigued by his sex life, or what he imagined it might be. His own tastes lay in the cool blondes he cast as his leading ladies, and he could not understand homosexuality. His enquiring mind wanted to learn more.

'He considered the actor something of an exotic,' Spoto continues.

> He found Clift's conduct difficult but psychologically intriguing ...
> In England Hitchcock had been almost wide-eyed over the discovery
> of the variations on sexual conduct, and his discoveries about actors
> like Ivor Novello, Henry Kendal, Charles Laughton and others were
> now repeated in the cases of Montgomery Clift and the German actor
> O.E. Hasse, who was playing the killer-sacristan. Hitchcock was
> not openly contemptuous, nor was he uneasy about their sexual
> conduct. He simply found the two men endlessly interesting.

At the end of the Quebec shoot the company returned to Hollywood to do interior scenes. Monty thought he had given a decent performance and Hitchcock, too, was optimistic. The director was a Catholic and had wanted to make a film on Catholicism for some time.

At the end-of-film dinner party which Hitchcock gave, Monty brought Mira who carried a single-stemmed rose. She kept it with her throughout the meal and regularly sniffed it, not contributing a great deal to the conversation. Hitchcock encouraged Monty to drink. Monty obliged and Hitchcock watched in sadistic fascination as his leading actor disintegrated before his eyes. 'The discomfort of the other guests increased as they watched Hitchcock enjoy Clift's swiftly diminishing sobriety, the systematic unravelling of his manner and coherence,' Spoto writes.

> Finally, after the actor had consumed a great deal of liquor and
> wine, Hitchcock poured him a full beaker of brandy and dared him
> to drink it in a single gulp. Anne Baxter and Karl Malden watched,
> motionless with horror, as the glass changed hands. Monty drank
> and, a moment later, fell to the floor, face down, in a perilous

alcoholic stupor. For a moment everyone stood more terrified
than embarrassed ... Karl Malden and his wife Mona sprang
to the moment and drove the unconscious actor home.

Hitchcock's feelings for Monty were summed up by another of the
director's biographers, John Russell Taylor.* 'Hitch's impatience with
the affectations of the Method actors was well known but he had
managed to do wonders with Eva Marie Saint [*North by Northwest*]
whom he liked and Montgomery Clift whom he didn't.'
I Confess did not do well at the box office and Hitchcock admitted
that, as a Catholic, his involvement with the subject matter had perhaps
clouded his judgement. He wondered if he was losing his touch and
whether, perhaps, Monty had contributed to that.

---

* *Hitch: The Life and Work of Alfred Hitchcock* by John Russell Taylor, Faber and Faber
Ltd, 1978

10

Before leaving Los Angeles Monty visited the Sunset Strip club where the anarchic Lenny Bruce was appearing. He never missed a Bruce performance if he could help it.

Back in New York he made the only political speech of his career. The presidential elections were coming up and he spoke in favour of Adlai Stevenson at a rally in Madison Square Garden. Stevenson had a glamour that appealed to many show business stars, and Henry Fonda and Lauren Bacall were also there. His brother Brooks went with him for support but their father Bill stayed at home. He was not a Stevenson supporter and had protested about Monty's appearance.

By this time Elizabeth Taylor had married Michael Wilding and given birth to her first son, Michael. Monty told her he envied her her child – which he did so long as it looked cute and did not cause too much inconvenience – and bought a tiny table and chair which sat ready in the duplex, waiting for Michael Wilding Jr to call with his famous mum. They did, quite often.

Libby Holman also came to visit. Not having met since *Mexican Mural* in 1942, they had bumped into each other again at Bobby Lewis's studios where they were both taking lessons, although in separate classes. Libby's town house was just a block away from his duplex on East 61st Street, and they resumed their friendship as though they had never been apart.

She was helpful to him on an artistic front and could, and did, offer valuable career advice. As Bobby Lewis put it, 'Libby wanted to own people and Monty wanted to be owned.'* A generation of teenagers was now in love with him, and it flattered Libby that he should seek her company.

They were an eye-catching couple, the highly made-up but fast-fading fifty-one-year-old torch singer and acquitted murder suspect and the eligible bachelor sixteen years her junior. There was something decadent about them. As Jon Bradshaw puts it: 'it remained an extraordinary alliance: a young homosexual who claimed to love women, and a middle-aged millionairess with a penchant for other women'.

Their relationship, in fact, was more wholesome than many. She discouraged him from smoking (she was down to four camphor cigarettes a day due to ill health) and drinking (Libby had ulcers and was virtually teetotal), which, as he was teetering into alcoholism, was no bad thing.

But they had much in common. Both were hypochondriacs with digestive problems which obliged them to drink pints of milk and eat raw meat. They spent whole evenings discussing ailments and medicines and would swap prescription drugs. Both, in the right company, were compulsive talkers. When Monty was on form, he could talk till dawn. Both were also insatiable readers, Libby almost compulsively so: in addition to books she read at least four newspapers each day. At the time she was converting to Zen Buddhism and devouring its literature, eagerly expounding its ethics to anyone who would listen. Both loved Europe and were excellent linguists, speaking fluent French and German. And both were emotional masochists.

In many ways she was a surrogate mother to him. Everything Libby stood for was opposed to Sunny. She courted notoriety where Sunny yearned for respectability. The aristocratic relations whom Sunny craved would have avoided Libby like the plague.

Libby was reputed to be a dope addict, and Monty was beginning to acquire a similar reputation, although the legend was yet to balloon into the proportions it was later to attain. It was gossiped that they indulged in narcotic orgies at Treetops, Libby's country mansion where she kept the Strawberry Suite permanently at Monty's disposal. If they ever descended into drugged degeneracy, as rumour had it, then Libby must have had the constitution of an ox as she was regularly giving recitals and receiving excellent reviews. Her songs demanded

* *Dreams That Money Can Buy* by Jon Bradshaw, Jonathan Cape, 1985

musicianship, memory and discipline, and no one bombed out of their mind could have sung them.

The Strawberry Suite was close to Libby's own suite and Monty was such an appalling house guest that he would keep her awake at night, tramping the floors and playing the gramophone. Libby had difficulty sleeping at the best of times, and when she did drop off did not take kindly to being woken. Her devoted maid Alice, who had been with her for years, was forever creeping into the Strawberry Suite in the dead of night to try to persuade Monty to keep the noise down. He was apologetic and she would stay with him, stroking his head until he fell asleep himself. Before leaving she would lock the door to stop him prowling about when sleepwalking, as he still sometimes did. When he stayed, Libby sometimes looked like death in the mornings, and it would have been easy to believe they had been indulging in undiluted debauchery.

Many people were convinced that Monty and Libby were having an affair, but, as with Elizabeth Taylor, his relationship with her was platonic. By this time Libby's face was heavily wrinkled from exposure to the tropical sun, and even the most predatory heterosexual would have had difficulty viewing her as an object of desire.

They did sometimes sleep together, for company, but not often. Both being insomniacs, they drove each other mad. Jon Bradshaw writes in his biography of Libby, 'the sexual act itself was not what captivated Libby. She sought instead the ensuing intimacy, its friendship and camaraderie. For Libby, making love was an act of solidarity and, for all her bravado, she was sexually insecure.'

That summer Libby toured Britain with her one-woman show *Blues, Ballads and Sin-Songs* – she was furious when the 3500-seater Lyric Theatre, Hammersmith, the climax of the tour, refused to allow the words 'Sin-Songs' to be illuminated outside the theatre, deeming them indecent. While she was away Monty continued to use Treetops as his own. In town he moved into her brownstone with Jeanne and Fred Green – Fred was still renovating his duplex including, at Monty's specification, the installation of a 14-foot medicine chest. He did not charge Monty a cent for his work, so as a thank you present Monty gave him a magnificent gold watch inscribed 'To a timeless friend'. Fred later found out it had been a Christmas present to Monty from MCA, the famous actor's agency. It was, nevertheless, a gold watch.

Libby returned from Britain and took her show on the road from Boston to New York. After the tour she joined Monty at Treetops and encouraged him to bring his friends there. Among those invited were

Roddy McDowall, Billy Le Massena and Jack Larson, the actor who is now best remembered as Jimmy Olsen, Superman's side-kick (pre Dean Cain days). Libby and Monty clearly adored each other, kissing and holding hands. They even began to look alike at a distance, although their faces could not be less similar, but both were lean and tanned. Monty spent hours sunbathing by her Olympic-sized pool.

Patricia Bosworth recounts how composer Alec Wilder was a member of Libby's pool party one weekend and, watching the nut-brown, thin Libby and Monty frolicking, remarked, 'Look, there's Mahatma Gandhi and her disciple.' It was well known that Libby donated generously to Gandhi's cause. There was always plenty of wit at Libby's, just as there were plenty of gays.

While Monty was in Quebec he had been visited by Vittorio De Sica. Although revered in Italy since the 1930s, it was not until a decade later that De Sica's neo-realistic direction began to be appreciated by the American film world, largely because of his award-winning 1947 film *Bicycle Thieves*. Using non-professional actors and a simple story, De Sica had achieved a movie which, as Halliwell's *Filmgoer's Companion* says, 'was an . . . absorbing and brilliant film which influenced film making in every country where it was seen'.

It had influenced Monty, who enthused over the director's stark technique and his European naturalism. He had agreed to do a film with De Sica when he had met him in Milan and now the details had been finalized. The film would be made in both Italian and English. Its Italian title would be *Stazione Termini*, while in America it was called *Indiscretion of an American Wife*. The original story was by Cesare Zavattini, the writer of *Bicycle Thieves*.

David O. Selznick was also impressed. The producer of *Gone with the Wind*, and much else, believed that by working with De Sica he would be able to gain a greater percentage of the all-important European market. He saw the film as a vehicle to give his new wife, actress Jennifer Jones, European status. As much as Selznick wanted to cash in on the European market, the Europeans wanted to cash in on Hollywood. Everyone thought they were on to a winner. Monty, and Jennifer Jones and the rest of the American party flew into a freezing Rome in the autumn of 1952.

Monty brought his boyfriend Dino, who spoke Italian. Mira was not with him, but he felt safe in De Sica's hands. This was false optimism – De Sica's hands were tied by Selznick, who was in Rome to supervise the film. De Sica was also the producer, but Selznick imperiously over-ruled him, firing off dozens of his memos famed for their quantity and frequency in the process. *Stazione Termini* was a disaster and one person was to blame – David O. Selznick.

The story was simplicity itself, which was what had attracted Monty in the first place – *Bicycle Thieves* had had very little story line. It concerned an Italian professor (Monty) and his adulterous love affair with an American housewife (Jennifer Jones) who was in Rome on holiday. It was set in Rome's new station terminus at night as they are about to part, marking the end of their affair.

De Sica intended to shoot in the sparse way he had shot *Bicycle Thieves*: 'neo-realism' was his hallmark. But Selznick would have none of it – he wanted European prestige but Hollywood know-how, and was appalled by the crude standards of the Italian technicians. He also supervised his scriptwriters and was unhappy with what they supplied. He had spared no expense and had commissioned both Paul Gallico and Carson McCullers to write the English script. Both were eventually paid off. McCullers was actually sacked (and immensely relieved to be off the job), and Truman Capote, then living in Rome, was hired to salvage things.

Capote had been Selznick's original choice but had taken so long to accept that by the time he had done so the job had gone. 'It would have been dishonest of me to have accepted it,' he later told his biographer Gerald Clarke*, 'for I did not feel at all sympathetic to the story they had outlined.' He was no more sympathetic when he did accept, and only took the job because he was broke and nothing else had turned up.

It seemed to Monty that the station was the coldest place in the Eternal City. By the time he arrived Capote was already hired but script skirmishes were still taking place daily. 'Again transformed into a frantic scribbler, he was in a constant huddle with the illustrious Selznick,' writes Clarke. The crew were having to work all through the night to make up lost time. While Monty and Jennifer Jones waited in one room, she in her Hollywood mink and he in a duffle coat, Capote and Selznick quarrelled in another, after which Capote would dash off a page of script for the actors to film.

De Sica's English was not good and he wanted to employ an Italian actor, whom he could direct, to act the scene out as he wanted it. Monty could then copy him. This went down with Monty as well as Carson McCullers' script had gone down with Selznick, and he was ready to catch the next plane home. They reached an unhappy compromise when De Sica hired an interpreter. This made Monty jumpy.

* *Truman Capote: A Biography* by Gerald Clarke, Hamish Hamilton, 1988

Selznick was constantly bombarding everyone with memos and advice. He was already disillusioned about European technical facilities but, as David Thomson writes in *Showman*, there was also another difficulty. 'More serious, he felt, was the photographic problem. The Italians were not trained in glamour, and De Sica did not favour close-ups. Realism required long shots and unadorned faces. Jennifer, David complained, was looking terrible . . .'* Selznick had imagined huge close-ups of Jones cascading on to the screen in the manner of *A Place in the Sun*. He was not getting them, so he brought in his own close-up cameraman. De Sica resisted futilely. To Selznick's bewilderment De Sica seemed more interested in the untrained actors than his two stars.

According to David Thomson, Monty and Jennifer Jones got along splendidly. Too splendidly for Selznick's liking. She was having marital problems and, like other powerful and beautiful women before her, confided in Monty. She felt she could trust him with anything. They spoke into the small hours of the night in the freezing station, snuggling together in a carriage for warmth, she talking more than him, as they waited for Capote to deliver their script.

She told him she was 'madly in love' with Selznick but found his 'emotional instability . . . almost as bad as her own.' Monty did not reveal too much of himself, which Jones did not notice in her need to explain her own difficulties. He knew, as did the crew, that she was developing a crush on him. He let it happen, as he always did. Monty could never resist people falling for him.

At one point Selznick interrupted a Clift–Jones nocturnal heart-to-heart by banging on the carriage window with a newspaper to deliver what he considered essential advice for the forthcoming shoot. In a fury, Jones leaped from the carriage and ran through the streets. Selznick followed in the limousine, yelling through the window for her to stop. De Sica watched silently as he set up his shots for his untrained, and bewildered, actors.

It wasn't the first occasion on which Jones had lost patience with her husband. Earlier, after she and Monty had played a love scene in both Italian and English several times, he arrived with rewrites and asked them to do it again. She belted Selznick so hard across his face that his glasses broke. He was almost blind without them and did not have a spare pair.

Monty knew the film was not going well, and feared for his

---

* *Showman: The Life of David O. Selznick* by David Thompson, Abacus, 1993

reputation. He was disappointed that things had not worked out with De Sica. Behind his back, David Thomson records, he called Selznick an 'interfering fuckface'.

Noting how close Monty and Jones were, someone thought it expedient to tell her he was gay. If she did not already know this she must have been one of the very few Hollywood people who did not. According to Truman Capote, however, it so upset her that she locked herself in a toilet, that being the most private place she could find, and could be heard sobbing. She was wearing her mink, a present from her husband, and is reported to have stuffed it down the lavatory bowl in frustration, pulling the chain.

De Sica shot all night and tried to sleep during the day. But this was impossible as Selznick, who seemed never to sleep, would summon him to meetings. As these were in English he barely understood them, so he was forced to hire a lawyer to protect his interests. The railway staff were constantly complaining about the disruption that the film crew was causing. The train drivers were dazzled by the arc lights which obliterated signals. Selznick was requested to speed things up or he would be asked to leave on safety grounds.

Monty and Capote formed a bond, which had by no means been a foregone conclusion. Although both were homosexual, this was no guarantee they would get along. Monty detested effeminate homosexuals such as Capote, but he respected writers and there was no doubt that Capote could write.

Capote had already met Monty casually in New York, but in Rome they became buddies. 'Monty was really gifted,' said Capote

He was serious about only one thing, and that was acting. He was an exception to the theory that a movie star has to be ignorant to be good. You have to be smart to be on the stage, but a film actor is just a conduit for the writer, the director and everybody else who puts something into a picture. He has to react to what they do. If he's too smart, he resists them and then he's no good. Brando never really made it as a movie star – he always resisted. Garbo, on the other hand, never had a thought in her head and she was fabulous! She was the perfect instrument for the writer and director. Monty was smart and good, but that was because he was also very shrewd: he knew just what he was doing.

I once asked him why he wanted to act in movies, why he didn't do something more interesting. He looked at me and said, 'You don't understand. It's my life. This is what I know

how to do.' He was an artist with all of an artist's sensibilities
and flaws.

Unfortunately their friendship was upset when Capote and Monty
quarrelled over Dino. A straight-looking former married man, he was
the same age as Monty and handsome as well. Capote, tubby, ugly
and camp, felt out of things, unable to compete. He could win Monty
over intellectually, but not physically. And physically was where he
longed to be. He resented, and envied, the physical magnetism Dino
exerted on Monty. Back in America Capote and Monty patched things
up. Monty and Dino went their separate ways: the pressure of Rome
finished things.

In Hollywood Selznick did what he could for the film with which
he had hoped to make his European reputation but which he now
hated. Whichever way it was viewed it was a boring mess. He cut it
down to sixty-three minutes, unworkably short for a main feature, and
discarded almost a third of De Sica's footage. Just to show his revised
opinion of neo-realism he added over the credits a love song, sung by
Patti Page, who was to have a hit the following year with 'How Much
Is That Doggie in the Window?' He retitled the movie *Indiscretion of
an American Wife*.

As everyone expected, it was a flop. Truman Capote thought it 'lousy',
according to Gerald Clarke – just two of his scenes remained in the
Selznick edit – and critics and public agreed with him. '*Indiscretion* is,
for the gifted men who made it, an indiscretion indeed,' wrote one critic.
Relegated to a second feature in both England and the USA, it turns up
on television now and then. Selznick did not, however, have control
over the Italian version. *Stazione Termini* ran for over two hours and,
although not considered De Sica's best, it is admired to this day.

Monty confided his disappointment to Elizabeth Taylor, who was
about to leave for a holiday in Copenhagen. She had replaced Vivien
Leigh in *Elephant Walk*. Vivien, as fragile as Blanche Dubois, had suffered
another mental setback and Liz was chosen because of their similarity.
They were so alike that some of the existing long shots of Vivien could
be used in the finished film – no one could tell them apart.

While on location a metal splinter had lodged in Elizabeth's eye,
necessitating surgery. 'Bessie Mae is the only person I know who
had more wrong with her than I have,' said Monty in Kitty Kelley's
biography of Elizabeth Taylor.

After *Elephant Walk* Elizabeth made MGM's *Rhapsody* for Charles
Vidor, who had directed Rita Hayworth in *Gilda*. *Rhapsody* was a

Technicolor romance, featuring some of the world's best-known classical music. Elizabeth's character was a socialite in love with a violinist and a pianist at the same time – the violinist was Vittorio Gassman, who had recently married Shelley Winters, while the pianist was John Ericson, Fred Zinnemann's *Teresa* discovery. Like Ralph Meeker, Ericson was a Brando casualty – they looked too much alike and their styles were similar. The handsome, gifted Ericson never rose to the top Hollywood echelon, something which has always puzzled Zinnemann.

Monty, Elizabeth and Wilding were invited to a party by TV chat show host Merv Griffin. Elizabeth had just been robbed of $17,000-worth of jewellery, but she ordered replacements from Bulgari and tried not to let it spoil the evening. Roddy McDowall was also there, as were Jane Powell and heart-throb crooner Eddie Fisher.

His next film was *From Here to Eternity*, a satisfactory treatment of which had finally been delivered to Columbia Pictures. Scriptwriter Dan Taradash managed to condense Jones's 800-page novel into 160 pages, which would edit into a two-hour film. Harry Cohn, founder and head of Columbia, was now in a position to go ahead. But not before he had made his considerable presence felt on cast and production staff.

From Here to Eternity tells the story of a group of soldiers, based in Schofield Barracks, Honolulu, during the time leading up to the Japanese attack on Pearl Harbor. Ever since he had met Jones Monty had wanted to play Robert E. Lee Prewitt, the bugling boxer soldier who refused to fight for his regiment because he had once blinded an opponent. He is bullied by a sadistic sergeant who attempts to coerce him into changing his mind.

As its director, Fred Zinnemann, put it in the documentary *His Place in the Sun*: 'To me it was the story about the spirit of a man who will not bow down . . . a man who will not box for reasons of his own no matter how great the pressure. In the end he gets killed because of that.'

Columbia head Harry Cohn, a former song plugger, was one of the most detested men in the industry. Hedda Hopper dubbed him 'a sadistic son of a bitch', and when he died Red Skelton quipped, 'Give the public something they want and they'll turn out for it.' Fred Zinnemann was not so vicious, and in his autobiography describes him as 'a gambler and extremely aggressive man whom I got to know and almost like – later on'. Photographs of Cohn often show him with a cigar jammed in his slit mouth. He looks as though he'd be more at home with Al Capone than with actors.

But he was a character and devoted to his trade. He had founded Columbia in 1924 and throughout the 1930s specialized in B pictures, small fry compared to MGM and Warner's. In the 1940s he had become more ambitious and made some shrewd judgements, including putting Rita Hayworth under contract and turning out hits like *Gilda*, *The Jolson Story* and *Born Yesterday*, which won an Oscar for its star Judy Holliday. Columbia was now a force with which to be reckoned.

When Cohn bought the rights to *From Here to Eternity* few people in the industry shared his enthusiasm for the book, which was referred to as 'Cohn's Folly'. The story required a cast of hundreds of trained soldiers and could not be made without the cooperation of the army. But it was unlikely that the army would cooperate as the novel depicted aspects of it in a bad light. In addition to this there were explicit sex scenes and foul language which would have been right for the army but wrong for the Hays Production Code – named after Will H. Hays, author of the code – the somewhat puritanical movie industry rules which were still in force at this date. There were other hurdles, of which Zinnemann writes in his autobiography:

> It is necessary to see the making of *From Here to Eternity* in the overall context of the time when it was shot. The year was 1953, long before the Vietnam War, Watergate and the era of disillusion. There was an automatic respect for Federal authority. To voice doubts about any of its symbols – the Army, Navy or FBI – was to lay oneself open to deep suspicion. McCarthyism was still very much alive, and filming a book so openly scathing about the peacetime Army . . . was regarded by many as foolhardy if not downright subversive.

It was thanks to Dan Taradash that Zinnemann was hired as director. Taradash had seen *Teresa*, liked the way Zinnemann portrayed soldiers, and recommended him to Cohn. But that was no guarantee that he would be hired. As Zinnemann says, 'I was still known as an "art-house" director, or a "director's director", meaning good reviews but no box-office.' After convincing Cohn that he could do the job, Zinnemann told him he wanted Monty for the part of Prewitt.

This was not good news. Cohn had already decided that Aldo Ray was to play the part. Ray, who had made a big hit with *The Marrying Kind*, Judy Holliday's follow-up to *Born Yesterday*, was under contract to Cohn, who could see no reason to hire another actor, particularly one less well cut out, on the face of it, to play a boxing soldier. Ray was tough and handsome, with the physique of a boxer. As Cohn said, the girls liked him. He was also a fine actor – perfect casting.

Not to Zinnemann, though, as he recounted in his autobiography. He asked Cohn why he wanted him.

"'What d'you mean, why?" Cohn exploded. "Because he's under contract here, he hasn't worked for ten weeks, his salary's mounting up."' Zinnemann told him he would prefer Montgomery Clift.

'That was when Cohn became very angry indeed,' Zinnemann writes. 'The sense of his tirade was that this was an idiotic suggestion. Clift was wrong for the part . . . He was no soldier and no boxer and probably a homosexual . . .'

Cohn countered by offering to let Zinnemann test John Derek, the actor built along Tony Curtis lines who had rocketed to fame in *Knock on Any Door*. Zinnemann would not budge and threatened to walk off the film if he did not get Monty. He gives his reasons for insisting on him:

'The first paragraph in Jones' book describes Prewitt as a "deceptively slim young man",' Zinnemann writes.

It was just that quality, the 'deceptive slimness', I needed to give an edge to Prewitt's character. I wanted Clift because this story was not about a fellow who didn't want to box: it was about the human spirit refusing to be broken, about a man who resists all sorts of pressure from an institution he loves, who becomes an outsider, and eventually dies for it. It was quite clear to me, if difficult to explain, what Clift would make of that character . . .

'I left him [Cohn] screaming', Zinnemann continues. 'But he did send the script to Clift the next day.'

As a goodwill gesture Zinnemann did test Derek, but this only confirmed what he already knew. Monty was his man. Cohn did not take that kindly, either, and upon being introduced to Zinnemann's wife greeted her with, 'Your husband is a louse.' His only hope was that Monty might turn down the script.

Cohn wanted the film in Technicolor. Although the cost worked out at about 1½ cents per foot more expensive than black and white, he wanted the prestige and, his sales department told him, he could expect to gross another million with colour. But Zinnemann objected to that too, on the grounds it would make the film 'soft and trivial'.

As soon as Monty heard from Zinnemann that he had the part he flew to see James Jones at his home in Arizona and grilled him about Prewitt until he knew exactly what Jones had had in mind. He already had a good idea as he had been talking to Jones about the character ever since they had first met. Jones, a former army man, had no reservations about Monty and had wanted him for the part from the start. Once he was back in New York Monty trained in earnest at his gym to get fit and look like an active soldier. He was up at six every morning jogging and taking drill practice.

His fee was $150,000, which resulted in some family arguments. Bill thought Monty should entrust the money to him to invest, and was convinced he could double it. But Monty would not allow his father to touch a cent. It was not that he did not trust his financial judgement, he simply did not want him interfering in his life. Bill was deeply hurt but Monty would not budge.

Other stars of the film included Donna Reed, who was to be Monty's love interest, Burt Lancaster, Ernest Borgnine, Frank Sinatra and Deborah Kerr. The latter photographed uncannily like a cool version of Marilyn Monroe.

Kerr had not been Cohn's first choice, either, for Karen, the adulterous wife. He had wanted Joan Crawford and made her a down payment of $100,000, but in addition she had insisted on her own house in Hawaii and her personal clothes designer. A row developed and she walked out. 'Fuck her!' said Cohn.*

While the role of Karen was still uncast, Kerr's agent rang Cohn suggesting his client. At a conference later, Cohn told Taradash and Zinnemann of the call. 'You know who this stupid son of a bitch suggested? Deborah Kerr.' According to Wiley and Bona's *Inside Oscar*, Zinnemann and Taradash looked at each other and exclaimed: 'What a great idea!' Kerr was aware of her debutante-type reputation and, wrote Zinnemann, when putting on her swimsuit for her beach love scene with Burt Lancaster quipped, 'I feel naked without my tiara.'

Sinatra was to play Maggio, Prewitt's weedy, mouthy friend. At the time he was married to Ava Gardner and his career was in the doldrums. Cohn thought he was washed up and, as with Monty and Kerr, had not wanted him. Unknown to Sinatra, Ava Gardner, who knew how important the part was to him, went to see Cohn's wife Joan and pleaded with her to try to influence her husband to give it him. She then went to Africa to film *Mogambo* with Clark Gable and Grace Kelly. Sinatra, having little else to do, went with her.

Joan did speak to her husband. Others, too, were enthusiastic about Sinatra, so Cohn reluctantly agreed to try him out. He phoned Africa and told Sinatra, with all the charm for which he was famous,

---

* *Bette and Joan: The Divine Feud* by Shaun Considine, Frederick Muller, 1989

that he could test for Maggio if he paid his own fare back to Hollywood.

Sinatra was back at Columbia almost before Cohn had hung up. Cohn and Zinnemann liked his test, but by now Eli Wallach was in the frame and Cohn wanted him. Then Zinnemann was told that Wallach had put himself out of the race by accepting an offer from Elia Kazan to play in Tennessee Williams's *Camino Real* on Broadway. Later, Zinnemann was told that this might not have been the whole truth: Wallach's agent had asked for too much money. This was certainly not so with Sinatra, who agreed to do the part for the insultingly small salary of $8000.

It was one of the wisest decisions he ever made. The film put his career together again. From then on he was taken seriously both as an actor and as a singer. He switched recording labels to Capitol and his singing career hit unprecedented heights.

Monty was awed to have the chance of working with Sinatra. He was one of his heroes, and in later years the singer's photograph stood on his mantelpiece.

Before filming, Monty intensified his preparation for the part. Mira flew with him to Hollywood and they worked on his scenes. Sinatra was also there and they worked together, overseen by Mira.

Unfortunately Mira and Monty had a serious argument while in Hollywood. His driving was as perilous as ever, and a few days previously he had drunkenly sent his car through someone's hedge. The police were called but because he was working with the influential Harry Cohn, who contributed generously to police charities, no charges were pressed. According to Mira, Monty was shaken and asked her to telephone Silverberg. But she was curtly ordered by Silverberg not to interfere between doctor and patient.

Monty was furious when he learnt she had phoned Silverberg, claiming to have no recollection of having asked her to do so. He told her to leave. Mira could always tell when he had been talking to Silverberg about her. He was hostile.

Filming started in Hollywood in March 1953, and then the company were to move location to Hawaii. 'Clift rose brilliantly to the occasion,' Zinnemann writes. 'The script required him to play the bugle, be a champion boxer and a well-drilled soldier. He knew nothing about any of these things but learnt them all.' He took boxing lessons – in *Red River* he had already learnt from Mushy Calahan how to pack a punch; 'Make me look like Sugar Ray Robinson,' he had told him – spent hours at bayonet practice, and learnt how to do perfect drill and studied the bugle with Manny Kline. 'By the time Monty was ready for the cameras,' Zinnemann continued, 'one could have sworn that he had bugled all his life and that he was a top soldier *and* a good boxer.' He spent hours searching music shops for a mouthpiece similar to the one Prewitt would have used. He had taken boxing lessons during the making of *Red River*; now that he had to play a boxer, with his customary dedication to his craft, he took further, more intensive coaching.

He stayed at the Roosevelt Hotel in room 928, where he would spend hours practising the bugle. Some believe he still does. According to the American television programme *Hollywood Hauntings*, the sound of a bugle can still sometimes be heard in the vicinity of that room. Several guests have reported it and a waitress named Teryl Valazza claims to have heard footsteps behind her in the corridor and felt an icy chill there. Patrick MacNee, who fronted the show, wondered whether Monty's spirit was still stalking the corridor.

In April the team moved to Honolulu. Military cooperation was finally agreed when certain changes were made to the script. Producer Buddy Adler, himself a former army man, had no option other than to comply if the film was to be made. Zinnemann's presence helped: he had treated army personnel sympathetically in three films, *The Search*, *The Men* (Brando's debut film) and his latest, *Teresa*. The theme of adultery had to be handled delicately so as not to offend the Hays censorship office.

Monty coached Sinatra as Maggio. 'Good dialogue simply isn't enough to explain all the infinite gradations of a character,' he told him.

'I learned more about acting from him than I ever knew before,' Sinatra commented. 'But he's an exhausting man.'*

In the evenings, after a hard day with Monty, Sinatra was ready to relax, and to telephone Ava Gardner who was still filming in Africa. But Monty, ever the idealist, would still be putting him through his paces.

He shaved his chest to play Prewitt. There are occasions in the film when he had to appear without his shirt, and he was self-conscious of his hairy body which he hated displaying on screen. He did not think Prewitt would have had a hairy chest. Hairy chests were associated with virility, and Prewitt's strength was hidden. In the main, Hollywood heroes did not have hairy chests – they were for the bad guys like Steve Cochran. The Hays office did not like them either, perceiving them as smacking of unacceptable eroticism.

---

* *His Way: The Unauthorised Biography of Frank Sinatra* by Kitty Kelley, Bantam Press, 1986

Deborah Kerr had just finished *Julius Caesar* with Brando. She and Monty talked about filming Shakespeare, and he told her his dream of playing Hamlet. But he would always return to discussing Prewitt. 'His concentration was positively violent,' she told journalist Michael Munn. 'We only had one scene together, I walked behind him and Monty was supposed to say to Burt "Who's that?" He spent two days figuring out how to say "Who's that?"'

Sometimes, Monty, Sinatra and James Jones would gather in one or other of their rooms for some serious drinking. All three might pass out and Burt Lancaster would put them to bed: 'Monty and Frank would get roaring drunk every night,' Lancaster recalls. 'And I had to carry them to their rooms every night, undress them and put them to bed. Frank took to calling me "mom" and still does.'*

Lancaster found Monty 'complicated' but revered him as an actor: 'I'll never forget when we shot our first scene together,' he told Michael Munn. 'It was the only time that I could not stop my knees from shaking because he had such power. His concentration was enormous. Just as well the camera was only shooting me above my waist as the world would have seen my knees knocking.'

Monty carried Jones's novel around with him all the time, referring to it whenever he had a query about motivation. He never stopped amending his script. He would ring his friend Patricia Collinge in New York to discuss Prewitt's character. They even went into Prewitt's parentage. He just could not get enough of Prewitt. His friend Jack Larson, who had been in *I Confess* with him, was also in the film. In the absence of Mira, Monty would play his scenes to him.

Donna Reed was Prewitt's girlfriend. Robert LaGuardia writes that she recalled Monty being aloof – probably shy – before they worked together, but when they were due to do a scene he telephoned: a long, friendly call so they could bond. When they came together on the set she felt his immense magnetism. 'It was a shock,' she said. 'No actor ever affected me that way. I was just stunned.' On one occasion Brando visited and stood by silently while Monty worked, filled with admiration.

Monty had one lapse, during a night shoot, when alcohol rendered him too drunk to say his lines. Sinatra tried to sober him up by slapping his face, but got no reaction. He took Monty to his trailer and whatever happened there, whether he cajoled, flattered or threatened, he returned to the set with a sheepish Monty who was able to continue.

* *Burt Lancaster: The Terrible Tempered Charmer* by Michael Munn, Robson Books, 1995

Although Monty coached Sinatra, Sinatra retained his own method, and Zinnemann had to reconcile their styles. Sinatra was at his best in the first or second take, whereas Monty needed more time. 'Clift would use each take as a rehearsal to add more detail so that the scenes gained in depth as we went on,' Zinnemann wrote in his autobiography. He added, 'By his intensity he forced the other actors to come up to his standard of performance.'

Ernest Borgnine was playing Fatso Judson, the sadistic sergeant who batters Maggio to death in the stockade and whom Monty, in revenge, fatally stabs in a fight. Borgnine was twice Monty's weight, but Monty was a match for him. No stunt man deputized for either of them. Borgnine complained afterwards that Monty had punched him black and blue. He was not the first actor to complain of Monty's realism during a fight, and he would not be the last. Clark Gable was to threaten to kill him for the same reason when later they made *The Misfits* together.

Towards the end of the shoot Harry Cohn arrived and stayed in a suite at the Royal Hawaiian Hotel. He did not interfere, except for one night shoot where Maggio and Prewitt are in a park. Maggio is drunk and attacks two military policemen. Zinnemann's intention was that Sinatra should jump up to attack, and this was how the scene had been rehearsed. But Cohn was warned by army PR that this would be unacceptably aggressive and ordered Zinnemann to shoot it with Sinatra seated. Zinnemann thought he could get away with it as rehearsed, but one of Cohn's spies telephoned and warned him what was going on. He arrived with a posse of military brass. Fearing that to do the scene his way could lead to the closing down of the entire picture, Zinnemann gave in to Cohn. As he says, 'It was a situation I could not win.'

James Jones was livid, but by that time his novel had been so diluted, particularly the sequences of prison brutality, that he barely recognized it anyway. He had never recovered from the initial insult when his screenplay had been turned down in favour of the Taradash version.

Sinatra, too, was furious, but for once Monty understood the director's problem and sided with him. Sinatra hit him. They got over it – what was a smack in the face between drinking buddies?

Nerves became more frayed as the shoot dragged to a close. Cohn was again summoned from his dinner table at the Royal Hawaiian one evening. In his white tuxedo and a black temper, he roared up to the set in a limousine and laid into everyone. How dare the actors not obey the director? How dare the director not follow the script? How dare the producer drag him away from his dinner and not sort things out himself? After giving them a thorough dressing down he drove away to resume his meal.

Almost everyone on the film noticed Monty's air of unhappiness. Deborah Kerr put it down to his chronic struggle with his homosexuality: 'He wanted to love women but he was attracted to men, and he crucified himself for it,' she told Patricia Bosworth. Miss Bosworth also records that James Jones added, 'Monty had a special kind of pain, a pain he could not release. He had a tragedy hanging over his head like a big, black comic-strip cloud.'

Jones later told Monty's friend Jeanne Green that, if it would have cheered Monty up, he would have had an affair with him himself. Monty was as sexually attracted to the cigar-smoking James Jones, in his silver jewellery and stupid cowboy boots, as he was to Alfred Hitchcock.

While tidy-up shots were being done back at Columbia, Monty, Sinatra and James again stayed at the Roosevelt. Occasionally the management had to reprimand them for obstreperous behaviour. James was no help in that department – heavy drinking was a part of his charisma. Sometimes, at night, Monty would wake him up by tapping on his window, having crawled down the fire escape with a bottle of scotch. Sinatra was having problems with Ava Gardner and, when drunk, threatened suicide. Monty, also drunk, long-windedly talked him out of it. He wouldn't have done it anyway.

One of the most moving moments in the film is when Prewitt plays the last post on his bugle after Maggio has been killed. He does not speak, but simply walks to his position and plays. His face says it all. The music silences the whole camp and the shot then cuts to Burt Lancaster, who mutters, 'I bet that's Prewitt'. It is in fact Manny Kline who is playing so poignantly, but Monty had mastered the movements of every muscle in his face, lips and throat in order to synchronise with him.

Zinnemann always remained unhappy about certain script changes he was forced to make to pacify the army. The one that particularly grated, he wrote in his autobiography, involved the promotion of the 'villainous captain to the rank of major. The Army would have none of that . . . it led to the worst moment in the film, resembling a recruiting short. It makes me sick every time I see it. Today most of the sardonic comments of the novel could be filmed without much trouble; to have tried using them in 1953 would have meant giving up the film altogether.'

The entire movie was shot in forty-one days, starting in early March and ending in early May. Even more incredibly, it was released only three months later. Cohn insisted that the finished print should not run one second longer than two hours. Zinnemann brought it in at 118 minutes.

One evening, while Zinnemann and his assistant were editing, Cohn arrived. He knew they would be working long into the night and, to boost morale, took them out for an expensive dinner – they would return to work afterwards. The restaurant stipulated that ties must be worn and none of them was wearing one. Cohn summoned a terrified wardrobe assistant from his studios and ordered him to get hold of three ties immediately. All the man could find were cheap, garish items and these had to do. After the meal Zinnemann was staggered when Cohn demanded his ties back.

The preview took place in front of an audience of two hundred in a specially adapted theatre in which the seats had been fitted with electronic levers that the viewers could move to the left if they did not like something and to the right if they did. Their reactions would be recorded on a graph.

No one made a sound during the movie, although the levers could be heard moving. Zinnemann anxiously paced the floor of the projection room and took the silence as disapproval. He thought the film had flopped. But Cohn had the graph in another room and came rushing in, waving it above his head so that it streamed after him like a bridal veil. The audience had loved it and he was sure he had a hit. 'It was eerie to see human reactions reduced to this 25 foot roll of paper,' wrote Zinnemann, Today, everything is reduced to a graph.

Cohn decided on immediate distribution and publicized the film in his own inimitable way. He made it known in the trade papers that he would open at Broadway's Capitol Theatre on 5 August 1953. Cinemas were not air-conditioned then, and no major picture ever opened in the sweltering heat of August. He decreed there would be no advertising and no glitzy premiere. He took out a full-page advertisement in the *New York Times*, signed by him as President of Columbia, stating how proud he was of his movie. Word of mouth got round that he had something special.

Zinnemann was in Los Angeles when the picture opened, and recalls that night in his autobiography: 'At 9pm Marlene Dietrich (whom I hardly knew) called from New York and said that it was midnight there but the Capitol Theater was bulging, people were standing around the block and there was an extra performance starting at one in the morning! I said, "How is this possible? There has been no publicity." "They smell it," she said.'

After the shoot Monty had gone to Cape Cod where he stayed with Kevin McCarthy's sister Mary. He swam, read and entertained in restaurants a little. As usual, he was not the most considerate house guest. While there he had another minor car accident, but remembered nothing of it. He would black out at times, though fortunately not at the wheel – yet.

He returned to New York for the opening of *From Here to Eternity*, which he attended with Sinatra. As there was no official premiere the management sneaked them in. He was disappointed in his performance. The critics were not. 'Montgomery Clift adds another sensitive portrayal to an already imposing gallery with his portrayal of Prewitt,' wrote Bosley Crowther in the *New York Times*. The *New York Herald* described Monty as 'taut and sensitive as he takes what is dished out to him, suppresses his love for the bugle except for one ringing "Taps" and transfers his emotions to a pretty prostitute. He makes himself indigestible to the Army, almost wilfully, but he always has sympathy on his side, even in an occasional murder.'

From Cohn's initial outlay of $2½ million, *Eternity* grossed $19 million. It turned out to be the biggest money-maker Columbia ever produced and the second-highest grossing film of 1953. In third place was George Stevens's *Shane*, which Monty had turned down.

Cohn wrote to the trade papers expressing his delight: 'It is heartening to us – and to the industry – to know that the payoff in our business still exists for fine entertainment. Give them the kind of pictures they want and the American public – bless 'em – will still beat down your doors.'

Some time after the film's release James Jones called unexpectedly, bringing a girlfriend. It was never wise to call unannounced on Monty – on a good day he might put out the red carpet, but on a bad day, he could be downright nasty. He resented any invasion of his space.

Although it was midday and sunny Monty had the blinds down and opened the door in his dressing gown. He was civil enough, for he liked Jones but, try as he might, could not disguise his irritation that they had called at an inconvenient time and had in fact woken him up. Jones was embarrassed, as he had told his girlfriend how close he was to Monty. Suddenly he felt a stranger. They never spoke again.

On the crest of *Eternity*'s success Monty gave an interview to Hedda Hopper. Patricia Bosworth records that Hopper took him to lunch at the Brown Derby, that eccentric Hollywood restaurant built in the shape of a derby hat, the American equivalent of a bowler. He was determined to win her over, a piece of cake for him, and arrived spruce, in chinos, loafers and sweater – everything that was wholesome in young America, everything that young America should be.

Hedda asked him that standard journalist's question, if he had not been an actor what else would he have liked to do? He told her he would have liked to be a bartender. While they were talking someone asked if he was Montgomery Clift and, if he was, could he give an autograph. He joked: 'Montgomery Clift is dead.' A touch sinister for Hedda, but she rode it out.

He poked one of her pencils into a bread roll and waved it around before leaving the restaurant in jubilant mood. The other patrons were enchanted; all eyes were on him and he could do no wrong. Outside, still in Hedda's line of vision, he did a few arm lifts for some nearby workmen who cheered him on, then ran to his car before he could be stopped for more autographs.

Hedda had some good copy. He fulfilled her expectations of a brilliant, whimsical but lovable Method actor. When her piece appeared it could almost be assumed that Hedda was a fan of Method acting. Not so Joan Crawford. Perhaps she was not best pleased with the success of *Eternity*, from which she had been ousted, for when commenting on the Method she had sniffed, as quoted in *Inside Oscar*, 'It's as if they're trying to impose their psychiatric difficulties on the audience.' It was a pretty sound assessment.

Monty had spent a lot of effort creating Prewitt and, as Frankenstein found with his monster, it was not so easy to destroy him. The character long outlived his usefulness. 'For many months after the end of filming Monty continued to be possessed by his own creation – Private Prewitt,' writes Zinnemann in his autobiography. 'He was quite unable to get out of that character.'

Brando had had a similar problem when appearing in *The Men*, which Zinnemann also directed:

> He was still very much the Stanley Kowalski of *A Streetcar Named Desire* [the stage version], stuck in that character, and he brought some of him into his performance in *The Men*. (It was fascinating to see how deeply the 'Method' actors would merge into the characters they were playing and how long it took before they could return to being themselves again ... An interesting film, *A Double Life*, was once made on this theme by George Cukor ...)

Perhaps Prewitt, still lurking in his psyche, may have been one of his reasons for turning down Elia Kazan's offer to play in Budd Schulberg's brooding screenplay of dockside union corruption, *On the Waterfront*. Monty declined the role on the grounds that he was 'unimpressed' by the script, and for a while it looked as though the resuscitated Frank Sinatra would do it. In the end it went to Brando, who won an Oscar, as did Kazan, Schulberg and the young Method actress Eva Marie Saint. Kazan, who still wanted to make a film with him, then offered him the part of Cal, the troubled teenager in *East of Eden*, which he was to direct. Despite the fact that Monty was now thirty-three Kazan regarded him as the perfect adolescent. In many ways he was still an emotional adolescent, for all his brilliance. Based on a John Steinbeck novel, the film is set in a farming community in California before the First World War. The action is centred on Cal, who turns against his austere father and discovers that his mother, whom he thought was dead, is running the local brothel.

Monty would not give Kazan an answer. In all probability he would have turned it down. In frustration, Kazan gave it to the largely unknown twenty-two-year-old James Dean. Dean had played small parts in movies and on television, and had had Broadway experience. After *East of Eden* he was likened to Monty, a source of irritation to Monty as he was not over-impressed with Dean, feeling that he had no range. But Dean hero-worshipped Monty, as he did Brando, and telephoned them both to tell them so. He admired them so much that he sometimes signed his name James Dean-Brando-Clift. He drew Cal's mannerisms from Monty's performances.

During the next few months Monty turned down over twenty movies and several Broadway offers. Two of the latter were Eugene O'Neill's *Desire Under the Elms* and Jean Anouilh's *Traveller without Luggage*, both plays which he admired. But he had lost his nerve. He did not want to risk his stage reputation, preferring to leave it as it was: intact.

Darryl F. Zanuck, meanwhile, wanted him to play a pharaoh in his CinemaScope Technicolor spectacular *The Egyptian*. Former vice-president in charge of production at 20th Century-Fox, Zanuck was now an independent producer. He had started his career writing stories for Rin Tin Tin.

CinemaScope was the new wide-screen process that Fox had copyrighted in 1953, a novelty to counteract the ever-encroaching threat of television. George Stevens commented: 'It's fine if you want a system that shows a boa constrictor to better advantage than a man.' But in its day it did its job and attracted huge audiences.

So far there had only been two CinemaScope releases. The first was the biblical spectacular *The Robe*, starring Victor Mature, Richard Burton and Jean Simmons. The critics had not been keen but the public had flocked to it, to see the enormous Roman sets startlingly featured by the new process and to hear the stereophonic sound that accompanied it. The second film was *How to Marry a Millionaire*, a comedy starring Lauren Bacall, Betty Grable and Marilyn Monroe. This, too, had been successful. Fox planned to release all future films in CinemaScope.

Although it was a commercial hit, actors and directors were doubtful. Many actors hated it, for it diluted the focus of their performances and did them no favours. There was too much else to watch on the screen at the same time.

Monty was not interested in appearing in Technicolor, stereophonic sound or CinemaScope. Of all the films he had made so far his favourite was the small-budget *The Search*, although he was warming to *From Here to Eternity*. Despite pleas from *The Egyptian*'s director Michael Curtiz and entreaties from his new agent Herman Citron, he turned it down. A great deal of money had been offered and Citron thought Monty had gone mad.

Zanuck turned to Brando, hot from *On the Waterfront*. He expressed interest, more in the salary than the role, as he was buying a cattle ranch at the time. Peter Ustinov then signed up, on the expectation of working with Brando. Unfortunately Brando decided not to do the film after all and accepted *Desiree* in its place. Instead of the exciting method actor, Ustinov found himself working with Edmund Purdom, a good-looking young man who had had a hit with *The Student Prince* in which he had deputized for Mario Lanza and mimed to his singing.

Other cast members included Michael Wilding and the beautiful Polish-French actress Bella Darvi. Zanuck had fallen heavily for Miss Darvi, whose stage name was derived from his own first name – she had been born Bayla Wegier. Unfortunately she did not have what it takes, and even with his backing her career fizzled out.

Bella Darvi, and nearly every other actor in Hollywood, would have loved the sort of success Monty had. Fans dogged his footsteps and sat outside the duplex waiting for him to come out. At first he had joked with them and even invited a few in, but now they frightened him. He could go nowhere without them following, and he came to dread them. He would go out of his way to avoid them, pushing past when they sat on his doorstep. His face would go pale if he saw a group of teenagers approaching. He developed a habit of looking over his shoulder, frightened of being attacked.

Cruising was difficult, and for a while he would give it up in despair. Then the need for sex would consume him and, if no one was outside, he would leave for the bars of Greenwich Village. He was rarely attracted to those who came to speak to him and preferred the meaner types, the sort who did not approach but just looked, dangerously, from across the room, although he was terrified that one of them might be a journalist in disguise. Yet part of him flirted with disaster. Like a nun, he needed to be flagellated for his sins.

11

Mexican Mural, which had done so much for Monty's reputation, had been staged over a decade earlier under the auspices of Bobby Lewis, whose classes at the Actor's Studio had spawned it. Lewis had now formed another group, with Mira as his assistant. Most of Monty's friends had joined, including Kevin and Augusta McCarthy. Another member was the young actress Maureen Stapleton.

The classes did not start until 11.30 at night, so that working actors could attend, and sometimes Monty, who had patched up his differences with Mira, would turn up. *From Here to Eternity* was showing everywhere and, as an acknowledged success, he was too self-conscious to act in the class. He was now public property, so fellow students would be looking for the slightest flaw in his acting. But he enjoyed the discussion sessions.

As he had turned down all offers of work he was free to join forces with Kevin and Mira to produce a definitive version of Chekhov's *The Seagull*, purely for their own satisfaction. They were very excited about this and decided to put in time and effort to make the play as near perfect as they could get it. All three loved Chekhov, and this was their chance to put it together as they had dreamed it could be.

First they would need an exact translation, as they felt that no published version quite captured Chekhov's exact nuances. Here Mira came into her own. As a Russian she could read the original. They gathered in the duplex, Mira translating and all three ponderously deciding on the precise shades of meaning. Both Thornton Wilder and Arthur Miller lent a hand on occasion. It took them months. Matters were further protracted because Monty had to keep flying to Hollywood for conferences as studios tried to persuade him to accept yet another film.

The Seagull was a formative play in Chekhov's career, incorporating his individual ideas on acting which also coincided with those of his contemporary Stanislavsky. These ideas now formed a part of Monty's own style.

Although Monty was never a pure Method actor, the basis of his work was rooted in Chekhov and Stanislavsky. Stanislavsky's ideas on acting Chekhov are as applicable today as they were when he devised them. They are the distillation of Monty's art: 'All those who try to "act", to "pretend" when taking part in Chekhov's plays, are making a sad mistake,' he wrote in *My Life in Art*. 'One should become part of his plays, one should live them, have one's being in them, and follow the deeply buried arteries through which their emotions flow as blood flows from the heart.'* This had been Monty's approach when working on Prewitt – pure Stanislavsky and pure Chekhov.

The Seagull, which Chekhov described as a 'comedy', in the manner of Dante, had had a chequered history. It had been a disaster when first performed in 1896 at the Alexandrinsky Theatre in St Petersburg. Chekhov had pleaded with the cast, 'everything must be simple . . . completely simple . . . the main thing is not to be theatrical.'

'This did not go down too well with the actors of the "old school"', Chekhov's English translator Elisaveta Fen notes†. Nor did it go down too well with the audience, who were accustomed to high-handed drama. Such was the jeering that a near-suicidal Chekhov left the theatre after the second Act.

But after this, in 1898, Stanislavsky and the writer producer Nemirovich-Danchenko created the now legendary Moscow Art Theatre, whose theories on acting were to influence the world. Stanislavsky abhorred artificiality and wanted his plays to be naturalistically performed. He was against the star system – as much in operation in Imperial St Petersburg, under the patronage of the Tsar, as it was to become later under Hollywood Tsar Louis B. Mayer. *The Seagull* was

---

* *Konstantin Stanislavsky: My Life in Art*, translated by J.J. Robbins, Little Brown, 1924
† *Plays* by Anton Chekhov, translated by Elisabeth Fen, Penguin Books

one of the plays selected for the opening season of the Moscow Art Theatre, not without some trepidation on the part of both Chekhov and Stanislavsky. It was an overwhelming success, securing the future of the company, and in gratitude the Moscow Art Theatre adopted a seagull as its emblem.

While Monty, Mira and Kevin worked on *The Seagull* a new student enrolled at the Actors' Studio. Marilyn Monroe humbly watched and listened to those who she assumed had a greater understanding of acting than she did, such as drama coach Lee Strasberg. Miller writes of Strasberg, 'Actors I respected ... revered him, although Monty Clift, a most astute analyst of acting and its problems, thought him a charlatan.'*

Marilyn had fallen in love with Miller and was seeking to improve herself. Her inferiority complex could not let her believe, let alone accept, that in addition to being among the world's most beautiful women, and a delightful and accomplished comedy performer, she was also a fine dramatic actress (as she had shown in *Niagara* in 1952). The fact that she had already achieved more than most people could ever aspire to did nothing to bolster her confidence. One of the greatest of Hollywood stars, she sat in the dingy studio too frightened to open her mouth, in Arthur Miller's words 'awed ... by Strasberg's weighty authority and the entire atmosphere of New York actor talk ...'

Word got around Bobby Lewis's classes that the trio had something special. Chekhov is a playwright open for psychological inspection, and there was much talk of the psychoanalytical research that had gone into it. Producers had long been trying to tempt Monty back on stage, and they thought that this might do it. Chekhov is not always safe at the box office, but at this stage in his career Monty could have read the New York telephone directory and filled the house.

Bobby Lewis offered to direct *The Seagull* in class so that Monty could see the piece taking shape, but Monty turned him down. Bobby was hurt and felt that Monty no longer valued his advice – that being a movie star had turned his head.

The idea of a special small production took root in Monty. He no longer had the nerve to appear in a Broadway theatre, but an intimate off-Broadway production with a limited run was a different matter.

There was another, selfless, reason for wanting to do *The Seagull*. He owed Mira a great deal. She had put his career above all else; in fact he had become her career. Although few people had seen her act

* *Timebends* by Arthur Miller, Minerva, 1995

she had become a legend in certain Greenwich Village quarters where she taught. With him as her leading man she would get the exposure he felt she had earned.

But for some unknown reason he then became the victim of a fit of depression and his enthusiasm died. Neither Kevin nor Mira was sure of the cause. He no longer called or attended meetings. When telephoned, he seemed to be drunk. Mira called round to check that he was well and vented her frustration on the doorbell. The place resounded to its echo. She was sure he was in.

Then he reappeared one day, full of enthusiasm again. No one mentioned the depression and rehearsals continued as though there had been no break. He announced that *The Seagull* would open in the spring, just two months away, at the small Phoenix Theater, for a six-week run. The director would be Norris Houghton of Theatre Inc. Monty had known him since 1945, when he had wanted to put him in one of his plays. Monty would play Konstantin, Kevin Trigorin, Maureen Stapleton Marsha and Mira would be Nina.

Nina was an innocent seventeen-year-old and Mira an experienced forty. She told Monty she was too old, but he waved her objection away. She was an actress, so she could play younger women. An accomplished actress can manage a wide range, of course, and many elderly actresses have played Juliet, including Sarah Bernhardt who had played Hamlet, too, and with a wooden leg to boot. The stage does not have the damning close-ups of the cinema. But there are limits, and Mira thought this part might stretch hers.

She was even more uncomfortable when Monty told reporters how much he owed her, raving that she was a unique actress. Now she had to prove it. It was not a prospect that anyone would relish.

Her voice did not help. Although the play was Russian everyone in it, bar her, was American and her accent stuck out like a sore thumb. Houghton expressed surprise at her casting, but Monty told him she was Laurette Taylor's successor. Monty had seen the great actress in *The Glass Menagerie* and been in awe of her ever since. Poor Mira began to feel extremely uneasy.

Monty had hoped to have Brando's teacher, the redoubtable Stella Adler, as the flamboyant actress Madame Arcadina. But after due consideration she felt she could not commit herself and was replaced by Judith Evelyn, who had just made an appearance in *The Egyptian*.

Mira was unable to rehearse a great deal with Monty as he was absent most of the time at business meetings. When in Los Angeles he stayed with the Wildings. Michael Wilding was unsuccessfully trying to build a Hollywood career. Elizabeth, pregnant with her second child, was trying to run a household. As usual, Monty was not the best of guests. There was an element of strain about these visits.

Back in New York he rehearsed with Mira, who had a permanent hollow feeling in her stomach. She would sometimes drive him to Silverberg's office after their sessions. When she picked him up afterwards he was aggressive. She could do nothing about it: if she tried to dissuade him from seeing Silverberg their friendship would be over. But she felt guilty that she did not try harder. Silverberg seemed to have a stranglehold on him.

Arguments exploded among the cast as nerves stretched beyond endurance. Thornton Wilder sat in at rehearsals and would huddle with Monty and Houghton afterwards, saying little to the rest of the cast. Sometimes he rewrote a scene.

Suddenly everyone realized it was not working. Mira was insipid, Kevin out of character and Monty tense. He wanted to walk out, and threatened so, but could not bring himself actually to do so. He could not abandon everyone at this stage – particularly Mira, for whom the play had been mounted. She herself would have loved to have abandoned it.

Meanwhile the Phoenix box office sold out and a queue formed for cancellations. It was the smart thing for which to book.

Monty's brother Brooks called to watch rehearsals and wished he hadn't: the atmosphere was heavy. But things were going well for him. He was now a TV director on the *Home* show, starring Arlene Francis. Later he was to direct *The Hit Parade* and *The Milton Berle Show*. He had found his niche, but in his heart he still wanted to be a star. Now married with several children – he went on to have a total of eight – all his life he was conscious of playing second fiddle to Monty.

On 25 March 1954 the Oscar ceremonies were televised live jointly from Pantages Theatre, Hollywood, and the NBC Century Theater, New York. For the third time Monty was nominated as Best Actor, along with Burt Lancaster, both for *From Here to Eternity*. Other Best Actor nominees included Marlon Brando and William Holden.

Monty did not attend. He would not have had to fly to Hollywood this time as several stars had made appearances from New York, including Audrey Hepburn who was starring on Broadway in *Ondine* and Deborah Kerr who kissed a security guard. But he could not bear to sit through a public ceremony again, waiting to see if he had won. Although he pretended he did not care, he very much wanted an Oscar. It was widely tipped that he would win this time, and he watched the ceremony at home on television.

Elizabeth and Wilding were at Pantages and jointly presented Walt Disney with his Oscar. Elizabeth had a new page-boy haircut. Paul Douglas, Monty's aggressive co-star from *The Big Lift* was there too. He was now making a fortune fronting commercials for Oldsmobile cars. Newly-weds Lana Turner and Lex Barker attended, as did Merle Oberon, Gary Cooper and Tyrone Power. Dean Martin sang his hit record 'That's Amore', and Donald O'Connor and Mitzi Gaynor duetted with 'The Moon is Blue'.

From Here to Eternity won eight Oscars, tying with the previous record holder, *Gone with the Wind*. Kim Novak, Harry Cohn's latest discovery who had just starred in *Pushover*, modelled some of the outfits that Deborah Kerr had worn in *Eternity* and which Joan Crawford had spurned. Zinnemann won an Oscar, presented by Irene Dunne, and Oscars were also awarded for the picture's screenplay and cinematography, editing and sound.

The Best Supporting Actress was Donna Reed, who ran to the stage for her statuette. She had already said that, for her, winning was a matter of life and death. It certainly helped her career: shortly afterwards she was given *The Donna Reed Show* on television.

The Best Supporting Actor was Sinatra. It was a popular decision, and someone patted him on the backside as he mounted the stage. He had made an entrancing entrance at Pantages with his thirteen-year-old daughter Nancy, all done up in ermine, and his ten-year-old son Frank Jr in evening dress. He thanked Zinnemann, Harry Cohn and Buddy Adler, the producer of *Eternity*. In his nervousness he forgot to thank Monty, but later made it known that he had meant to do so. He was so overcome at winning that he skipped the party afterwards and went for a walk, still clutching his statuette. He was stopped by the Beverly Hills police who mistook him for a burglar.

Monty was hurt that Sinatra had forgotten him but there was an even bitterer blow awaiting. William Holden won the Oscar for Best Actor for Billy Wilder's *Stalag 17*. In a letter to the author Zinneman described what happened: 'The problem was that both Monty and Burt Lancaster were nominated for the award and split the vote, so that neither got the Oscar.'

Monty thought he was jinxed. Later, as Zinnemann left the theatre, he told the press, with typical courtliness, that he owed much of his success to Monty. He added in the TV documentary *His Place in the Sun*, referring to Sinatra, 'Monty inspired him and got his performance up to a level that would have been impossible – I could not have gotten that out of Sinatra without Monty's help.'

For all his disappointment, Monty telephoned to congratulate Zinnemann. He got Mrs Zinnemann, and told her that Fred was a deserving winner. She had a miniature gold trumpet mounted for Monty on an Oscar-like stand, and he was moved to tears when it arrived.

In glum mood, work continued on *The Seagull*. Monty knew it was going to be a disaster. He, Kevin and Mira were now working privately together in the hope that their scenes might save the play. This caused resentment among the rest of the cast, who thought, with justification, that they were being neglected.

No one had yet seen these scenes, but as the preview date approached the trio were forced to perform openly. With great curiosity the rest of the cast watched. No one could hear them, so Norris Houghton urged them to speak up, but Monty was deliberately scaling down his voice so as not to swamp Mira.

In crucial scenes he turned away from the audience, saying that these were too personal to share. He had become Konstantin. This may have worked in a film, but on stage it was lost. Mira felt helpless and humiliated. She had been railroaded into something beyond her grasp.

The preview, in front of an invited audience, increased the cast's foreboding. In the interval Dorothy Parker expressed the opinion that Judith Evelyn looked like a drag act. Someone else complained that Mira lacked direction. Most complained that they could not hear. Bobby Lewis thought the whole thing a shambles, as did many of the others. Monty's dream of the perfect Chekhov had turned into a nightmare.

At Monty's request Arthur Miller stepped in. In his autobiography *Timebends*, MIller noted the play was so shapeless that he assumed, at first, there was no director. He addressed the company: 'My first note is the audience can't hear . . . My 150th note is the audience can't hear.'

He wrote of the production:

I thought this well-meant effort had no concise center . . . it never lifted off. I talked to the actors a couple of afternoons, searching out some consistent metaphoric line they might follow, but nothing took except one remark that Monty repeated for years to come, even into the shooting of *The Misfits* some seven years on. As [Konstantin] Treplev, he was not quite sure why he commits suicide, and I suggested that he think of Treplev aiming the revolver through his own head at Arkadina, his mother. This idea absolutely delighted him and made him wish his suicide occurred onstage instead of off.

For the next few days Miller gave master classes. He told Monty to stop slouching and to act like the aristocrat he was playing.

Miller had problems of his own. He was preparing to go to Belgium where his play *The Crucible* was being premiered, its first foreign production. He discovered that his passport had expired and Monty went with him to the Wall Street passport office to try to sort it out. But Miller's departure was viewed, he wrote in *Timebends*, to be 'not in the national interest', a reference to the 'lump of left-wing entries' in his government file. He was being punished for past political misdemeanours.

In the final days before opening night Miller tightened things up. The cast felt easier although Monty was still tense, nervously chain smoking all the while, using the gold lighter that Sinatra had given him for Christmas. He knew the best that Miller could do would be a salvage job.

If anything, the rumours that things were not going well increased interest at the box office. Tickets could not be had. On opening night, 11 May 1954, so many celebrities turned up that it looked like an Oscar ceremony. Among them were Marlon Brando, Marlene Dietrich, Patricia Neal (who by this time had forgiven Monty for standing her up in London) and Fred Zinnemann.

Squeezed among the celebrities was an unknown twenty-two-year old actor, sexy in his gangling way. He had made a brief appearance in his first film, *The Actress*, the previous year, but it was to be another two years before he really made the grade with an appearance in *Friendly Persuasion*, for which he received an Oscar nomination. This was Anthony Perkins, who in 1960 was to make *Psycho*, the film with which he will always be identified. He was gay and had a crush on Monty, which was why he had gone to such trouble to get a ticket. Monty was everything Perkins wanted to be, and he even copied his halting delivery. Although Perkins did not presume to try to speak to him that night, in time they got to know each other and he proved a good friend. They were probably lovers for a while.

Opening night was not such a disaster as had been feared. The production was knocked, as were Mira and other players, but Monty was praised. His magic redeemed even this fiasco. Walter Kerr wrote in the *Herald Tribune*:

> Mr Clift does not really work any more openly, any more showily, than the others. But there is a secret, and very clear, line of emotion behind the terse facade. The actor's edgy anxiety before the performance of his adventurous play; the elusive contempt with which he tells the novelist his works are charming; the management of a difficult soliloquy in which he edits his own work – all are casual bits of playing and completely telling ones. And Mr Clift's groundwork is firm; when the play rises to its few passages of explosive emotions – the boy's rage with his mother, his abandoned gratitude for a compliment – the performance enlarges without effort, expands into furious fire.

In the *New York Times* Walter Kerr also praised Monty but had little good to say of his fellow cast members.

> Montgomery Clift's lonely, brooding Konstantin is beautifully expressed without any foolish pathology . . . Without a good Nina and a good Trigorin, a performance of *The Seagull* is imperfect. That is the situation here. Mira Rostova, as Nina, is handicapped by a heavy accent. She is further handicapped by a florid style alien to the whole spirit of Chekhov. And Kevin McCarthy's amiable, weak Trigorin has none of the worldliness or lazy corruption of the part. These important parts are inadequately played, which is a pity . . .'

Harold Clurman of the *New Republic*, however, was nastier.

> As an earnest actor he [Monty] believes he can pay his debt to his ideals by attempting a challenging role for four weeks out of ten years. He needs ten years of work on stage to act as well as he potentially can in the kind of parts he aspires to. It is not idealistic and it is certainly not healthy to reserve oneself for certain rare occasions to do what one wants to.

Although Monty had been praised by most reviewers, it was he who took the criticism the hardest. He blamed Mira for a great deal of it and left her in no doubt as to how he felt. There was an after-show party, a brittle and artificial affair. He moved about accepting compliments and smiling grimly. Mira, whose triumph this should have been, hardly got an encouraging word. She was crippled with humiliation.

The show ran to packed houses for its six-week run, improving all the time, and was extended by a further two weeks. He stayed in his dressing room when not on stage, distancing himself from Mira.

She took it on the chin, as she had taken so much else on the chin since she had fled for her life from Russia. Monty never gave a thought to her misery. Every night she had to appear before a packed house which had come exclusively to see Montgomery Clift, knowing that she was miscast, out of her depth and despised. She did it without self-pity and never missed a performance.

Mira's performance is, of course, lost. It was never recorded, but photographs exist. Judging from these her style is florid, with extravagant attitudes and widespread arms reminiscent of Nazimova. But her frail face is that of a naive girl, the eyes enormous, and there is drama in her stance. It is possible to believe that she would be memorable in the right part. As she had tried to warn Monty, Nina was not the right part.

He was a star, in jeopardy of losing all that a star could lose, but she had a reputation too. He could have been aware of her problems and shown a little sympathy. 'I felt that Monty was in a frame of mind like if he could choose he wouldn't do it,' she later said. 'So one remembers it as something that should have been much better.'

He now became close to Maureen Stapleton. Then nearly thirty, she had already had a life full of vicissitudes and philosophized that it was, after all, just a play and not the end of the world. Her attitude was illustrated during rehearsals, when she was criticized for moving about too much during one scene. 'It's harder to hit a moving target,' Robert LaGuardia says she quipped.

With the ignoble demise of The Seagull Monty knew he would never go back to the stage. The confidence he had mustered for his return was shattered. He went to Ogunquit, in the Maine countryside, for a holiday. Silverberg had a house there and he saw him every day. He felt he needed therapy after The Seagull. Monty also studied film scripts and books that could be turned into films and kept a meticulous ledger, in his small, neat writing, of what he had read and the date he had read it.

The knowledge that he was there soon spread and the locals asked him to a dance; he was polite, but did not turn up. They were determined to get to know him and a group of about half a dozen returned, drunk, later the same night. He was out, but they waited until he came back. As he was staying for a while he thought it better to make friends than enemies and was good-natured, inviting them in for more drinks. Later he went on fishing trips with some of them.

There was a gay community and he accepted an invitation to one party, assured that there would be just a few guests. In the event it was like Coney Island. Straight women were at the party too, which he had not expected, but he was charming to them all. He got drunk and fell through a mesh screen, but retained his humour. So did the host, surprisingly.

Monty was not eager to start work, but had to. He had taken on a financial adviser, more to spite Bill than anything else, but his investments had not been successful. He would have done better to have deposited his savings in a building society. He also had to pay substantial back income tax for which he had not allowed. He had earned half a million dollars the previous year and tax was due on that. He also owed $10,000 to MCA, his agents. Once again he was in debt.

He needed someone to organize his life and hired a secretary, Roddy McDowall's sister Virginia. But she was married, with a family, so could only work part-time. This was not enough. Then Marge Stengel came into his life.

Marge was not sure, at first, how Monty and she would get along. She was even less sure when, on their first meeting, he came out of the kitchen chewing, vampire-fashion, on a piece of raw meat. But she warily took the job and stayed with him for seven years. She was a godsend.

It was as well she did not witness his farewell to Ogunquit, or she might have given notice there and then. New tenants were expected the day after his departure, so the estate agent drove to the rented house to check the inventory. The place was filthy, the furniture upturned, there were bottles everywhere and a naked Monty drunk in the middle of it all.

He was dragged to the porch, where someone threw a blanket over him while order was restored. Suddenly he came to, gave a horrified yell, ran into the house and put on some clothes. Then leaped into his car and drove madly back to New York. He had had a therapy session with Silverberg the day before.

Now that he had Marge, Monty would sometimes, when the mood was on him, enjoy entertaining. She organized the invitations and he still had his cook. The duplex was tidy and the new stereo, of which he was inordinately proud and which gave the best sound reproduction of its time, was invariably playing Ella Fitzgerald or Frank Sinatra. He had a vast record collection, but all that anyone can ever remember hearing was Ella or Sinatra. Somebody recommended Billie Holiday, but he could not bear to listen to her because she tore his heart out.

The evening usually started off well, and those who knew him hoped for the best. When on form there was no more genial host in New York. Sometimes he could go for an entire evening without losing his cool. This, however, was never certain. It was like dining on the rim of a volcano. One drink too many and he could erupt.

Then, anything could happen. He might decide they must all go out to a club, or he might prance around giggling as he broke the furniture. The food could go anywhere but down his throat, and frequently over his guests. Heads of big conglomerates like MCA were as liable to get it as anyone else, particularly if they were pompous. If he felt like dancing he would whirl them around. That part of the evening could be pricelessly satisfying to some.

Friends like the McCarthys or Maureen Stapleton could cope, and recognized the danger signals. He would be less likely to attack them as he genuinely liked them, and also they did not stand for too much. But the McCarthys were wary of inviting him to their home now, since Monty had nearly dropped their baby on the kitchen floor one day. He was mortified when they told him what he had done.

It could be a relief when Paramount's most eligible bachelor collapsed unconscious. Sometimes he would drop to the floor like a corpse, while at other times would stagger to the couch and sleep there. On one occasion his rear was on the couch while his dribbling head drooped on to his feet like a human hairpin. Polite conversation continued around him. At least, when he was out cold, people were spared the humiliation of being attacked or, worse, becoming the subject of wild accusations containing just enough truth to make people wonder.

Afterwards he would have no recollection that he had been unpleasant. When told what he had done he would over-compensate, making apologetic phone calls and sending flowers and presents.

He could still be impulsively kind, particularly, it must be said, to handsome men. One day he encountered a young black writer, Bill Gunn. He introduced him to Mira, whom he was slowly coming to terms with again, and spent hours going through scripts with him. 'He was the teacher and I was the boy learning.' Gunn told Robert LaGuardia. 'After a while almost every idea I had about style and attitude came from Monty. He was so full of wit . . . he had a vast knowledge of literature, and a great command of the language.' Although he expected Monty to make a pass at him, he never did.

He showed Gunn some of his own writings. Although nothing was ever published, Monty would often scribble away in his study. He had written books for children and read some of these to Gunn.

Sometimes, if they both got drunk, Gunn would spend the night. Like anyone who spent nights in Monty's company, he became accustomed to the shouts, sudden wakings and wanderings. Monty telephoned friends throught the night – a star's prerogative. When he was at his own home Gunn, too, was a regular recipient of small-hour calls. Sometimes Monty would fall asleep while talking; then Gunn would hang up and try to get back to sleep himself. He came to realize that there were times when Monty hated to be alone and times when he could not bear company.

Meanwhile, his films were now influencing a younger generation, including many actors who would achieve fame. Among these was the ten-year-old Robert De Niro. His biographer Patrick Agan writes:[*]

Bobby became a movie freak and . . . began spending as many hours as possible in the rundown cinemas that dotted the neighbourhoods of lower Manhattan . . . his knowledge of the movies and their stars gave him a crash course in acting. And happily it was a time of great movies. He saw them all, and in doing so witnessed the screen explosions of the top new actors of the time, including Montgomery Clift, Marlon Brando and, a bit later, James Dean.

Monty's name was still inexorably linked with Brando. On 26 April 1955 the following item had appeared in *Reveille*:

Hollywood and one of its top stars – Montgomery Clift – don't like each other at all. Because Monty likes to lead the life of an average American man, Hollywood accuses him of being eccentric – and in return Monty says he thinks the film city is artificial.

Hollywood thinks Monty is crazy not to buy himself a mansion befitting his star status and not to surround himself with such luxuries as swimming pools and Cadillacs. But the star's argument is that as soon as he succumbs to these things he will cease to be a 'real' person and become as artificial as many other stars.

So he makes his home in New York and stays in Hollywood only long enough to make a film. While he is in Hollywood he shuns swanky hotels and either takes a cheap flat or lives in a second-rate boarding house . . .

[*] *Robert De Niro* by Patrick Agan, Robert Hale, 1989

He drives around in his 1940 car, he doesn't associate with well-known people and he wears old and comfortable clothes. This last habit again makes Hollywood furious. People argue that the words 'movie star' used to mean glamour and leopard-lined limousines – but that Clift (with plenty of assistance from Marlon Brando) has helped to make the words mean old flannels, torn T-shirts and tennis shoes. He looks like a stevedore rather than a star, they say.

More arguments arise when Monty finishes his films. The usual procedure is for stars to be available for interview and personal appearance tours to help publicize the film. Studios say that the public is quite as interested in the off-screen lives of the stars as in their performance – and that all stars should work at their profession twenty-four hours a day.

But Mr Clift says he feels his job is finished when the cameras have stopped and disappears to relax in the wilds, leaving the film companies to manage as best as they can without him. He is, Hollywood declares, a male Garbo.

In the film city Monty is reputed to be eccentric, shy and unfriendly. The fact that he seldom dates film actresses and that he shuns cocktail parties and premieres adds to his legend as a mystery man. Monty, in return, says he prefers not to let success turn him into an artificial person, adding that the reason he makes films is because of the high salary he gets. 'It gives a guy wings,' he says.

In New York Monty has a well-furnished apartment. He has a maid to clean it and a cook who, twice a week, prepares meals and leaves them in the refrigerator to be warmed when wanted. Monty never has lunch because he feels better with one big meal a day, and most evenings he warms a meal at home rather than dine out. When he dates a girl he takes her to a quiet, out-of-the-way restaurant because he feels it is an intrusion on their privacy to be seen and written about in the gossip columns the next day.

He likes his dates to be dark, soft and feminine types like Jean Simmons, Pier Angeli or Audrey Hepburn. He says he doesn't like women who are 'blonde, brittle and driving and who have had to struggle hard for success because this always shows in their faces and makes them hard.'

Another of Monty's hates are 'posed pictures'. When a photographer takes shots of him Monty always insists that the pictures should not be retouched. 'I like them to show me and all my pores,' he says. When he's in New York he likes to spend his days reading plays and film scripts. While he's doing this he usually chain smokes and continuously drinks cups of coffee. Most days he goes to a local gymnasium to exercise and keep in shape and when he wants entertainment he goes to the cinema – often accompanied by his close friend Marlon Brando.

A New York typist says she and a close friend went to see a Marlon Brando movie recently and they discussed him during the film. 'Suddenly', says the girl, 'there was a tap on my shoulder and a voice said, 'Listen, honey – do you mind keeping quiet. What do you see in this Brando fellow anyway?'

I looked round and was speechless. Because it was Montgomery Clift, and sitting beside him was Marlon Brando.

As far as Monty's own appeal is concerned one girl fan sums it up by saying: 'He's got such expressive sad eyes that he arouses terrific maternal instincts in women.'

Monty had never been to a movie with Brando in his life, any more than he had dated girls like Pier Angeli or Audrey Hepburn.

He continued to live off advances from MCA. The agency let the debt mount, hoping it might be an inducement for him to pick up the phone and accept a movie. But he continued to turn down all scripts, including *The Tinker's Wedding* which he could have done with Maureen Stapleton.

He was beginning to slip from the public eye. *Modern Screen* listed its most popular actors of 1954 and he was not among them – they were Rock Hudson, Marlon Brando, Tony Curtis, Tab Hunter, Robert Wagner and William Holden. Among the women were Debbie Reynolds, Grace Kelly, Elizabeth Taylor, Doris Day, June Allyson and Marilyn Monroe.

Brando was making *Guys and Dolls* and he sometimes rang Monty to discuss his role. Like Monty, he had turned down *East of Eden*. Kazan had dreamed of them playing brothers, but ended up with Dick Davalos and James Dean.

Dean had seen *A Place in the Sun* and been mesmerized by Monty. As Paul Alexander writes in *Boulevard of Broken Dreams*,*

He simply couldn't take his eyes off Montgomery Clift who loomed before him, his luminous face sometimes filling up the whole screen.

* Warner Books, 1994

Of the actors whose work he respected, Clift came closest, or so Jimmy said, to doing what *he*, Jimmy, wanted to do. When the picture was over and the full impact of Clift's performance had sunk in, Jimmy felt overwhelmed. He had loved Clift before; now he adored him. Jimmy was so swept away that he insisted on watching the picture a second time.

Some said Dean's screen arrival damaged Monty's career. Author Michael Munn is one; in *Hollywood Rogues* he wrote: 'For Clift, Dean's arrival in Hollywood was a setback in his own film career. After *From Here to Eternity*, his choice of films often left much to be desired, he was constantly being compared to Brando, and vice-versa, which outraged him, and now Jimmy Dean was being hailed as the new Clift *and* the new Brando.'

It is difficult to judge Dean's potential box office viability, because the adulation of him after his early death has made it impossible to be objective. But the extent of his talent is there for all to see and, for all his ravaged appeal, he was not in the same league as either Monty or Brando.

Meanwhile, Monty continued to reject scripts. He turned down Tennessee Williams's *Cat on a Hot Tin Roof*, which Paul Newman later made with Elizabeth Taylor and for which both received Academy nominations. He was wary of the character Brick because Williams suggests he is homosexual, although this was played down in the film.

He also rejected *Friendly Persuasion*, the story of a Quaker family, although he could have brought much to the film – Sunny, after all, was a Quaker. It was a success for Gary Cooper and Anthony Perkins, the young actor who had come to see Monty in *The Seagull* and on whom he had based much of his style. The film was nominated for an Oscar.

He also rejected Carlo Ponti's production of King Vidor's *War and Peace*. This may not have been a bad thing as Henry Fonda, who took the part, wrote of it 'All the genius of Tolstoy went out the window.'

Much of the summer of 1954 Monty spent with Libby by the pool at Treetops. In October she opened with *Blues, Ballads and Sin-Songs* at New York's Bijou Theatre, just across the road from where Tallulah Bankhead was starring in *Dear Charles*. 'She's in between murders,' Tallaluh remarked. Either critics were bored with Libby's Sin-Songs by now, or she was off form, for her reviews were not good.

In order to focus attention on the songs everything else was stark.

She wore black and there was no backdrop, just a piano, a pianist and a chair which she sat on, posed with or used as a prop. One critic was so unkind as to suggest that she should balance it on her nose to cheer things up. Another wrote that she 'seems to be listening to something the audience can't quite hear'. Yet another commented that she lacked the common touch – and he put his finger on the trouble.

Like Monty, she would not compromise, and he backed her all the way. The audience had to reach up to her, she refused to reach down. She had searched diligently for her repertoire and had painstakingly rehearsed. She believed in her work, but there was something futile about it. She knew that had she not been notorious she might have played to empty houses; as it was, they were barely half full.

Due to the strain her ulcers became inflamed. She took too much medication and hallucinated. While in this state she attempted suicide with a Seconal overdose. It was not her first attempt and it would not be the last.

The Seconal did nothing for her ulcers. Her maid, Alice, nursed her back to health and made her promise she would never do such a thing again.

Monty, who had been in New York at the time, rushed to her side, crying and chiding her for wanting to leave him. He was profoundly shocked, having thought her too strong for such a thing. Her strength was part of her attraction. The papers took up the story and wrote of the Holman Curse and how it affected all who came near her. John Bradshaw adds:

'Be careful,' she told him sardonically. 'Something terrible will happen to you.'*

* *Dreams That Money Can Buy* by Jon Bradshaw, Jonathan Cape, 1985

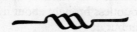

12

Monty and Libby spent Christmas together in Key West, soaking up the sun and occasionally fishing from a yacht. They gave each other gold Zippo lighters which they both continuously lost and replaced. Monty had 'GO AHEAD AND LOSE IT' inscribed on one of her replacements.

Back at Treetops he had a car crash. Libby had taken possession of a new Simca, a small French car which had taken her eye. Monty wanted to put it through its paces and see what he could do with it. He rammed it into a tree and landed up in hospital, frightening himself so badly that he gave away a green MG he had recently bought. The two of them featured regularly in the newspapers and such was their notoriety that they were the subject of a play, *Single Man at a Party*, at the Theater Manque.

While rooting around at Treetops he came across an X-Ray photograph of Libby's skull. This delighted him and he pinned it in the kitchen of his duplex, telling friends it was his steady girlfriend. According to Jon Bradshaw, Alec Wilder, who had dubbed them Mahatma Gandhi and Disciple, now called them Flotsam and Jetsam, the Tortured Twins.

To the relief of his tortured MCA agent, Edie Van Cleve now, he now agreed to film *Sons and Lovers*. The offer came from British stage director Peter Glenville. Monty liked D.H. Lawrence's novel and, when

Glenville told him he wanted to shoot it in England, considered that a plus factor.

He had turned down the chance to work in England only recently when British director John Boulting had offered him the film of H.E. Bates's *The Jacaranda Tree*. Rather undiplomatically, Boulting asked why he had done *Indiscretion of an American Wife*, pointing out that it had already been done, rather better, in *Brief Encounter*.*

After nearly a decade of thinking about it, Thornton Wilder finally come up with a play for him. Originally called *Alcestis*, it was later retitled *A Life in the Sun*. It was set to open on 22 August 1955 at the prestigious Edinburgh Festival, with Irene Worth as leading lady. There was international excitement. But as he and Wilder worked on the script they had inevitable differences of opinion. In the end Monty walked out in a huff, doubtless brought about by nerves at the thought of appearing live at Edinburgh.

He also cancelled the film, to the cost of Edie Van Cleve's nerves. This was probably all to the good, for Glenville had not yet made a film. His first, *The Prisoner*, was released the following year. A virtual two-hander in which a cardinal is tortured, it was a dreary piece with little flair.

Libby had left for Florence that August and he decided to join her, but first he went to London to do the theatres. He was interviewed by journalist Thomas Wiseman, whose piece was published in the British press after Monty had left for Italy:

> After a certain amount of psychological warfare, I got Montgomery Clift to tell me his plans. They are, if you will forgive the sensationalism, to lie in the sun somewhere in the Adriatic. To fulfil this programme Mr Clift this week took an airplane from London to Italy, where he is now, presumably, absorbing more ultra-violet rays than an embryonic banana. This is precisely what he has been doing for the past two years. When I called on him at his hotel he looked worn out by all this strenuous inactivity. While Mr Clift has been lotus eating – and from his frail appearance one would think that is all he does eat – the movie moguls have been inundating him with offers . . . But Mr Clift has said 'No' so often as to make Mr Molotov, in his heyday, sound like a yes man by comparison.
>
> His latest 'No' has been to the Edinburgh Festival where he was

* *Montgomery Clift: Beautiful Loser* by Barney Hoskyns, Bloomsbury 1991

supposed to appear in a play by Thornton Wilder . . . He gave me his reasons: 'I had a disagreement with Thornton Wilder about how my part should have been written. I was not prepared to play it the way it was written and he was not prepared to write it the way I could play it.'

Other parts Mr Clift has turned down as 'unsuitable' include: Starring role in *Ben Hur*; Starring role in *Joseph and His Brethren*; The Brando role in *Desiree* . . . The James Dean role in *East of Eden* . . .

Montgomery Clift was at one time running neck and neck with Marlon Brando in the race for stardom. What makes him now so particular about films that he would rather make none than one which would not satisfy his fastidious tastes? The story was that he had a private fortune and did not need to work. Mr Clift denies this. 'I don't have any private money,' he said. 'My attitude . . . Well, I as an individual would be deeply uninterested in seeing some of the films I have been offered.' I suggested: 'But you would be paid to make them. Not to see them.'

'I'm just not interested, like Marlon is, in being a business man and making money, I've got nothing against it, it just doesn't interest me . . .' he insisted. What, I asked, did he think the Hollywood bosses thought of his high-principled attitude? Was he not, in the politest possible way, telling them all to go to hell?

'I don't know,' he said. 'I really don't. I don't have much occasion to meet Hollywood tycoons. I don't live there. Living there is like living in a hot house . . . the breezes are all so gentle and the temperature is ideal. And I'm not just discussing the climate when I say that. Nothing to stimulate you there.' He paused, considered my question again. 'I suppose,' he said, 'the tycoons must think I'm either an idiot or a genius.'

Mr Clift, I would say, certainly does not regard himself as an idiot. Nor do I. Nor, on the other hand, would I say that he was a genius.

Libby's health was going from bad to worse. She actually screamed out at times when the pain from her ulcers was too crippling. In her room she put the radio on loud so that Monty would not hear. Many people who saw her cringing assumed this was the wages of a dissipated life, but in fact her life was positively abstemious and her diet consisted largely of milk.

She was a fan of Garbo's, and photographs of the great lady adorned

Treetops. Knowing that Monty knew Garbo and, unlike most people, got on with her, she pressed him to invite her to dinner at his duplex. The whole world wanted Garbo as their dinner guest, but as a token of her affection for Monty she accepted.

Libby was full of excitement. They had actually met once, briefly, when Libby had been going to the hairdresser's – the salon was in the block in which Garbo lived. As Libby entered the swing door Garbo came out and their eyes locked through the glass. Libby squealed with excitement and rushed to shake Garbo's hand, admiring words tripping from her lips. She didn't get much of a chance to deliver them. The reclusive Swedish actress's hands jerked to the collar of her mackintosh which she pulled up to her nose. Her trilby hat was pulled almost down to her nose anyway. She nodded in terror and scurried into the drizzle. For Libby it was a meeting with an angel.

Now she was to meet her at Monty's. Other guests included the McCarthys, Thornton Wilder, Arthur Miller and Garbo's friend, businessman George Schlee.

Schlee, who bore a striking resemblance to Mauritz Stiller, the director who had brought her to fame, was rumoured to be her lover but in fact was merely part of her coterie. That select group included dietician Gayelord Hauser and Schlee's wife, dress designer Valentina. These three were planning a return to the screen for Garbo. Hauser had devised a health diet to make her look younger and Valentina was designing her costumes, while Schlee was acting as manager. She let them get on with it. Who knows if she wanted to return or not? She least of all.

Monty was in good form, probably due to the austere presence of Garbo. The same could not be said for Schlee, who became drunk and started taunting Libby about her husband's murder. It was difficult for Monty because he did not want to offend his guest of honour's escort.

Garbo solved the problem herself. She had not spoken much during the evening – she rarely did – but now she looked up over her wineglass, from which she had taken just two sips, glared at Schlee and said, 'Shut up!' It had the effect of an H-bomb landing on the table, and he complied at once.

She did not speak much more during the evening, apart from enthusing about the local hardware store and how she enjoyed hunting for bargains there. Neither she nor Monty mentioned movies. Although Garbo as a rule spoke little, and when she did it was only about everyday matters, people were always conscious of being in the presence of a star. Meeting her was one of the highlights of Libby's colourful life.

Another star had his colourful life stamped out on 30 September 1955. Monty was staying with Libby in her townhouse, and she came into his bedroom that morning with newspapers bearing grim headlines. James Dean had been killed at the wheel of his silver Porsche Spyder, the joy of his life.

Monty was no fan of Dean's – if anything, he despised the younger actor's cashing in on characterizations based on his style. Dean had phoned him several times but Monty had always refused to meet him. Yet the shock of his young life being ended so violently made him throw up all over the bed. As he later said, 'I don't know why.' It was as though he had some premonition of his own fallibility. Since the accident in the Simca he had not driven much, and he was even less inclined to do so after Dean's death.

That autumn he went skiing in Canada, and when he came back he told friends he wanted to play a private eye. He had been reading Micky Spillane novels and fancied himself as a gumshoe.

He had discovered cocaine by this time and seems to have been a mild user. According to Patricia Bosworth, Bill Gunn recalled Monty asking him to share a line with him. Gunn refused, and Monty never brought up the subject again. 'He wasn't a junkie, contrary to rumour,' says Gunn.

If his mother heard the rumours she refused to acknowledge them. But she could not refuse to acknowledge his friendship with Libby, for the gossip columns were full of it. She never approved of Libby and warned Monty against her. Her disapproval rather pleased him. Their relationship had settled down, but he was always slightly antagonistic towards her, although he kept in touch. He was conscious of how she had guided his early career, and was now determined to prove he was his own man and made it clear he was brooking no professional interference. He never missed a chance to snub her snobbery, hence his pleasure at her disapproval of the scarlet Libby.

Libby's health continued to deteriorate. On 1 January 1956 Monty took her to New Haven Community Hospital where she underwent an operation for the removal of nearly all her stomach. Her looks deteriorated even more drastically afterwards and her formerly lustrous hair, her last bastion of glory, thinned to grey wisps. She was forced to give up her four camphor cigarettes a day, and Jon Bradshaw tells us that when a visitor asked how she was coping she replied: 'Every time the doctor puts a thermometer in my mouth I'm tempted to light it.'

Monty stayed with Libby at Treetops after her operation. Despite his unconscionable habits as a guest, the place was big enough to accommodate the two of them without driving either too mad. Her staff all liked him, as did Libby's two adopted sons, particularly nine-year-old Timmy. They shared a birthday.

While Libby recuperated Monty played hide-and-seek with Timmy and swam with him in the pool. On one occasion they deliberately turned all the dining room pictures upside down before Libby came down to lunch. She played the game and pretended to be horrified.

It was over three years since he had worked. Basically he did not want to work – he could have taken his pick of several attractive offers. But money was running out and his debt to MCA increasing. Something, reluctantly, had to be done.

That year, in Britain, Winston Churchill resigned and the murderess Ruth Ellis became the last woman to hang. In America superstars Bruce Willis and Kevin Costner were born. The big movie of the year was Hitchcock's *To Catch a Thief*. Montgomery Clift was being forgotten.

He resumed studying scripts, realizing he must make a film. He would be competing against himself. He knew he had been good in *From Here to Eternity*, so in his new picture he had to be better. It was a terrible responsibility. Friends suggested he play Hamlet, which he still talked about, but he replied he was not ready. He was thirty-five and ought to have been ready.

About this time *Guys and Dolls* was released, starring Brando and Sinatra – both singing. He went to the preview and left before the end, having made several loud and disparaging remarks during the show. When leaving he punched the advertising display case in the foyer, shattering the glass. He apologised, then ran down the street laughing.

He thought both Sinatra and Brando had sold out by making the film. When Brando asked him what he had thought of it he told him, 'Well, I was watching the picture and . . . you know what I saw? . . . this big, big, big fat arse!'* His remark reportedly did not go down too well.

That October he told Libby that he had decided to make a new film. She did not take him too seriously – he had been saying that for a couple of years now. But this time he was earnest. The film was *Raintree County* and his co-star would be Elizabeth Taylor. Her marriage to Wilding was in difficulties, and when she was in New York she often

---

* *Brando* by Peter Manso, Orion, 1994

stayed with Monty. She slept in his bedroom and he walked the block or so to Libby's townhouse and slept there. She urged him to accept this new film so they could be together.

Raintree County was to be the most crucial movie of his life. He was never to feel the same way about things again, and it contributed to his early death. But he did not know that as he read the Ross Lockridge novel upon which it was to be based. He was not particularly impressed by the story, and neither was Elizabeth, but MGM agreed to pay him $300,000 and he would be with Elizabeth. She needed him, and he liked to be needed.

A sprawling saga of magic and madness, *Raintree County* had been a best-seller in 1947. But the author did not live long enough to enjoy its success, as he committed suicide the following year. Set during the American Civil War, the action revolved around an unbalanced Southern belle (Elizabeth) and the man she loved, Johnny Shawness (Monty), an idealistic schoolteacher. Shawness is searching for the meaning of life. Legend has it that this will be divulged to the man who finds the legendary Raintree. It took courage to search for the Raintree, for tragedy followed those who did not find it. Shawness has the courage to search, 'for,' as he tells Elizabeth in the film, 'it opens all locks'.

MGM saw *Raintree County* as a latter-day *Gone with the Wind*, and certainly in Elizabeth and Monty it had worthy successors to Vivien Leigh and Clark Gable. It was to be shot in Panavision and Technicolor on revolutionary 65mm film, which provided the sharpest focus yet for a colour movie. It had a budget of $5½ million and was planned to run for three hours. In fact it came in fourteen minutes short. The director would be Edward Dmytryk.

Dmytryk had been in films since the 1920s, achieving a measure of success during the 1940s with thrillers. One of these had been RKO's Oscar-nominated *Crossfire*. Based on the novel *The Brick Foxhole* by Richard Brooks, it was one of the first movies to cover the controversial theme of anti-Semitism. The novel's original theme had been even more controversial, the murder of a homosexual, but homosexuality was beyond the pale in the 1940s, so a heterosexual Jewish victim was substituted.

Dmytryk was to find out, at first hand, all about persecution. In 1947 he was tried by the Un-American Activities Committee for Communist activities. He had fought his way back and in 1954 had had a success with *The Caine Mutiny*, starring Humphrey Bogart.

Jack Larson asked Monty if he found his part in *Raintree County* exciting, and talked about their conversation in *His Place in the Sun*. 'Exciting. No,' he had replied. 'But it's good enough, I'd be a coward not to do it.' Then Millard Kaufman's screenplay arrived. Kaufman had just completed *Bad Day at Black Rock*, starring Spencer Tracy and John Ericson, for which he had received an Academy nomination, so Monty was expecting great things. He was disappointed, as always, and decided to rewrite his part. Sheets of manuscript were piled all over the table.

The film was to be made in Hollywood and he flew there in March 1956, well in advance of shooting. MCA found him a house on Dawn Ridge Road in the Hollywood Hills, which came with a butler and cook. A chauffeured car was also at his disposal. It was about twenty minutes' from Elizabeth and Michael Wilding's home on Beverly Estate Drive, off the lethally steep and winding Benedict Canyon. Now it's a popular site, but fewer people lived there then.

Shooting was to start on 2 April 1956. His first scene was to be a dialogue with Eva Marie Saint, who had won an Oscar for *On the Waterfront*. He did not know her, so, using the technique that had worked so well on Donna Reed, he telephoned beforehand. They agreed to have lunch.

They were both shy and awkward and the meal turned into an ordeal. There was no bonding this time, for they seemed to have absolutely nothing in common. 'As long as we were engaged in work – everything went smoothly,' Saint said. 'When we tried to relate one-to-one offscreen, we had trouble. We never made another lunch date.'*

Raintree County spanned many years, and in this first scene he had to play a twenty-year-old. He joked with the make-up man as his facial lines disappeared, but he was worried about his eyes. They were his best feature and he took trouble to ensure they were clear – not always easy when he had been drinking heavily the night before. His eyes looked fine but they pained him, particularly under lights. He fretted that something was wrong with them. Whatever it was it did not show – this was his first colour film and he was photographing a dream. The medium suited him. He'd never looked more handsome.

As usual when filming he got up at six every morning and slept in the back of the car while his driver took him to Culver City. That always happened. His driver knew to keep quiet.

When not working, he spent much time, with Elizabeth and Wilding,

* *Liz* by C. David Heymann, Heinemann, 1995

sometimes separately. After his initial reservations he took to the genial Englishman. They were both heavy drinkers. Sometimes a tipsy Wilding would be driven to Dawn Ridge Road where he'd open his heart to Monty. He was a good listener. After a session of this kind Wilding would leave even more drunk.

He also become friends with Millard Kaufman and visited him and his family at their home. Kaufman had a six-year-old daughter called Mary, and Monty was always buying her presents. He remained friends with her for the rest of his life, telephoning her from time to time. There was a whole list of people whom he kept in touch with by phone, such as Lillian Hellman, some of whom he had not seen for years.

Despite their cosy social relationship he did not baulk at rewriting Kaufman's script. He would badger Dmytryk most mornings, having worked on the script through the night. Although the director called him 'one of the greatest actors I've ever worked with', he naturally found this irksome. He also noted how Monty shied clear of the homosexual extras. There was a ballroom scene and many of the extras were obviously gay; Monty gave them a wide berth.

On Saturday, 12 May 1956 Elizabeth gave a small dinner party to celebrate the end of the Hollywood shoot before the company moved off to locations in Louisiana, Tennessee and Kentucky. In addition to Monty the guest list included Dmytryk and his wife, Kevin McCarthy (who was in Hollywood shooting his most famous film, *Invasion of the Body Snatchers*), a young priest whom Elizabeth had met and who had admired Monty in *I Confess*, and Mr and Mrs Rock Hudson.

Mrs Hudson was the former Phyllis Gates, sometime secretary to his agent Henry Willson. Rock, and his studio, had had a fright the previous year when *Confidential* magazine had threatened to expose his homosexuality. A deal was done involving money and the scuppering of lesser stars, and the story was shelved. Rock's multi-million box-office appeal remained intact but he was jolted. Marriage quickly followed.

Monty had not wanted to go at first – he was tired and felt like an early night, so had given his driver the night off. If he went to the party, he would have to drive himself. Jack Larson came round earlier in the day and cheered him up so he changed his mind, intending to leave early.

He was nervous as he drove up Coldwater Canyon. He had not driven for some months and the big American car was not the most manoeuvrable of vehicles. The MG he had given away would have been better. When he got to Elizabeth's house he found Wilding sprawled out on a couch. He had slipped a disc and was under sedation from painkillers.

The death of James Dean was in everyone's mind. It had happened the previous year but both Rock and Elizabeth had worked with him on *Giant*, not yet released. He had been at Elizabeth's house the day before he died, raving to Stewart Granger and Jean Simmons about his car. Granger, the proud macho owner of a new Mercedes, recalls bandying good-natured insults with him and warning him not to hit anything as the Porsche was rear-engined and offered little protection at the front.*

There was one guest short: the priest could not make it in the end. Monty did nothing to lighten the atmosphere, Phyllis Gates recalls: 'Clift lived up to his reputation: he was brooding and sullen. McCarthy seemed bright and intelligent. He kept the conversation alive, meanwhile eying Monty to make sure he didn't consume too many drinks.'†

By all accounts Monty drank very little that night – just two glasses of rosé wine, well within the permissible driving limit even today. He may, of course, have been drinking with Larson earlier in the day, but if so he did not appear drunk. But he was having trouble with his ever-nagging dysentery problem and taking medication. This could have reacted with the alcohol.

Elizabeth made her entrance after everyone had arrived, magnificent in white and gems. She sat next to Monty on a couch and 'they conversed almost in whispers,' Gates continues.

Most of their conversation concerned *Raintree County*. Monty thought that Elizabeth might steal the film, but said it was worth it just to be working with her. Like Monty, she adored Sinatra, and was up and down all evening putting his LPs on the stereo.

By 11p.m. the party was breaking up. Dmytryk and his wife had already left. Kevin, who was flying to New York in the morning, said he had better go too. Monty was leaving and told Kevin he was nervous of driving down Coldwater Canyon. Kevin told him he knew a short cut to Monty's road and offered to lead the way.

When the two men were alone by their cars, after the Hudsons and Wildings had gone back to their drinks, Monty returned to the subject of *Raintree County*. He confided to Kevin that he was worried about Dymtryk's editing: he had been cutting out certain mannerisms that Monty considered essential to his character.

Both cars left, Kevin's in front. It was silent, and the desert stars shone, as only desert stars can shine, in the jet sky. As Kevin drove

---

* *Stewart Granger: Sparks Fly Upward* by Stewart Granger, Granada, 1981
† *My Husband, Rock Hudson* by Phyllis Gates and Bob Thomas, Headline, 1986

down the canyon he noticed Monty's car coming up behind him much too fast. He thought his companion was playing one of his dangerous practical jokes.

In order to dodge Monty, who he thought was going to nudge his bumper, Kevin accelerated round a bend. There was a house nearby, and for a second Kevin feared Monty might crash into it. To avoid being tailgated further he accelerated again until he was about a hundred yards ahead. In his mirror he saw Monty's lights veering from side to side. He still thought his friend was playing around.

Suddenly the lights disappeared. He was sure, now, that Monty was joking. He waited, expecting the lights to reappear. They didn't.

He parked his car and ran back. The engine of Monty's car howled through the night as though Monty were racing it. He could not be far away – perhaps he had got stuck somewhere.

When Kevin reached the car he was horror-struck. Monty had collided with a telegraph pole, and the huge box of electrical circuits attached to its top was dangling overhead. Had it fallen it would have demolished the car.

The engine sounded as thought the accelerator was jammed and there was a stench of flooded petrol. Terrified that the car might burst into flames, he turned off the engine. There was no sign of Monty. He called, but there was no answer.

Kevin ran back to his own car and turned the headlights on to Monty's. He found him slumped unconscious under the dashboard – it was the weight of his body on the accelerator which had caused the engine to howl. The driver's seat was soaked in blood.

As Kevin frantically tried to shift him, Monty's head collapsed on to his sleeve to reveal the face. It was truly dreadful – a morass of pulp and blood. As Jack Babuscio put it, the crash 'was to drastically alter one of the most photogenic faces since Garbo'.

13

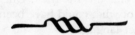

Kevin rushed to the house on the corner, the house that he had feared Monty might crash into, and banged on the door. But it seemed to be unoccupied. He was terrified that another car would come down the hill and crash into Monty's, but there was no alternative other than to leave it. He drove back to the Wildings, hammering on the door like a madman. Wilding limped to the door and opened up.

'Monty's had a terrible accident!' Kevin blurted out.

Elizabeth rushed out in panic, shouting that she was going to Monty. Wilding called for Hudson to ring the police and Dr Rex Kennamer, a well-known Hollywood doctor. Then all of them followed Kevin's car back down the hill.

In their headlights Monty could be seen in the car as Kevin had left him, blood pouring from his face. The driver's door was jammed, but the men levered a back door open and Elizabeth pushed past and forced herself in, clambering across to the front seat and cradled Monty's head in her lap. As she attempted in vain to stem his blood with a silk scarf she had been wearing, her dress gradually turned scarlet.

He was choking. Elizabeth put her fingers in his mouth and found an obstruction lodged in his throat. She pulled it out. It was two of his front teeth. Her action saved his life and his breathing steadied. He later had the teeth mounted and gave them to her.

Then the press arrived. Reporters were always stationed at the Beverly
Hills police station – it was the best place to get a story on the stars –
and one of them had heard Rock Hudson's call for an ambulance. They
scrambled down the hill, pushing each other aside in their eagerness
to get pictures of Monty. But Wilding, Hudson and Kevin formed a
bulwark in front of the car to protect him. Elizabeth screamed that if
any of them took a single shot of Monty like this she'd never let them
near her again.

Hudson later told Kitty Kelley, 'Elizabeth prevented the photographers from taking Monty's picture by the foulest language I've ever heard.'
And he'd certainly heard some. According to the same source she ended
her salvo with the warning that, if they did attempt to take a picture, 'I'll
kick you in the nuts!' This did the trick. One of them, disappointed
at not getting a photo of what could have been Monty's death throes,
reprimanded her for her language.

Then the doctor arrived, eventually followed by the ambulance,
whose driver had had difficulty finding the accident spot. Hudson
and Kennamer helped the crew manhandle Monty from the wreck
while Elizabeth still cradled his head. Phyllis had some tissues and
tried to mop up the blood. Kennemar did what he could to staunch
the haemorrhage – Monty might have died from loss of blood alone.

He was conscious by this time and the doctor gave him a painkilling
injection. His face had swollen to twice its size; as someone later told
him, 'The only normal thing about you was your ears.' For all his distress
Kitty Kelley records, he had not lost his humour. 'Doctor Kennamer,'
he said. 'Meet Elizabeth Taylor.' No one could quite believe he had
said it. Then panic set in and he cried out that he would be unable
to complete the film.

Finally the police arrived.

He was taken in the ambulance to Cedars of Lebanon Hospital.
Phyllis went in the front with the driver while Elizabeth stayed in
the back with Monty. Wilding followed in his car. Rock Hudson went
home. 'I never once saw her [Elizabeth] hysterical or break down that
evening,' Wilding recalled to Robert LaGuardia. 'Elizabeth could be
remarkably strong in a crisis.'

Monty was seen by Dr Nathan Hiatt. As he had been drinking alcohol
the doctor could not use anaesthetic. By 2a.m. he was finished. Monty's
head was covered in bandages and looked like an Egyptian mummy.

There were no injuries to his body, not even bruising – his face had
taken the entire impact. Several teeth had been knocked out, including
the two which Elizabeth had scooped from his throat, his nose was

broken in two places and his jaw in four. There was a vicious vertical slash from his cheek to his lip, covering a cracked cheekbone which had splintered his sinus cavity.

Despite the facial injuries his brain appeared at that time to be undamaged, but there is now doubt about this. John Huston, the director with whom he was later to make two films, was convinced he had brain damage. Certainly his behaviour became more erratic after the accident. Jack Larson, who had been with him earlier on the day, said, 'I don't think anybody knows how brutal the accident was, what a terrible condition he was in.'

Dawn had long since broken by the time the Wildings drove home, listening to the news of the accident on the car radio. By now it had flashed round the world. Phyllis Gates left the hospital at 7a.m. She had been questioned by reporters, as had the whole party, and answered as best she could. Ironically, Monty's tragedy was to have repercussions for her marriage, for when she returned home she was greeted by a furious Rock Hudson. Why had she gone to the hospital? He had left as soon as he knew there was nothing more he could do, knowing his presence would only add to the circus.

'Rock didn't talk to me for days,' she writes in her memoirs. 'He acted as if I had been guilty of some transgression. Was it because I had been in the spotlight and he hadn't?'

That was doubtful. Rock could get all the publicity he wanted, and much of what he did get he did not want. It was Phyllis's naiveté that had upset him. Phyllis was unused to being in the spotlight; marriage had given her a position that she would never otherwise have occupied, and she was human enough to enjoy it. Rock accepted publicity as part of his job, but only ever publicized his movies. The studios were hard pressed to get him to pose at his home, and he knew that comments would be misconstrued. Like Monty, Rock had secrets to hide, and did not want Phyllis attracting attention.

Monty was, of course, besieged by the press, none of whom could get near him as he was too ill. When he did recover sufficiently to give a press conference he referred to the cause of his accident as 'a blink too many', meaning he had fallen asleep at the wheel. 'That was his sense of humour,' said Dmytryk, whom Elizabeth had telephoned from the hospital, in *His Place in the Sun* He continues, 'That's actually what happened, I'm sure he just closed his eyes and fell asleep very quickly and on one of those curves, instead of making the curve he went off and hit the telephone post.'

Later, in 1962, Monty gave a television interview to publicize his latest film, *Freud*. It was the only TV interview he ever gave. He talked about the accident and, although it had happened eight years previously, the circumstances were still crystal-clear in his memory. With tremendous dignity he wryly related:

> When they showed me in the hospital a picture in the paper of the car I couldn't believe I was in the hospital bed. It was so demobilized . . . and it was a result of just plain tiredness after shooting . . . I was so tired . . . I'd gone down a winding road in Beverly Hills – they're very dangerous – I just sort of went like that [he nodded his head] half asleep. That was enough to run right into a power pole. If the big box had come down on me I would not be here to talk with you [he laughed]. In the hospital I saw the picture of the car and, I must say, my face was about as disfigured . . . I was all bloated. A friend of mine who came from the East said . . . I wouldn't recognize myself.

It does seem incongruous that a man as nervous about driving down the hill as Monty had been could actually doze off while doing so. It seems more likely that the alcohol he had consumed that night, discounting what he might have drunk with Larson earlier, reacted with the medication he was taking and caused him to black out. He had a history of blackouts.

It has been suggested that he might have taken drugs at Elizabeth's, but there would be no reason to do so. He was going home to bed because he was tired – surely no one would take a sedative when about to drive at night down a precipitous canyon? And there would be no reason to take an upper for the day was over.

While Monty lay in his hospital bed Libby Holman was stuck on the Long Island Expressway trying to get to the airport. In *Dreams That Money Can Buy* he explains how Jack Larson had telephoned her with the news as soon as he had heard it on the radio. She had booked a flight to Los Angeles to be with Monty, but it was Mothers' Day that weekend and the freeway was jammed solid. She had no alternative other than to go back and fly out the following day.

She took a taxi from Los Angeles airport and moved into the hospital, spending her nights on a couch at the foot of Monty's bed.

She and Elizabeth did not get on, which was not surprising since they were both strong-willed, successful women. In *Liz* David Heymann quotes nurse Betsy Wolfe as saying, 'the two nearly came to blows while Monty, his face swaddled in bandages, lay helplessly in bed'.

A huge arrangement of flowers stood in his room: when the crew had heard the news a whip-round had been organized. He was deeply touched, wrote a letter of thanks, and kept the flowers there until they were dead. As soon as he could he hissed his thanks through his wired up jaw down the phone to the crew.

The hospital quickly discovered the sort of patient they had. Although sedated, the night after he had been brought in he had left his bed and sleep-walked into another patient's room. She was a woman suffering from a heart condition, and her scream brought a nurse who discovered a zombie-like creature apparently staring at her. No one could be quite sure, as his eyes were masked by bandages. He was steered back to bed. Next day, when told of what he had done, he apologised to the patient. Fortunately for the hospital she was quite flattered that she had had a brush with a movie star, and took no further action.

He was given cortisone to reduce his swelling and speed the healing process. As his mouth was out of action he could not devour solids, only liquids, which he drank through a straw.

A few days later his bandages were removed. His face was disfigured and bloated but, contrary to what is now legend, he did not need plastic surgery. His teeth were reconstructed and his jaw wired into position. As Jack Larson is recorded as saying in *Dreams That Money Can Buy*, 'He looked as though he'd been stuffed.' Libby screamed and begged him to come to Treetops where she would get him the best nursing money could buy.

A cluster of MGM executives soon homed in, among them Dore Schary, head of production. Schary had been worried about Monty from the first, and before filming had started had asked him point blank whether his drinking would cause trouble. Monty had promised he would stay sober and, give or take a little, had stuck to his word.

Due to the big budget of *Raintree County* Schary had taken the precaution of insuring the film against delays. He had taken out a $500,000 policy on Monty alone. It was the first movie to take such insurance, which is now standard practice.

Schary had to make a decision. Either the film could be aborted, in which case, even with the insurance, MGM would lose around $2 million; or, if the film continued without Monty, his scenes could be junked and reshot with another actor, although this would cost almost as much as starting from scratch. The third choice was that the film could be suspended until he was fit to face a camera again. A glance at his face indicated that this might take some time – possibly forever.

Libby went ballistic at the last proposal. She would not hear of him resuming filming. Jon Bradshaw writes: 'Libby detested the movie executives who simpered and fawned at Monty's bedside, but reserved the brunt of her rage for Elizabeth Taylor. She had long been jealous of the twenty-four-year-old actress. Libby thought her "sensual and silly – rather like a heifer in heat. There's no telling," she said, '"where her lust will lead her next . . ."' That was rich coming from Libby. Dr Hiatt walked into Monty's room one afternoon while Libby and Elizabeth were fending, and hastily left.

Monty pleaded with MGM to let him complete the film, and Elizabeth backed him up. She feared that if he was discarded he might fall into a lethal depression. No one knew how his face would heal, although Hiatt was optimistic. Beneath Monty's resolutely cheerful facade he was terrified he might never work again. He had to continue. Schary agreed to the postponement.

Libby left the hospital in a fury, says Jon Bradshaw. 'As long as I can help him, I'll do it,' she said, 'but he's acting foolishly. I've got two little boys. They need me more than Monty does. I love Monty, but the boys have first call.' She made her exit on that rather noble speech.

Monty left hospital on 22 May to convalesce at his rented home. His life has been described from then on as 'the longest suicide in Hollywood'. At first he was exceptionally brave. When he saw his face in a mirror, which had been denied him in hospital, he could barely recognize himself. The left side was worse than the right. A nerve had been severed in the cheek, leaving it immobile; it never regained full mobility.

His visitors, too, were shocked. They tried to conceal it, but he registered their embarrassment. He had plenty of visitors, among them Kevin, who flew from New York, as did Monty's father, Bill. But Monty would not allow Sunny to come: he knew her reaction would be hysterical and he made Bill promise not to tell her how disfigured he was.

Elizabeth spent much time with him, and Dmytryk called regularly. Monty clearly wanted to start work again as soon as possible, and had no wish to end his career: he needed the money. It was one thing to turn down films, another not to be offered them. Worries preyed on his concussed mind, one of which was that a good script might turn up while he was committed to *Raintree County*. This was one of the reasons he wanted to get it over and done with.

He sat by the pool, believing the sun would help heal his face. He was still taking nourishment through a straw and existed mostly on soup. Sometimes he augmented this diet with a martini, although this was against doctor's orders.

He wrote lots of letters, particularly to Ethel, Brooks and Sunny. Brooks told him about his own career in TV, and Monty did his best to advise him.

After three weeks it was discovered that his jaw would have to be reset. This was excruciatingly painful. Equally painful, and of longer duration, was the dental treatment which from then on he was to be subjected to all his life. Miraculously, none of his upper teeth had been hurt. He developed a gum abscess while his jaw was wired and underwent painful sessions of canal drainage and implantation of new teeth. He was in pain most of the time and suffering from delayed shock.

When he was able to fend for himself, Elizabeth and Wilding went for a weekend's cruise on the yacht of Broadway producer Mike Todd. Todd was fifty-two and engaged to actress Evelyn Keyes. He was now producing *Around the World in Eighty Days*, the only film he would ever produce. It was a staggeringly expensive project, shot in Todd-AO, a wide-screen process named after him – at that time Hollywood was obsessed with wide screens.

There were 69,000 extras and 75,000 costumes, and among its stars were David Niven, Shirley Maclaine, Marlene Dietrich, Ronald Colman, Noël Coward, John Gielgud, Trevor Howard, Glynis Johns, Peter Lorre, Victor McLaglen, George Raft, Frank Sinatra and Red Skelton. It was to win several Oscars.

'He [Monty] was back on set within six weeks of the accident,' recalled Dmytryk in *His Place in the Sun*. Everyone, including Monty, realized it was too soon. He had written to Brooks and told him he was not looking forward to the first couple of weeks because of the pain he was in, but knew he had to get on with the movie. The delay had cost MGM $2 million and no one was anxious to increase this debt. He was worried about his looks, particularly if the press photographed him before he was made up. MGM promised a closed set.

Dmytryk thought that he could overcome the problem of Monty's lopsided, swollen and still far from recovered face by concentrating on his right profile. That way much of the paralysis could be avoided. But the accident had aged Monty and he had also lost weight.

People were as reassuring as they could be, but when Monty saw the rushes he realized he would never look the same again. His face would settle down and his speech become less slurred, but his heart-stopping handsomeness had gone forever. The actor that now stared from the screen was middle-aged, weedy and haggard and had a lop-sided face.

It would be difficult to integrate the new footage with what had already been shot. The man in glowing colour, shot in the new sharp-focus process, was an unwelcome stranger.

Natchez was the first location site. He did his very best, arriving on time and struggling to learn his lines. But it was clear that he was under pressure, in pain and disoriented.

'There was an enormous difference in his behaviour after the accident,' said Millard Kaufman in *His Place in the Sun*. 'I think – I may be wrong, I don't know, indeed, nobody does – but I think that reaction came about as a reaction to medication. I think he was heavily sedated.'

Another actor in the film, Nigel Patrick, later commented in the *Sunday Express* of 1 June 1959, 'He looks quite different . . . he was in great pain though he never once complained.' No one can remember him ever complaining. 'He was unable to work most afternoons,' Dmytryk recalled in *His Place in the Sun*. 'He would wear out and run down very quickly.'

Monty had been able to resume work so quickly thanks to painkillers. But he was always careless about prescribed amounts and overdosed at the best of times. Due to the pressure he was taking vast amounts. He was also drinking heavily – he always drank under stress. He found the best medication was to crush pills and mix them with vodka and orange juice. He drank this concoction guiltily, in private, nervous of being discovered.

He would pour the lethal mixture into a hip flask and take it on to the set with him in a leather bag. It acted as his security blanket, and he became upset if anyone moved it once he had put it down to do a scene. However, a few people had seen his flask and he told them it contained orange juice, which was partly true.

It was clear, however, that he was under the influence of something stronger than fruit juice and much sniggering went on, particularly when anyone caught him sneaking behind the set to have a quick swig after he had blown takes because he was drunk. But without the flask he could not have mastered any takes at all.

'He simply was drinking too much,' said Dmytryk in *His Place in the Sun*,

> I think it was because of the pain . . . because he was trying very hard. When he was misbehaving, as I put it, it was never meanness, never nastiness, it was just because he didn't know what the hell he was doing. He'd just fall apart, he couldn't do anything, you know, but would never get mean. I could sit here all day and tell

you stories of actors I worked with who got mean when they got drunk.

Monty took amphetamines to give him strength, and sedatives to help him sleep, all washed down with booze. Dmytryk tried to reduce the amount of pills he took and stole some from his dressing room, replacing them with vitamin pills. Monty never noticed, but was taking so many that it made no difference. His goal was to get through the film, and medication and alcohol was the only route he knew.

His sleepwalking increased. Twice he was found wandering naked through the streets. To try to curb this he took an increased dose of sleeping pills. Consequently he had to take more uppers in the morning to get through the day, creating a vicious circle. He had no armour against his moods. He would sometimes cry over trifles, while at other times he would react boisterously.

In one scene he had to drive a horse and carriage but kept falling out of the carriage, laughing hysterically as the hours ticked into overtime and there was still no take. He was panic-stricken but could not remain upright, try as he might. Realizing that Dmytryk was losing patience, as was everyone else, he tried to win them over by playing the buffoon. It did not help that the scene was being played in front of local people, most of whom could not believe their eyes. He pulled faces for them, trying to turn it into a joke. The crowd clapped and asked for more. Eventually Dmytryk had to tie him into the carriage, which pleased the crowd enormously.

'When he wasn't drunk or under the influence of dope and drugs, he could be a wonderful person and actor,' recalled Dmytryk in *His Place in the Sun*. 'But whenever he turned to alcohol and pharmaceuticals he tended to go out of control.'

He hit the papers in New Orleans, where there was a plane change between locations. Stories of his bizarre behaviour had circulated and unsolicited reporters were waiting for him. He took one look at them with their raised cameras and panicked, but they chased him like a pack of hounds. He shook them off by hiding behind a pile of luggage.

He saw a bar and made for it, downing a few vodkas to steady his nerves. The reporters later found him there, long after his flight had been called, drunk, out of control and terrified. He could not have done them a bigger favour. The photos were splashed across the papers the next day.

He chain-smoked – nicotine was mild compared to the other sedatives he was taking. Sometimes he went to sleep while he was smoking and was discovered one day, when he had failed to turn up on the set, in a drug-induced stupor, with scorched fingers. His cigarette had burnt right through the flesh and he had felt no pain. It was agonizing, though, when he awoke. But he was back on set as soon as he was woken, as usual falling over himself to apologise to everybody. The gates of hell opened for him on *Raintree County*.

Now he had got used to his new face he did not say much when he watched the rushes, but sat slumped while well-meaning people told him how well he was doing. He was fed lies, but knew the truth. All his physical imperfections were magnified in diamond-sharp close-ups, while his acting was stilted.

To try to counteract the negative publicity, MGM's press office set up interviews for him. He would agree to them, but at the last moment lose his nerve and not turn up.

For all Monty's addiction to medication, Kevin McCarthy never considered him as a drug addict. There was no evidence that he was taking hard drugs.

Libby made it up with him and came to visit. According to a press report of the time, 'They'd get drunk together. She seemed to want to control him.' If they had indeed got drunk together Libby would have been dead – she had drunk only moderately for years, and since her operation had become virtually teetotal.

For all his distress he was helping Elizabeth with her performance, as he had done in *A Place in the Sun*. Millard Kaufman thought he was more benefit to her than Dmytryk. But not all actors were inspired by him. Anne Baxter, who liked him as a person, had not found him particularly helpful when working on *I Confess*. Lee Marvin, who was also in the new film, was another.

Marvin told Michael Munn, as reported in *Hollywood Rogues*, 'I've got to know what he's thinking, right? I got to react to him. But all he ever looked at was my forehead . . . I couldn't understand that kind of fascination with my forehead . . . it threw me having those tormented eyes of Clift staring just above me.'

Another unfortunate incident occurred at an airport. News had got out that the stars were leaving, and a crowd had gathered to watch Monty and Elizabeth arrive. Monty, doped and confused, shot the crowd an unmistakably hostile stare, grabbed Elizabeth and bolted into the plane. They were booed.

Realizing they had made a mistake, the stars reappeared, waved, posed for photographs and even signed autographs. But it was too late and the harm was done. Even the British *Daily Mail* carried the story. 'Elizabeth Taylor and Clift booed by angry fans . . . Deep Freeze Stars Sneer!'

By the time they reached Kentucky, the last of their locations, Monty had deteriorated even more. Dmytryk gritted his teeth and carried on, desperate to get the cursed film over with. Monty felt much the same.

As always at the end of a shoot, everyone was tired. He had a tiff with Elizabeth one night and walked out on her. She rang his rented house but could get no answer. Frightened, she drove there, to find the bathroom full of blood and the shower glass broken. She phoned Dmytryk, who in turn called the police. A search was organized. Then Monty strolled in. Knowing that Elizabeth would come looking for him, he had deliberately broken the shower glass and splattered prop blood on the floor. He thought it a great joke.

As he did when an MGM executive visited while he was filming in a swamp. He hugged the man, even though he was covered in mud. As they parted, the executive now in his filthy suit, Monty told him to pass on his best to Hedda Hopper and thank her for telling the world he was a drug addict. Apparently she had interrupted him when he was injecting himself with a vitamin supplement, which he did from time to time. He still could not chew, due to the pain in his jaw, so shot up vitamins.

He did not behave strangely all the time, however. Millard Kaufman recalls times when he was as rational as any man and, when Kaufman was ill with pleurisy, Monty nursed him. He loved a patient.

The company returned to Hollywood for a final week of filming. The last shots were actually taken on Monty's birthday, 17 October. The film had been a nightmare, with Monty as the demon king. 'I said I would never work with him again,' Dmytryk recalled in *His Place in the Sun*. 'Much as I admired him as an actor . . . I'd never go through that agony again.'

Fred Zinnemann and his wife were in town, and Monty gave a party for them and to celebrate his birthday. Among the guests were Jean Simmons and cameraman Bob Surtees. He made a little speech telling them how much he loved them, but became upset when they had to leave. Apart from his physical appearance Zinnemann could not help noting how Monty had altered emotionally since *From Here to Eternity*. It was as though he had had a layer of skin peeled away.

Surtees gave the Zinnemanns a lift to their hotel. As he turned the car out of the drive Monty tumbled off the roof, hit the bonnet and rolled into the main road. Surtees had to brake hard to avoid running him over.

But he was unhurt, and the men helped him up and sat him on his lawn. He hugged them and told them he knew he would never see them again. He said he knew they loved him and didn't want them to go. He would not be reassured, and as they were driving away was still crying.

Utterly exhausted, Monty stayed in California for a while. It was autumn and New York would be cold – he could not face that. Jack Larson found him one day sobbing in the bathroom. His system had had no chance to recover from the trauma of the accident, and depression would fall suddenly, unexpectedly and lethally.

The swelling lessened and his face improved. It was still lopsided, but the paralysis had eased. He looked better than he had during the filming of *Raintree County*, and it was no longer a fright mask that stared back from the mirror. It sank in that he would be able to continue to work. He tried to pull himself together. Very hard.

14

In the spring of 1957 he went to a private screening of *Raintree County* and thought it a 'monumental bore'. Of his own performance, he said, according to Patricia Bosworth, 'excepting a couple of moments I'm horrific – wooden, frozen, walking through. In my beard I look like Jesus Christ in a union cap.' Despite this he knew it would do good business – audiences would queue to see his smashed face.

While still in Hollywood he was visited by Brando, who first sent one of his entourage to see if it was convenient. Monty agreed, but was not too flattered. Jack Larson, who was with him at the time, recalled 'Monty was a little bit offended and he said to me, "He wants to see how I am, whether to come up or not, so he sent somebody to reconnoiter . . . to see if I'm drunk, worth talking to.'*

Brando had, in fact, heard a whisper that he might be making a film with Monty. But this was not the main reason for his visit. He had heard how precariously Monty was behaving and believed he could help. When Brando arrived, eyebrowless from filming *Teahouse of the August Moon*, Larson made himself scarce. The two actors spoke together for a couple of hours. 'I had a feeling that Brando was giving Monty a vote of confidence,' said Larson.

* *Brando* by Peter Manso, Orion, 1994

After Brando had left Larson drove Monty to his doctors, where he was still having treatment for his jaw. He was crying, drunk but moved by Brando's concern. Larson recalled their conversation. 'What Brando had come to say,' he told Peter Manso,

> was that he had always admired him, that he had been rooting for Monty to win the Oscar for *A Place in the Sun*, the same year he was up for *Streetcar*. He also said he'd always been jealous of Monty, always envious – that he'd go to see his movies and say, 'How can he do that? How can he be that good?' As Monty related it, Marlon ended up telling him, 'You're what I challenge myself against. Take care of yourself for me so that you can keep challenging me because you're all I have.

Brando later confided to Maureen Stapleton that he had also urged Monty to join Alcoholics Anonymous, and promised to go with him if it would help. Monty told him he wasn't an alcoholic and could stop drinking any time he wanted.

The truth was that he had by now given in to his alcoholism. He could not get through a day without drinking, not even for a couple of hours. The pain in his head never lessened.

He telephoned Silverberg regularly – the psychiatrist, of course, did not view alcoholism as a threat – but sought additional help while in Los Angeles. He consulted Bob Buckley, described by Mickey Rooney as 'an internist who has also had considerable training in psychiatry'.* Rooney was one of his patients, and Buckley had also treated Howard Hughes and James Dean. Rooney was trying to get Judy Garland to see him. Rooney claimed that Monty was helped by Buckley. He took solace from any source that was offered.

Monty returned to New York in November 1956, travelling to Texas first to see his sister Ethel. He told her how relieved he was that he was still able to work. As always, he took presents for her children.

By now *Around the World in Eighty Days* had been premiered, to enormous success. Elizabeth confided in Monty how greatly she was taken by Mike Todd. Monty did not like him, but she did not want to hear his reservations.

Whilst Elizabeth and Wilding had been cruising on Todd's yacht, he and Elizabeth had been thrown together. It rang the death knell for the Wilding's marriage. She and Wilding had drifted apart

---

* Account taken from *Life is too Short* by Mickey Rooney, Hutchinson, 1993

by this time anyway. Within a short time they parted and she married Todd.

Giant opened on 10 October 1956. Warner's initiated an enormous publicity campaign concentrating on Dean's death and the fact that this was his last film. Audiences queued around the block. Dean's sometimes beautiful face (depending on which angle it was shot) was tailor-made for tragedy. People wept openly – there had not been such grief expressed since the death of Valentino.

The film received ten Academy nominations although only its director, George Stevens, received an Oscar. It was his second – his first had been for *A Place in the Sun*. Monty did not look much like George Eastman now.

He spent a lot of time at Treetops with Libby. With the protection of her estate around him, he rallied. 'The old Monty in disguise,' she dubbed him encouragingly. It was like the old days: they studied dozens of scripts, and among the rejects was John Huston's *Moby Dick*, which went to Gregory Peck.

He became friends with Nancy Walker, the late, diminutive actress now most famous as the maid in *McMillan and Wife*. When they became friends she was not so well known, although she had appeared in the 1946 film *Best Foot Forward* with Lucille Ball and June Allyson. He saw her in a play in New York and called backstage afterwards to congratulate her. He told her he thought she was marvellous. They had already met briefly, in a bar, some years previously before Monty had made a movie. He kept returning to see the play, bringing friends, and called on Nancy every time. They went to dinner and visited each other's homes. He introduced her to Roddy McDowell and Kevin. Noël Coward was in town at the time and they both knew him, so sometimes he would join them too. She had a black, gutsy sense of humour that matched his own. He came to adore her.

There was talk of him filming Graham Greene's *The Quiet American* with Laurence Olivier, to be directed by Joseph L. Mankiewicz. Olivier had already agreed, and Monty was thrilled at the thought of working with one of his heroes. The project, however, fell through. According to Mankiewicz's biographer* this was because the director refused to send a draft script and Monty would not commit himself. When one was eventually sent, Monty was committed elsewhere. Audie Murphy was substituted for Monty, and Olivier pulled out as he refused to work with the replacement. Michael Redgrave took

* *Pictures Will Talk*, Kenneth L. Geist, Frederick Muller Ltd, 1974

Olivier's place, and both actors were eventually commended for their performances.

Monty finally got to act with Brando in 1957 in Edward Anhalt's adaptation of Irwin Shaw's Second World War novel *The Young Lions*. There had been great interest in the book since its publication in 1948. Producer Al Lichtman was to make it for 20th Century-Fox.

Edward Dmytryk asked him to be in the film – the same Dmytryk who had vowed never to work with him again. So likeable was Monty that Dmytryk was only one of many who had had horrendous experiences with him, yet forgave him.

Fox originally decided to make the film with inexpensive actors – worthy people who were not stars – and a draft script had been sent to Dmytryk. The director recalled in the TV documentary *His Place in the Sun* how he persuaded Fox to have a change of heart:

> It wasn't on the basis of the script, actually, but because I had read the book and I thought it would make a great film . . . they were going to make it very cheaply with a cast of second-rate . . . I shouldn't say second-rate – second-category actors . . . I said, 'Hell, you've got to get the best people, it'll make a great picture out of it. The first one I thought of for Noah was Monty Clift. I called him on the phone and shipped the script off to him. He read the script and I still have the telegram – he sent me a wonderful telegram – it simply said YES. That's all and I was stuck with Monty Clift again [he laughs].

Dmytryk had, in fact, already booked Brando. With Fox's agreement to upgrade the actors to stars the budget had been raised from its original $2 million to $4 million. There had been talk for years of coupling Brando with Monty – Kazan had tried to do it in *East of Eden*.

Monty was receiving the astonishingly high fee of $750,000, more than his co-star, for Brando was being disciplined for walking out on *The Pharaoh*. So much for Monty's fears that he might never work again. As a result of the accident he was enormous box office now, probably bigger than he had ever been.

The Young Lions was a war story told simultaneously through the eyes of two American GIs and a German soldier. Monty was Noah Ackerman, an American Jew who finds he is fighting prejudice from both the German and American armies.

He and Libby worked on the script at Treetops every evening. They felt that Ackerman had become lost in the transference from book to screenplay. 'What else can you expect from men with a genius for mediocrity?' spat Libby (according to Jon Bradshaw), referring to executives at Fox. Ever since the MGM conferences around Monty's sick bed she had been violently opposed to film executives, who had done nothing for her career anyway. She and Monty would find Ackerman.

Libby knew he was frightened of filming again. This would be his first film since the accident. *Raintree County* had merely been a mad dash to get the film done before he collapsed, and he had taken anything to keep himself going. He had been an automaton, for all his flashes of brilliance. But this was his chance to prove he was together again, and he absorbed himself in his part. That he was playing opposite Brando concentrated his mind profoundly: there was no way he was going to play second fiddle.

To play Noah he decided to alter his features. He had never resorted to character make-up before, but he wanted Noah more Jewish-looking and weedy. He would use putty to alter the shape of his nose and push out his ears. He also determined to lose 20 lb in weight – weight he could ill afford to lose since the accident.

This was the first film in which he could not rely on his looks. The real Monty was to be hidden, locked away, and the public would be presented with Noah Ackerman – thin, undistinguished, with protruding ears and a crooked nose. He would be judged purely by his performance. It was a terrifying challenge.

He took pride in telling his mother he was playing a Jew – she was prejudiced against them. She made a few sounds of disapproval, but by and large kept quiet. 'Why do you do this to me?' Sunny had once pleaded. The answer was because she set herself up for it. She must have been anguished by the damage the accident had done him, but kept quiet about that too. He never spoke to her about it.

Bill, a racist in his passive way, approved of neither blacks nor Jews and was appalled at Monty playing a Jew. Monty, who had no racism in him at all, would tell him he had been chosen because everyone assumed he was Jewish since he looked it.

In his determination to lose weight he exercised in the grounds at Treetops and in Central Park. He was virtually starving himself, eating only tiny amounts of raw steak and dry bread. He did not enjoy dieting but believed it to be right for Noah who, in Method analytical style, he had decided had been a clerk at Macy's before signing up with the army.

The third soldier in *The Young Lions* was to be played by singer

Dean Martin. When Dmytryk told Monty he was thinking of casting Martin, Monty, who only knew him from the Dean Martin/Jerry Lewis comedies, was aghast. Dmytryk told him not to worry and that Martin was only a suggestion from the singer's agent at MCA – the agency that represented Monty and Brando. He had thought *The Young Lions* might elevate his career, rather as *From Here to Eternity* had Sinatra's. Dmytryk told Monty that actor Tony Randall was first choice, and that he had merely been thinking about Martin.

The lightweight Randall had just completed his first film, *Oh Men, Oh Women*, with the forty-six-year-old Ginger Rogers and David Niven. Monty went to see it. He rang Dmytryk next day, telling him, 'If it's still alright, I'll go with Dean Martin.'*

Martin received the small fee of $20,000, less than he received for one week's cabaret in Las Vegas and less than he had received for his first film in 1949. Like Sinatra he was prepared to gamble for the sake of his career.

Stories circulated that MCA had bullied Buddy Adler, producer of *From Here to Eternity* and now head of Fox, into accepting Martin or losing Brando and Monty. *The Hollywood Reporter* and *Confidential* both carried the story. Things came to a head and Dmytryk had to testify that he had booked Martin solely on instinct after his recommendation by MCA. He suggested that the rumours might have been started by Randall's agent.

Martin, awed at the prospect of working with Brando and Monty, told his friend, lyricist Sammy Cahn, 'I'm so scared.' Cahn could see this, as Martin had broken out in a nervous rash, and sagely observed, 'Do you know what Marlon Brando and Montgomery Clift would give to be able to do what you do? Walk out on a stage and charm an audience out of their skins? These fellers have to do what a director tells them to do. You are in charge.' Monty, who had quite a fair singing voice, would love to have done what Martin did.

Peter Manso records that Monty flew to Paris, the first location, in May 1957, and checked in at the Hotel Raphael. Later, there would be filming in Berlin. When Brando arrived, early in June, Dmytryk took them to dinner with Maximilian Schell, the Austrian actor who, like Brando, was playing a Nazi officer. Monty was hyperactive, clearly excited and talked animatedly. Brando told Dmytryk he thought Monty should see a psychiatrist. He had of course been doing so for five years.

Brando's weight had increased by 20lb to 190, but he was still as

---

* *Dino* by Nick Tosches, Minerva, 1992

svelte as a leopard. He was soon a startlingly improbable platinum blond, too, almost a parody of the Aryan image he was portraying. He had tried various wigs but found them unconvincing so had gone to Carita-Alexandre's salon in Paris and had had his hair bleached.

It was not only the Brando hair that had undergone shock treatment. He was teetotal while in Paris and, when drinking tea, had spilt boiling water over his crutch. He was taken to a hospital and treated for a blistered groin. He had complained to Carlo Fiore, his drama coach, 'This would have to happen to me now in the middle of Paris in the spring, with my prick in a sling.' He phoned his girlfriend, Anna Kashfi, with the news and she suggested that the papers might run the story headlined: 'Brando Scalds Balls.'*

Brando was able to practise his French with Monty and France Nuyen, the beautiful Franco-Chinese model who appeared in *South Pacific* and with whom he had become friends. Monty was not always the most encouraging partner in these exercises – he spoke better French than Brando and would sometimes poke fun by exaggerating his American accent. *Dino* tells how Dean Martin and Monty shared many scenes together, and Martin nicknamed him Spider because of his jerky movements. Unlike Monty, Martin loathed Paris, and told reporters he'd tasted better food at Barney's Beanery in Los Angeles. When asked whether he had visited the Louvre, he replied, 'I had a guy once who did my house in two days, he was a better painter than those guys.'

According to Brando's memoirs, *Songs My Mother Taught Me*, during *The Young Lions* he developed a new technique for delivering his lines. Rather than waste time memorizing them, he pinned them on the backs of other actors. That way he could concentrate on spontaneity and not be over-rehearsed.

There had been great interest when it was announced that Monty and Brando were to co-star. As Brando's biographer, Peter Manso, puts it, 'The news that Brando was to be teamed up with Clift, his most respected rival, sparked the imagination of those who hoped for a Method-Acting duel.'

They were disappointed, for it never took place. Monty and Brando shared just one scene together, in which neither of them spoke. This was a great relief to Dmytryk because, as he put it in *His Place in the Sun*, 'I can tell you, right now, that if I ever had Montgomery Clift and Brando in the same scene that would have been the end of the picture

* *Brando* by Charles Higham

. . . I knew that Monty was good for one or two takes and after that he got mechanical.'

This was the opposite of what Zinnemann had said on *The Search*. Then Monty had improved with each take. But by now his technique had weakened. He could no longer hold his concentration, or remember, and if he did not get what he wanted quickly he floundered.

He and Brando assessed each other's moves like champion boxers. During one scene Monty noticed Brando standing behind a camera watching him. 'Tell Marlon he doesn't have to hide his face when he's watching me act,' he told Dmytryk. Monty later told Jack Larson, according to Peter Manso, that Brando was 'using about one tenth of his talent'.

As Dmytryk knew, Monty was at his best in the mornings and he arranged his schedule accordingly. Monty still brought his little bag, containing his flask, on set with him. The flask was the reason he was not so good in the afternoons, but he could not get through the day without it.

Brando knew what was going on because he once innocently picked up the flask, after Monty had told him it contained orange juice, and took a swig. Being on the wagon at the time he choked when the pungent liquid coursed down his throat. As usual when embarrassed, Monty pulled faces and tried to laugh it off.

There were further humiliations. He had a boyfriend with him and he knew the crew was whispering about it. Cameraman Duke Calahan recalled for Manso the feeling on the set about Monty's homosexuality: 'The theory was that when he was sober he fought it, but when drunk submitted.' Every morning he was sober. Every afternoon he was drunk.

Perhaps his biggest humiliation was when he bumped into Alfred Lunt in a hotel lift. Monty slumped drunkenly to the floor in front of his disbelieving eyes. Lunt never spoke to him again and never returned his calls. In Lunt's view actors did not get drunk in public.

Sometimes he would revert to childlike behaviour, constantly repeating swearwords in a mantra like a child who had just learnt them, or crawling around on all fours. It was clear he was sick. As Dmytryk said, 'There was nothing evil in it.' But he would not seek a cure anywhere other than with Silverberg, who did not seem to be helping him.

Occasionally he would go missing and Dmytryk would have to reschedule the shoot. Monty had two passports, one in another name, so was able to leave the country without difficulty. He was once discovered in a brothel in Italy. Many people assumed he was trying to prove he was not homosexual. On another occasion, when drunk, he danced on the roof of a car.

For all this he knew his lines in the mornings, clearly having worked on them overnight. But if lines were altered he would have difficulty learning the new script. He sometimes complained to Dmytryk when Brando altered his lines.

Certain women thought they could straighten out Monty's sexuality. Robert LaGuardia explains how one, a friend of Edward Anhalt's, was determined to have him and conned her way into his hotel room. The management had to be sent for and she was escorted from the hotel. When Anhalt learnt of the encounter he apologised to Monty. 'Gee, she scared the life out of me,' was all he said, laughing. Dymtryk recalls, as recounted by Peter Manso, 'The women on the film wanted to meet both Marlon and Monty, but about Monty they'd say, "I can help him." Which was a great mistake. Nobody could help him.'

There were interruptions during the shoot. Actors walking about in Nazi uniforms stirred unpleasant memories and there were some rough encounters. Once, Brando had his uniform coat torn off. From Paris the company moved to Berlin, then back to Los Angeles where Brando's death scene was shot in Charlton Flats.

Brando had various ideas of how this should be done. One was that Monty should carry his corpse away on his shoulders, but Monty refused to do so. 'Despite his precarious state, Clift put his foot down,' Manso writes. 'Openly refusing to sanction Brando's polka dot Nazi . . . "I don't know how he's going to get his arse down the road," he commented to Jack Larson. "But my character's not going to carry him."'

An alternative suggestion of Brando's, which Dmytryk liked, was that he should die straddled against a barbed wire fence, arms outstretched like a crucified Christ. 'Clift was outraged,' Manso notes. 'If Marlon's allowed to do that, I'll walk off the picture,' he said.

In the end he died face down in a puddle, which was OK with Monty. Before dying, Brando had to fall into the puddle. To do so he had to collide with a tree, then roll downhill. He insisted on doing the stunt himself and dislocated his shoulder. No one realized he had hurt himself until after the shoot, when he tried to move and yelled in pain.

Monty, after some hesitation, produced his flask. Although people had guessed what its contents were he had rarely owned up to it. But he could not bear to see Brando suffer when he had the means to lessen it. It contained his usual cocktail of painkillers and alcohol and it did ease Brando's pain until a doctor could get there. He was scarlet-faced with guilt but no one said a word.

Edward Anhalt was another who, Robert LaGuardia recounts, had tasted the contents of that flask. He was sitting with him in his trailer one day when Monty poured him a drink. Within minutes Anhalt felt woozy and asked Monty what he had poured him. 'It's a mixture of bourbon, fruit juice and Demerol,' he confessed disarmingly.

No matter how high Monty became on his cocktail there were never any complaints that he had made an uninvited pass at any man on the set, from his co-stars down to the runners. Not even in the privacy of his trailer. Some of his heterosexual colleagues might have taken a leaf from his book.

Dmytryk had detailed his production manager, Ben Chapman, to ensure that Monty got to the set on time each morning. Chapman had worked on *Raintree County* so knew Monty and liked him; compared to *Raintree County* this job was a piece of cake.

One morning, when Monty was leaving his hotel, he saw Chapman waiting for him by his car. It was not Chapman's lucky day. Monty kept going round in the revolving door until Chapman, driven to distraction, had to go and grab him. Monty was behaving as though he was high, but the only substance he had had that morning was his breakfast. It was a joke on Chapman who burst into laughter, probably out of relief. But others witnessed the scene and gossip abounded that the actor was out of his mind again. So the legend grew, fed by Monty.

He made a friend of actress Hope Lange, who was playing his wife. He would coach her in their scenes together, as he did with all his leading ladies.

As in *Red River* and *From Here to Eternity* there was a fight scene. Although he could punch pretty well by now he wanted to make sure he did not make a fool of himself, so he took lessons from prizefighter Johnny Indrisano. Indrisano was a great character who had been Mae West's lover-bodyguard and chauffeur. Miss West had doted on the black champ, showered him with gifts and even put him in her movies. There was no doubt that the masochistic side of Monty enjoyed his punishing sessions with Indrisano. Each bruise was a pleasure.

Sometimes he was unable to remember long tracts of dialogue, but he knew the sense. Dmytryk would shoot Monty's improvised, abbreviated versions, not insisting on the full speech and realizing he would never get it anyway. But what he got rang true.

As with *Raintree County*, the actual last day of the shoot fell on Monty's birthday. Dmytryk gave him a party. Monty was touched and made one of his speeches, for which he received a round of applause.

It was well deserved, for, although he had had his moments during the shoot, he had tried hard to pull himself together and by and large had succeeded. Dmytryk knew that. There was no comparison between his misbehaviour on *The Young Lions* and *Raintree County*. Neither was there a comparison between his performances. It was clear from the rushes that he was in fine form again. All he had to do now was sustain it.

15

Raintree County was premiered in New York in December 1957, for which Elizabeth and her new husband Mike Todd returned to America from Europe. She had agreed to take the part of Maggie in *Cat on a Hot Tin Roof* opposite Paul Newman's Brick, the part Monty had turned down. She told the press, 'The opportunity to appear in a production based on a work by our greatest living playwright, Tennessee Williams, precludes the possibility of refusal.'

Raintree County was, as Monty had predicted, a colossal success. The public flocked to it out of morbid curiosity, and conversation revolved around Monty's before and after shots. He shrugged it off, but it stung to the quick. 'When people saw my face on the screen,' ran a piece in the *Sun* on 25 July 1966, 'they shrieked, "Oh God, Poor Monty! What's happened to his face!" No one, man or woman, who has once been beautiful easily comes to terms with losing it, particularly when the loss is quick and violent.

Unfortunately his opening scene, with Eva Marie Saint, focused on his puffy, battered face, and even today it shocks. As Jack Babuscio wrote 'the screen persona that Clift had carefully crafted . . . was one which, in essence, was youthful – and this was a quality which the actor no longer seemed able to convincingly embody.'*

The film received universally bad reviews, *Time* magazine dismissing it as an 'opulent, emotional circus'. This did not stop Oscar nominations for Elizabeth, art direction and the music – the theme song became a hit for Nat King Cole. Nor did the contemptuous reviews distress MGM's accountants, who were raking in the profits. Demographs proved that Monty was the main attraction – pre-release research had indicated this, and it was one of the reasons he had secured such a substantial fee on *The Young Lions*. For all the inconvenience he had unwittingly caused he was now making the company a fortune. But for the accident the film, in all probability, would have been a failure.

The Young Lions was to premiere on 2 April 1958 at New York's Paramount Theater as a benefit for the Actors' Studio, so many of his peers would be there. He was more nervous about this than he had been about the opening of *Raintree County*, which as far as he was concerned had already been written off. The accident had left him with a deep inferiority complex and he was frightened that no one would want to see him any more.

A week before the premiere, to which he was taking Libby, Elizabeth was widowed. Todd's plane, the *Lucky Liz*, had proved very unlucky indeed and crashed over a mountain range in New Mexico, killing him. She was distraught beyond comfort.

The funeral was in Chicago, where Todd had been brought up, and Monty flew there out of respect for Elizabeth. He left messages telling her he was there if she needed him, but she had more offers of help than she could accept. He stood silently on the fringes of the VIP guests; no one recognized the thin, middle-aged man in the battered hat and raincoat.

Elizabeth, heavily shrouded in black, flew in from Los Angeles in Howard Hughes's private plane in the company of Dr Kennamer, who had attended Monty immediately after his accident. Among her entourage was Eddie Fisher, a talented young Jewish singer who had adored Mike Todd. His wife, actress Debbie Reynolds, stayed behind with Michael Wilding to look after their, and Elizabeth's, children. Debbie and Eddie had a daughter, Carrie, then a three-year-old, who went on to make her mark by playing the Princess in *Star Wars* and writing *Postcards from the Edge*, a sharp exposé of Hollywood and its star mothers.

Putting his hurt to one side, Wilding had done all he could to help Elizabeth. Probably, at the back of his mind, was the forlorn hope that she might return to him. The odds were long.

The cemetery was jammed with onlookers sitting on tombstones and

1956 still from *Raintree Country* after the accident – not so handsome, but no freak.

Monty,
Katharine
Hepburn and
Elizabeth in
*Suddenly Last
Summer*, 1959.
(*Columbia,
courtesy The
Kobal
Collection*)

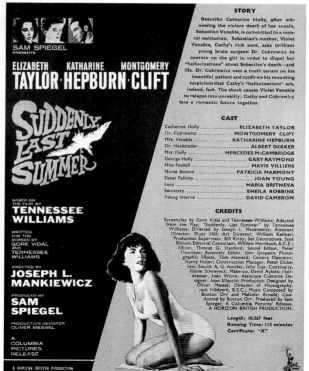

SAM SPIEGEL PRESENTS

ELIZABETH TAYLOR · KATHARINE HEPBURN · MONTGOMERY CLIFT

SUDDENLY LAST SUMMER

BASED ON THE PLAY BY
TENNESSEE WILLIAMS

WRITTEN FOR THE SCREEN BY
GORE VIDAL AND **TENNESSEE WILLIAMS**

DIRECTED BY
JOSEPH L. MANKIEWICZ

PRODUCED BY
SAM SPIEGEL

PRODUCTION DESIGNER
OLIVER MESSEL

A COLUMBIA PICTURES RELEASE

A HORIZON BRITISH PRODUCTION

STORY

Beautiful Catherine Holly, after witnessing the violent death of her cousin, Sebastian Venable, is committed to a mental institution. Sebastian's mother, Violet Venable, Cathy's rich aunt, asks brilliant young brain surgeon Dr. Cukrowicz to operate on the girl in order to dispel her "hallucinations" about Sebastian's death—and life. Dr. Cukrowicz uses a truth serum on his beautiful patient and confirms his mounting suspicions that Cathy's "hallucinations" are, indeed, fact. The shock causes Violet Venable to relapse into unreality; Cathy and Cukrowicz face a romantic future together.

CAST

Catherine Holly	ELIZABETH TAYLOR
Dr. Cukrowicz	MONTGOMERY CLIFT
Mrs. Venable	KATHARINE HEPBURN
Dr. Hockstader	ALBERT DEKKER
Mrs. Holly	MERCEDES McCAMBRIDGE
George Holly	GARY RAYMOND
Miss Foxhill	MAVIS VILLIERS
Nurse Benson	PATRICIA MARMONT
Sister Felicity	JOAN YOUNG
Lucy	MARIA BRITNEVA
Secretary	SHEILA ROBBINS
Young Interne	DAVID CAMERON

CREDITS

Screenplay by Gore Vidal and Tennessee Williams; Adapted from the Play, "Suddenly, Last Summer" by Tennessee Williams; Directed by Joseph L. Mankiewicz; Assistant Director, Bluey Hill; Art Director, William Kellner; Production Supervisor, Bill Kirby; Set Decorations, Scot Slimon; Editorial Consultant, William Hornbeck, A.C.E.; Editor, Thomas G. Stanford; Sound Editor, Peter Thornton; Assembly Editor, John Jympson; Photographic Effects, Tom Howard; Camera Operator, Gerry Fisher; Construction Manager, Peter Dukelow; Sound, A. G. Ambler; John Cox; Continuity, Elaine Schreyeck; Make-up, David Aylott; Hairdresser, Joan White; Associate Costume Designer, Joan Ellacott; Production Designed by Oliver Messel; Director of Photography, Jack Hildyard, B.S.C.; Music Composed by Buxton Orr and Malcolm Arnold; Conducted by Buxton Orr; Produced by Sam Spiegel; A Columbia Pictures' Release. A HORIZON BRITISH PRODUCTION.

Length: 10,267 feet
Running Time: 114 minutes
Certificate: "X"

Advertising
poster from
*Suddenly Last
Summer*.

Monty and Lee Remick in *Wild River*, 1959. (*20th Century Fox, courtesy The Kobal Collection*)

Group shot of *The Misfits*, 1960, the film Arthur Miller wrote for his wife Marilyn. Monty, Marilyn, Gable, John Huston (second row, far right), Eli Wallach, producer Frank Taylor and Arthur Miller at back.

Judgement at Nuremberg (1961) with Maximilian Schell. Both Monty and Judy Garland took cameo roles for which they both received Academy Award nominations – Monty's fourth.

Freud, 1963. (*Universal, courtesy The Kobal Collection*)

His last film, *The Defector*, 1966. Only done as a preparation for *Reflections in a Golden Eye* in which he planned to star with Elizabeth the following year. Brando took over. (*Warner Brothers/Seven Arts, courtesy The Kobal Collection*)

trampling over graves. They drank cola and ate hamburgers, crisps and ice creams bought from nearby vans, the sound of whose speakers sprinkled over the tombs like musical rain. The litter was ankle-deep and the shouts for Elizabeth nearly drowned out the funeral service.

The crowd frightened Monty, as it did Elizabeth and every other celebrity there. There was a distinctly sinister feel to it. As Elizabeth was helped to her car after the service she collapsed and Mike Todd Jr helped her along. The crowd jammed her progress, shoving autograph books and pieces of paper at her. It seemed people were seizing the opportunity to pay her back for her beauty, wealth and charmed life. It was like something from *The Day of the Locusts*. Neither Monty nor Elizabeth ever forgot that ugly crowd.

The premiere of *The Young Lions* was imminent, but at the last moment his nerve went and he told Libby they were not going. She made him pull himself together, so he put on his detested tuxedo – he hated wearing evening clothes – and faced the cameras. The film itself lasted two hours and fifty minutes and was in black and white CinemaScope.

He received an enthusiatic welcome, but once the film had started – he knew he was good, as he had already seen a rough cut – a woman in the balcony screamed in horror at a close up. 'Is that him?' she yelled, and fainted. It reeked of a set-up, just as the appearance of the female fan in his hotel room in Italy had. He hated anything like that. But the scream did nothing to dull the enthusiasm of the audience. When the lights came on he was surrounded by well-wishers, stars among them.

The reporters concentrated on his reaction to the scream from the balcony. He blustered, smiled and joked. But he felt most uncomfortable and it brought home to him the awareness that from now on, no matter how good his performances, he would be remembered for surviving the accident. The *Sunday Express* summed up the mood: 'To those who have seen his earlier films, the face of Montgomery Clift in *The Young Lions* looks distinctly odd.'

There was a reception at the Waldorf, and he and Libby paired with Hope Lange and her husband Don Murray, the actor who had made a hit with Marilyn Monroe in *Bus Stop*. He liked Murray and almost began to enjoy the evening. Everyone was waiting for the early editions of the papers, assuring him he was a success.

The party finished before the papers came out, or so Monty thought, so he, Libby, Lange and Murray went to Reuben's bar to wait for them. But Hope Lange carried a horrible secret which she was forced to reveal. The *New York Times* had already been published, and she had a copy. Monty could sense something was wrong and, guessing what it was, demanded to see the paper. Critic Bosley Crowther had stabbed him in the heart: 'Mr Clift is strangely hollow and lacklustre as the sensitive Jew,' he read. 'He acts throughout the picture as if he were in a glassy-eyed daze.'

Publicist John Springer was at Reuben's when Monty read that and recalled, as he told Robert LaGuardia, 'I never saw a face fall like that . . . he said, "I don't understand it . . ." Hope Lange . . . burst into tears . . .' Other reviews followed, and all were enthusiastic. The *Herald Tribune* was full of praise:

> Clift is superb in his inarticulate anguish as he walks with his girl's father who has never met a Jew. He is no less so in the trying and brutal scenes in the training camp . . . By far the most engrossing of the romantic episodes is the courtship of Montgomery Clift and Hope Lange, which, despite the presence of Marlon Brando, made Clift's performance for me the most outstanding in the movie.

Newsweek considered him 'virtually flawless' and *Time* 'wonderfully funny and touching'. But none of this soothed the Crowther wound. 'The reviews were all terrible,' Monty told people.

Later, at Libby's, says Patricia Bosworth, he burst into tears. 'Noah was the best performance of my life,' he told her. 'I couldn't have given more of myself. 'I'll never be able to do it again. Never.' He was right. He never did. Recently, *Variety* magazine wrote of *The Young Lions* that it 'rates as one of the greats in the ranks of motion pictures'.

In May 1958 Noël Coward was in New York and he and Monty saw each other several times. When Coward sailed back to England Monty, Nancy Walker and Roddy McDowall went to the harbour to see him off. Coward, who loved a boat trip, took the opportunity to keep his diary up to date. His entry for 25 May reads, 'Sailed on Friday, seen off by Monty Clift, Nancy Walker . . . and Roddy McDowall, a curious little group.'* A curious little quartet, with the addition of Coward.

Although Libby was wonderful at building Monty's confidence, she was worried that his damaged looks would affect his appeal. She called him 'the same old Monty' but confessed to friends that everything was different now except, joltingly, his eyes. They remained the same and

---

* *The Noël Coward Diaries* edited by Graham Payne and Sheridan Morley, Weidenfeld & Nicolson, 1982

seemed out of place – ghostly beautiful youthful lanterns in his hollow face. They seemed to belonged to someone else, a young man's eyes transplanted into his sockets. His weight loss accentuated this. He could not put the weight back on.

Libby was depressed over the loss of her own looks. Due to her operation she was like a living skeleton with only a bit of thin hair still attached to the scalp. Monty spent much of the summer of 1958 with her at Treetops. Both formerly stunning in their different ways, they were now spectral parodies of what they had been.

Dreams That Money Can Buy records that composer Ned Rorem came to stay. A friend of Jean Cocteau and Leonard Bernstein, Rorem thought Monty a 'spoiled, cantankerous drunk'. He added that there was a 'kind of translucence to his skin, a sickly sheen. The former pretty boy looked like a sexagenarian.'

In New York Maureen Stapleton was in a TV version of *For Whom the Bell Tolls*. She introduced Monty to the cast, which included Maria Schell (sister of Maximilian), Jason Robards and Christopher Plummer. They would gather at Monty's duplex and talk the night away.

If left alone he had panic attacks, the residue of shock from the accident. When these happened he would telephone anyone he knew, begging them to come round. Bill Gunn was working in Massachusetts at the time and received a call one night. Monty begged him to come back to New York. A short time later a car and driver arrived to take him to the airport, where he would be flown by charter to New York. It was morning by the time he arrived, so he took a taxi to the duplex. He could get no answer. Knowing of Monty's pill-induced comas, he telephoned from a call box. Eventually, a befuddled Monty answered. What was Bill doing in New York? He had no recollection of arranging transport. Apologetically, he arranged for a helicopter to take him back to Massachusetts.

Marge Stengel spoke to Silverberg about Monty's addiction to drugs. As usual the man would not be drawn into a discussion, telling her that the psychiatrist's couch was confidential. For a while Monty was hospitalized with what he believed was hepatitis, but was really a ruse to dry him out. He bribed staff to smuggle in bottles. He was diagnosed as having high blood pressure complicated by an enlarged thryroid gland. He still suffered the head pains from which he had never been free since the accident and which, he told Fred Zinnemann, were worse than migraine. There was an added pain when filming, as strong lights hurt his eyes. He worried that he was going blind.

That autumn he flew to Hollywood to star in *Lonelyhearts* for independent producer Dore Schary, about whom, according to *Halliwell's Film Companion*, John Simon wrote, 'A man whose few successes were even more distasteful than his many failures.' Based on Nathanael West's allegory *Miss Lonelyhearts*, the film tells the story of a journalist's disenchantment at the work he has to do when he becomes an agony aunt.

Monty was beginning to get over the Bosley Crowther snipe and take a pride in *The Young Lions*. He believed he was on course – not as a pretty boy now, something he had rather despised (although snatching at the benefits), but as an actor, his true vocation. He admired West's bitter novel and hoped it would translate to the screen. So far, Schary's treatment seemed to be along the right lines. The cast included Maureen Stapleton who was making her movie debut, Robert Ryan, veteran star Myrna Loy and Dolores Hart, who eventually had enough of the rat race and gave it all up to become a nun.

Nancy Walker flew down to visit, as did Libby, with whom he spent Christmas in Key West. He had also acquired a new boyfriend, a Frenchman called Giles. Despite her own many lovers, and the fact that she had a new boyfriend herself, Libby always suffered a pang of jealousy whenever Monty took up with anyone new, viewing it as an infidelity.

Giles wanted to move in with Monty lock, stock and barrel, but he would have none of it. He had had a hard time getting Dino out when their affair was over and did not want to fall into that trap again. It suited him to have men around when he wanted them, and that was not all the time. Few of his friends were introduced to his lovers – he kept them all compartmentalized.

Before accepting *Lonelyhearts* he had nearly landed himself the role of the preacher in the Hecht-Hill-Lancaster film of George Bernard Shaw's *The Devil's Disciple*. On Shaw's own admission this is not his greatest play, but Monty was keen to do it. Burt Lancaster had bought the rights for $60,000 and was its producer as well as appearing in the film.

But as producer he found he could not insure Monty. Talk of his alcoholism and drug dependence was widespread. According to Lancaster's biographer, Michael Munn, he found insurance companies refused to cover Clift for a film part. This problem was to pursue Monty for the rest of his life. Clearly some insurance companies were prepared to cover him, otherwise he could never have made another film; but it was an uphill battle, and sometimes Monty was not aware quite how uphill that battle was.

Marilyn Monroe, then thirty-two, was in Hollywood making *Some Like It Hot* for Billy Wilder, her first Hollywood film since *Bus Stop*, although *The Prince and the Showgirl*, shot in London, had come between. The press were hounding her, something which she had not wholly discouraged in the past but which at times had its drawbacks. She and Monty had dinner together and commiserated on the trials of being stars.

Monty was a hero of Marilyn's, one of her role models when she was aspiring to become a serious actress at the Actors' Studio. He was a fan of hers too, and had loved her in *Bus Stop*. He had actually been offered the Don Murray part first and, after seeing the film, wished he had taken it.

One evening she and Monty got drunk together, he on scotch and she on rum. Monty visibly disintegrated, slurring his words and knocking things over. If anything, the experience endeared him to her. Powerful, beautiful women regularly fell for Monty's lost boy charm. He and Marilyn formed a bond that was to sustain them both in the future when they co-starred in her husband Arthur Miller's *The Misfits*. After they got drunk Marilyn remarked, 'He's the only person I know who's in worse shape than I am.'* When the final script for *Lonelyhearts* arrived Monty was disappointed. He thought it had lost much of its bite and that the satire had been diluted by sentiment. Maureen Stapleton agreed, although she was later to win an Academy nomination for her part. Nancy Walker told him it was a mistake to do the film. 'I'm used to being disappointed,' he told her.

It was never intended to be a big movie. Schary, making it for United Artists, had a budget of $1 million and out of that Monty's fee was $100,000. The director was Vincent J. Donehue, who came to Hollywood specifically to work with Monty. This was his first movie; he had only done stage work before. He was sensitive to Monty's problems, and they got on at once. The fact that he was a theatrical director immediately elevated him in Monty's eyes. At rehearsals at the Goldwyn studios the cast discussed their parts at length, as though they were doing a live drama – just the sort of thing he enjoyed. Robert Ryan soon came to appreciate Monty's qualities. Monty had read all of West's novels and Ryan came to value his advice. They would huddle for hours.

Marilyn was also at the Goldwyn studios. They visited each other in their dressing rooms and planned to do *Cat on a Hot Tin Roof* together one day. Marilyn was keen both to do a Williams play and to work

* *Goddess: The Secret Lives of Marilyn Monroe* by Anthony Summers, Sphere, 1986

with Monty. She wanted to concentrate on drama now, and at the time Arthur Miller was actually working on *The Misfits* predominantly as a vehicle for her.

There was a fight scene in *Lonelyhearts* between Monty and actor Mike Kellin. Monty punched Kellin so hard that he nearly knocked him out, providing a brilliant take. When Kellin recovered, and had been checked out at the hospital, he took it well. But Monty had enough technique by now to know that he did not need to throw a real punch. It was taking advantage.

He was sorry for hurting Kellin but had not been able to stop himself. He started to cry, and something broke inside and he could not stop. It was afternoon and Donehue had a good take, so he sent him back to the Bel Air Hotel, where he was staying, for the rest of the day. Whenever he made a film he paid Silverberg a retainer. This meant he could speak to him on the phone as often, and for as long, as he wanted. He phoned him in New York that afternoon.

Like Dmytryk, Donehue came to realize that Monty could only work in the mornings – by the afternoon he was spent. He had tried to keep going, but the results were dire. He would stay and watch the others for a while, offering to do anything that was required, but returned to the Bel Air at about 3.30.

He had trouble memorizing lines. This had been a problem on *The Young Lions* but he had managed to struggle through. Now he found it was worse. He made jokes about his problem and did his utmost to underplay his panic. However, this affected the way Donehue had to shoot, as there had to be plenty of cutaways to cover Monty if he dried. The dreaded, but by now familiar, panic attacks would surge up and he could feel the part slipping from his grasp. At rushes what he saw on the screen was not always what he had intended. No one criticized; in fact everyone was full of praise. This was not hypocritical – the rest of the cast could see he was shaping a fine performance. But it was not totally the shape he intended, and that unnerved him.

The crew downright spoilt him, even when he stomped around the set the worse for wear and caused delays. Like Dmytryk, they knew there was nothing evil in him. Quite the reverse – he was often fun.

He made another friend for life in the down-to-earth form of Myrna Loy. Known as the Queen of Hollywood during the 1930s, she was now in her fifties and had shifted painlessly to character roles. She had no delusions about film-making and possessed a caustic wit. She often had lunch with Monty in his dressing room, along with Nancy Walker and Maureen Stapleton. The butch Robert Ryan looked on indulgently as the ladies flocked to Monty's room. Peals of laughter could be heard coming from inside.

Monty was by now addicted to Seconal, Tuinal and Doriden among other drugs of a similar nature. According to Dr William Russell, MB, MRCGP, writing in 1996 in a letter to the author;

> Seconal and Tuinal are quinalbarbitone and a mixture of amilobarbitone plus quinalbarbitone respectively. These drugs are now regarded as dangerous because of their ability to make patients dependent upon them and are in fact covered by the Dangerous Drugs Act at the moment. However, in the 1950s and '60s they were widely prescribed. Doriden was a sleeping pill developed from a different compound in an effort to overcome the dependence but in fact it also had the potential for dependence and was eventually taken off the market.

Fred Zinnemann had noticed a complete personality change in Monty since the accident. The concussion had had far-reaching and unrecognized effects and, in his haste to get back to work, these had not been fully treated. It was ridiculous that he, a hypochondriac, should not seek further treatment. He had always been eccentric but had long passed that boundary. His endless telephone sessions with Silverberg reassured him that it was good to drink alcohol – it demolished barriers. To live without alcohol was impossible, and he was not strong enough to struggle.

The Swinging Sixties were looming and it was becoming fashionable to shoot up all manner of mind-blowing drugs. He would not entertain any of them. Patricia Bosworth relates that Brooks, as emotionally unbalanced as Monty and now on his third wife, told him he was thinking of experimenting with LSD.

Monty was appalled. 'If I were paid $500 I wouldn't take lysergic acid,' he wrote to Brooks in alarm. 'You are dealing with a terrible unknown and I say this caring for your love life.' On this occasion he sent Brooks $1000 – he regularly sent money to Brooks and others.

No sooner had he sent the cheque than *McCall's* magazine published an article in which Monty allegedly criticized Brooks's louche lifestyle. He had never made the remarks and had never mentioned his family to journalists. This sometimes annoyed Brooks, who would have enjoyed the publicity. Brooks cashed in, although in a non-malicious way, on Monty's name whenever he could. He even appeared on TV talking about his famous brother. This upset Monty, who could not bear his private life being aired in public. He was truly a star who despised personal publicity.

Lonelyhearts was completed in forty-five days and he returned to New York, relieved, as always, to be rid of Hollywood. By now film-making had become a chore rather than a pleasure, although socially he had enjoyed this one more than any other film to date. But he was depressed, and he felt the film was not particularly good. He later modified this opinion and would, on occasion, even recommend it. But not always.

Like others, Arthur Miller thought the source of Monty's unhappiness was his homosexuality, or rather his struggle against it. 'I thought later on that if he had been born ten years later, he would still be alive,' he was quoted by Robert LaGuardia as saying in 1977. 'This struggle that he secretly fought caused him great guilt. He never discussed it with me but I could sense it, because he wasn't that inscrutable.' James Jones thought that he was simply too sensitive for this harsh world.

Like many sensitive people, however, he was not always so sensitive to the suffering he caused others. Most of his friends suffered a barrage of insults or unfair treatment at his hands throughout the years, admittedly only when he was drunk – but he was drunk a great deal of the time. If he remembered what he had done, or it was brought to his attention, he would apologise sincerely. This was usually accepted, though had he not been a star he might not have received such understanding.

Psychoanalysis was Monty's answer to any problem, and he embarrassed Nancy Walker by buying her an emerald necklace to celebrate her first year of analysis. For Monty this was something of which to be proud.

Film companies were not falling over themselves to offer him work now. He had received only $100,000 for Lonelyhearts, less that one-seventh of what he had received for The Young Lions, and it was not a major film. A regular trickle of scripts was submitted by upstart producers, but these were unacceptable, low-budget horror films and thrillers. Although he had worked dedicatedly on The Young Lions and Lonelyhearts, his reputation had defeated him. Word was out that Lonelyhearts would not do good business – which was right, for it didn't. When released in March 1959 it was damned – not for his performance, but the film itself. The Herald Tribune summed it up: 'Lonelyhearts is a bit hard to take even though Montgomery Clift works every hesitant eyeball-rolling moment to the bone.'

He was now an unreliable has-been. His looks were gone and the curiosity which had brought audiences to Raintree County had been sated. The great promise he had shown was burnt out and there was nothing much left. MGM rejected him for *The Brothers Karamazov* and Yul Brynner got the part. He was considered by David O. Selznick for *Tender is the Night*, to star opposite his wife Jennifer Jones who had been so smitten by him in *Stazione Termini*. The director, John Frankenheimer, thought he would be ideal. Selznick, on reflection, reconsidered and wrote to his wife, 'Monty Clift has, I think, become impossible to work with . . .' She recognized the truth of this. It was Elizabeth Taylor who saved him.

16

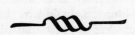

Elizabeth had chosen to star in the Columbia Pictures production of Tennessee Williams's one-act play *Suddenly Last Summer*. This was a fashionable piece, originally part of a double bill of two one-acters entitled *Garden District*. Its off-Broadway production in 1958 had caused a sensation, becoming the most talked about event of the season. The film was adapted for the screen by Gore Vidal, with bizarre decor by Oliver Messel.

Tennessee Williams was at the height of his acclaim and this was to be a prestigious production. In addition to Elizabeth the cast included Katharine Hepburn. The director was Joseph L. Mankiewicz, who had made such hits as *All About Eve* with Bette Davis, *Julius Caesar* with Brando and *The Barefoot Contessa* with Ava Gardner. Mankiewicz had not wanted Monty for *Suddenly Last Summer*, scared he would let him down, but Elizabeth had insisted. Given her bankability – her fee of $500,000 made her the highest paid actress in the world at that time – Columbia agreed to go ahead with Monty, even though there was a problem with his insurance. No doctor would pronounce him fit.

The film was to be shot at Shepperton Studios in England, which worked out cheaper even though the principals had to be transported and accommodated there. So Monty flew to London with Marge, arriving at Heathrow on 14 May 1959. He did not receive the most reassuring

of welcomes from the British press. He was discomfited, and annoyed,
by the barrage of questions about his marital status. Why wasn't he
married? the reporters wanted to know. They knew exactly why.

Trying to build on his somewhat repaired reputation for reliability
after *Lonelyhearts* – and he had tried hard to be reliable – he was
determined to be on his best behaviour. He personally delivered a
bouquet to Katharine Hepburn, which delighted her. Worried about
the health of her alcoholic lover Spencer Tracy, she was not feeling
at her brightest. She had not realized until after she had signed her
contract that the film was to be made in England.

Hepburn told Monty that Mankiewicz was ill, and he called on the
director to pay his respects. He stayed to dinner, which was a mistake.
The veneer cracked. He had taken medication but started to drink. He
knew the effect the combination would have, but was unable to resist.
Mr and Mrs Mankiewicz were not best amused as their haute cuisine
was thrown about the room. Monty thought it hysterical while it lasted,
but was full of remorse in the morning.

When Mankiewicz started to work with Monty, before Elizabeth
arrived, there was, understandably, some coolness. Monty felt ostracised.
In order to work well he needed support, such as he had received on
Lonelyhearts.

The theme of *Suddenly Last Summer* was not conducive to jollity,
either. The story concerned the death by cannibalism of homosexual
Sebastian Venable, who had preyed upon the available youths of a
Spanish resort. Mrs Venable (Katharine Hepburn), Sebastian's wealthy
mother, consults Dr Cukrowicz (Monty) to try to persuade him to
perform a lobotomy on her niece Cathie (Elizabeth), who, she says,
is perpetuating 'a hideous attack on my son's moral character'. If
Cukrowicz performs the lobotomy she will finance a new wing for
his hospital. In truth, Cathie had been used by Sebastian as bait for
the youths after Mrs Venable became too old to attract them, and
Cathie had witnessed his murder when a gang of boys tore him to
death in revenge and ate him alive. She had told what she had seen
and Mrs Venable, in order to protect Sebastian's reputation, had had
her committed to a lunatic asylum and requested Cukrowicz to excise
the incident from her memory by surgical means.

It was the most ornately barbarous story that Williams had ever used
for a play. In 1973, well after the film was finished, Mankiewicz described
it as 'a badly constructed play based on the most elementary Freudian
psychology and one anecdote'. That seems a rather harsh judgement.

According to critic Kenneth L Geist, the cannibalism is meant to recall the martyrdom of St Sebastian – in the play, a painting of the saint hangs in the conservatory. Cathie's final monologue, in which she recalls the incident, parallels 'the learned speech of Saint Catherine of Alexandria'. Few in the audience would have picked up on that.

Lobotomies, now largely discredited, were newsworthy at the time. The technique involved manipulation of the brain with a sharp instrument, which resulted in formerly troublesome patients becoming placid. The most notorious case had involved film star Frances Farmer, who had been arrested on a motoring offence, caused uproar at her trial and committed to jail. When she continued to give trouble she was submitted for surgery. She emerged a shadow of her former self and lived the rest of her life in docile submission. A similar operation had been performed on Williams's own beloved sister. It was a subject painfully close to his heart. In his memoirs Williams testifies to the autobiographical content of *Suddenly Last Summer*.

Mercedes McCambridge, also in the cast, remembers the movie as an unhappy experience. The stage doors marked CLOSED SET, NO VISITORS ALLOWED seemed to set the mood. Messel's jungle-like set was oppressive: the script called for a Venus Flytrap – an insect-eating plant – and macabre fun was had by the crew who fed it meat.

Mankiewicz, still unwell, was suffering from a condition which caused the skin on his fingers to split and had to wear gloves the whole time. Hepburn, who had just learnt that Tracy was now suffering from emphysema, was not at her best either.

Kenneth L. Geist, then a student, had permission from Mankiewicz to visit the set and later, in *Pictures Will Talk** recalled his reaction to Monty:

> It was a considerable shock to see this sensitive actor's deplorable condition . . . he was now a mass of tics and spasms, constantly snorting from an ever-handy inhaler . . . My curiosity about how Clift could be photographed in this condition, let alone act, was soon satisfied . . . Mankieciwz grasped Clift by the shoulders and began to impart his directorial suggestions. While riveting Clift's attention with a piercing gaze, Mankiewicz surreptitiously started to massage Clift's neck and shoulders. The result was astonishing. Clift's tremors subsided and, despite the annoyance of a malfunctioning fountain, he maintained his composure through a series of repeated takes.

* *Pictures Will Talk* by Kenneth L. Geist, Frederick Muller Ltd, 1974

Mankiewicz's massages may have helped Monty physically, but could do nothing to induce him to act in a way he felt wrong for. According to Geist Cukrowicz would say, 'What's wrong with him?' and Mankiewicz would snap, 'He acts like he doesn't hear me.'

He was having trouble, as usual, learning his lines, and Mankiewicz was not as understanding as Donehue had been on *Lonelyhearts*. It was not laziness. He tried to learn the words but they would not stick in his brain. When he dried on the floor of the set, the panic attacks flared up.

Elizabeth had just married Eddie Fisher in a blaze of publicity. Mankiewicz, having heard how close Monty was to her, assured a worried crew that things would improve when she arrived. Actress Pat Marmont, also in the movie, recalled in a conversation with the author:

> It was a hard time for him [Monty] and we were aware of it. But we were assured by Joe Mankiewicz that as soon as Liz arrived he would be all right. And he did improve. But it was difficult working with him. We shared a scene, just half a page or so of dialogue, but we took over thirty takes on that one scene alone and then started again the next morning – he just could not remember his words. But he was very likeable, although he was all over the place. And very shy. I just wanted to get him through it. It was very difficult.
>
> There was a strange arrangement on that film. All three principals would go to their caravans and have their lunch and the rest of us would have lunch in the canteen. It was two distinct camps and they never mixed. The non-principals formed a little repertory company.

Monty took greatly to Gary Raymond, the handsome young actor playing George Holly, Cathie's brother. He had a photograph of him and put it on the mantelpiece. He was clean-cut, punctual and line-perfect, an example for Monty. Raymond liked him too, and still has warm memories as he explained to the author:

> He was a delight. There was no question of not getting on with him – his whole attitude was getting on with us. He was wonderful. He met my [then] fiancée Delina [actress Delina Kidd] and visited us at her flat in Westminster. We both liked him enormously.
>
> Katherine Hepburn was extremely good with him, too. She knew

**everything there was to know about the play and she was very
protective of him. We all liked him. He was very popular.**

Known for her short fuse, Hepburn was patience personified with Monty.
When he forgot his lines and spoilt a scene she had done superbly, she
would simply do it again. 'He used to have the most peculiar expression
on his face,' she recalled in her biography. 'Whenever we'd shot a scene
big beads of sweat would pop out on his forehead.'* She invited him to
spend the weekend with her and tried to talk him off the bottle – after
all, Tracy was also a drinker. 'None of my arguments,' she continued,
'did any good. I thought he was weak. Simpatico but weak.'

Mankiewicz had envisaged long takes between Monty and Hepburn
but had to abort the idea, as had Donehue. He just had to adapt to
what Monty could give.

Producer Sam Spiegel wanted to replace Monty, particularly on those
days when his insecurity jeopardized the film. But then Monty would
have a good day and all was forgiven: 'I was fond of him,' Spiegel told
Robert LaGuardia. 'I spent hours and hours . . . practically nursing him
– postponing the shooting until I knew he was calm.' Later he added,
as recorded by David Heymann in *Liz*, 'We would have been better
off casting Monty as one of the mental patients in the film rather than
a doctor.'

It was not Spiegel's affection that kept Monty employed. Anne
Edwards says he had mentioned to Elizabeth that he thought of
replacing him with a young actor called Peter O'Toole and she had
snapped, 'Over my dead body!' In *Starring Roles* Ron Base writes that
O'Toole had actually tested for the part, during which he had mimed
performing an operation, then turned to camera and quipped, 'Your
son will never play the violin again.'

In her biography *Elizabeth Taylor* Kitty Kelley explained, that,
according to writer Max Lerner, Elizabeth felt a degree of guilt since
Monty had suffered the accident after leaving her home. 'Elizabeth
talked to me a great deal about Monty Clift and the car accident . . .
She felt very responsible for that accident and said she felt she had let
Monty down.'

In her biography of Katharine Hepburn, Anne Edwards says Liz's
language was so profane during the shoot that she 'terribly offended
the British crew'. If that was so, British crews were a sight more
easily offended then than they are today. Elizabeth was severely tried

---

* *Katharine Hepburn* by Anne Edwards, Hodder & Stoughton, 1986

at the time. Her new husband, Eddie Fisher, had been married to Debbie Reynolds and the press blamed her for the breakdown of that marriage.

The assistant director was Bluey Hill, married to actress Chili Bouchier. Monty was playing a brain surgeon and Miss Bouchier recalled in conversation with the author her husband seeing the funny side of this. Monty's hands were shaking so much in the mornings that he could barely hold his coffee cup steady, let alone a scalpel. In keeping with the rest of the cast, Hill liked him. 'He was very fond of him,' Miss Bouchier says, 'and he was great fun, a great sense of humour.'

For all the support Monty received from the cast, he could not break through with Mankiewicz. All the director could see was his project being ruined by an incompetent actor who had behaved preposterously at dinner. As Spiegel put it, 'Mankiewicz is an excellent director but devoid of a great many human considerations when it comes to weaker beings than himself.'

Monty's driver, Roy Pryce, used to arrange cushions in the back of the car so that he could snooze comfortably in the hour or so's drive from London to Shepperton. He was in the car with Mercedes McCambridge one rainy morning when they drove past Wormwood Scrubs. They thought the prison summed up their feelings. Laurence Harvey, the swashbuckling leading man, was on another set and swaggered in to visit them one day, wearing a silk dressing gown and conscious of the honour he was bestowing. Monty whispered, 'Wormwood Scrubs' to Mercedes, and they fell about. Harvey left looking puzzled.

Hepburn grew increasingly hostile towards Mankiewicz who, she thought, in addition to favouring Elizabeth to her own detriment, was being too hard on Monty. One day, when she had suggested a certain way of doing a scene, Mankiewicz sarcastically told her he had sent for her director's ticket. She walked off the set.

According to Anne Edwards's biography, when the last shot had been taken she asked, 'Are you quite sure we're finished?' He said he was. She spat in his face. Later she commented, 'When I disapprove of something, it's the only thing I can think of to do. It's a rather rude gesture, but at least it's clear what you mean.' Some have interpreted her action as a comment on the harsh way Mankiewicz had treated Monty. She put the record straight by emphasizing that it had nothing to do with Monty but was entirely in response to the way Mankiewicz had treated her.

Both the editor, William Hornbeck (a friend of Monty's, with whom he had worked on *A Place in the Sun*), and the cinematographer, Jack Hildyard, aver that Mankiewicz did not ill-treat Monty. But Hornbeck testifies Mankiewicz asked him to sit with Monty in his dressing room to ascertain if he was taking drugs – Mankiewicz could think of no other reason for Monty's memory lapses. Hornbeck never saw him take anything suspicious.

Knowing of Hornbeck's affection for Monty, Mankiewicz delegated him to persuade Monty to dub some lines that had been spoilt due to extraneous traffic sounds. Monty refused, insisting that the lines in the film were right. When Hornbeck persevered, he flew into a rage, In *Pictures Will Talk* Kenneth L. Geist quotes Hornbeck as saying: 'He [Monty] did the strangest thing. He lay down and rolled around on the floor like a naughty child. He was so infantile and so nasty that I grew very irritated with him. I said, "It's really a shame you can't behave like an adult."' He finally agreed to the dub, with ill grace, and parted bad friends with Hornbeck. Next day he sent him a pound of caviar with an apology.

He got his own back on Mankiewicz, Gerist reports. Monty was frequently late and Mankiewicz was understandably furious. One morning he arrived at 8.30, but instead of going to the set sat with Hornbeck in his cutting room. He refused to leave until 9.30. When Mankiewicz opened his mouth to protest, he snapped, 'I've been here since 8.30.'

Due to the vogue for Tennessee Williams's plays, the sensational subject matter and the illustrious cast, *Suddenly Last Summer* did well at the box office, rather to Columbia's surprise. Now it is regarded as a trail-blazer, opening the gates to a flood of sexually explicit films. Both Katharine Hepburn and Elizabeth Taylor received Academy nominations: 'If there were ever any doubts about the ability of Miss Taylor to express complex and devious emotions, to deliver a flexible and deep performance, this film ought to remove them,' gushed the *New York Herald Tribune*. Britain's C.A. Lejeune felt differently: 'I loathe this film, I say so candidly. To my mind it is a decadent piece of work, sensational, barbarous and ridiculous.' *Variety* was less vitriolic, but still not impressed, calling it 'Possibly the most bizarre film ever made by a major American company.'

Also in uncomplimentary mood was Bosley Crowther in the *New York Times*: 'Mr Williams and Gore Vidal have indulged in sheer verbal melodramatics which have small effect on the screen and are barely elevated from tedium by some incidental stories of inmates of a mental institution.' *Film Daily* was more approving: 'Tennessee Williams' brooding, probing study of a set of introverted people and how they use each other in a devouring way is here brought to the screen with striking theatrical flair.' Finally, Noël Coward committed these waspish observations to his diary: 'Suddenly Last Summer, beautifully acted by Kate Hepburn, Liz Taylor and Monty Clift, was poor Tennessee Williams at his worst. It was full of horrors, so many really that it was idiotic. Madness, brain operations, queerness, cannibalism and a few high-flown observations on life, no particular shape and badly directed by Joe Mankiewicz.'

When the film was over Monty was glad to return to New York. By his standards he was in fair physical condition and as happy as he could be. He liked London and had had some fun, but New York was home.

On 24 September 1959, Libby Holman was driving down East 61st Street when she saw fire engines outside Monty's duplex. Smoke was billowing out. Fearing the worst, she left her new fiancé, Louis Schanker, in the car and, forcing her way through the crowd, made her way in. She found Monty in bed with Giles. Workmen had accidentally caused a fire in the lobby. Monty and the Frenchman, unable to do much about it, had remained in bed. The blaze was a gift of a story to the press. Rumour had it that Monty had set fire to himself.

The fire caused considerable damage, leaving the place filthy, but he refused to move to a hotel and lived in it as it was until it could be redecorated. He felt secure there.

In November, a bare two months after Suddenly Last Summer ended, shooting began for 20th Century-Fox on Elia Kazan's Wild River. Monty had taken the film simply for the money, and did not really want to do it – in fact he told the author he did not want to make any films at all.

Elizabeth was working on Butterfield 8 in which Eddie Fisher had a part – he was a busy man, filming in the daytime and appearing in the evenings at the Empire Room of the Waldorf Astoria. An inexperienced actor, he asked Monty for help, which he was pleased to give.

Monty was delighted to be working with Kazan again, even though the director's career was in one of its periodic troughs. After directing A Streetcar Named Desire and East of Eden he had not had a film released since A Face in the Crowd in 1957.

Kazan had been working on Wild River on and off for years. Set in 1933, in a Tennessee valley, it is about a matriarch, Jo Van Fleet (who had received an Oscar for East of Eden) who refuses to leave her home although it is about to be deliberately flooded by the water authorities. Monty was Chuck Glover, the official from the Tennessee

Valley Authority who tries to evict her and, while doing so has an affair with her granddaughter, Lee Remick.

'I'd conceived of this film years before as homage to the spirit of FDR,' Kazan wrote in his autobiography *A Life*. 'My hero was to be a resolute New Dealer engaged in the difficult task of convincing "reactionary" country people that it was necessary, in the name of public good, for them to move off their land . . . Now I found my sympathies were with the obdurate old lady who lived on the island that was to be inundated and who refused to be patriotic . . . I was all for her.'

Monty had not been Kazan's first choice; he had wanted Brando.

> Then I began to see how the part could be played as a rather uncertain and inept social-working intellectual from the big city, dealing with people who were stronger and more confirmed in their beliefs than he was. I'd known Monty for many years, directed him sixteen years before in *The Skin of Our Teeth*, remembered him even before that as an insecure boy who'd curl up on the floor at the foot of the chair where Molly [Kazan's wife] was sitting and confide his problems to her . . . Monty's sexuality was of a child waiting for his mother to put her arms around him . . .
>
> He was no longer handsome, and there was strain everywhere in him – even, it seemed, in his effort to stand erect. As far as my story went, he'd be no match for the country people whom he'd have to convince of the 'greater good', and certainly no physical match for any of them if it came to violence. Pictorially, the story would be the weak against the strong – in reverse . . .

Kazan was in no doubt that the chemistry between the matriarch and the man from the Authority would work:

> 'The old lady of the island . . . was played by one of the great character actresses of that day, Jo Van Fleet, aged thirty-seven, as difficult and dear a woman as a director in need of a performance could hope for. I . . . knew her strong will and knew its purpose: to excel. Full of unconstrained violence, she'd eat Clift alive, and I was prepared to let her . . . Whereas Clift, sleepy and shaky, had something wobbly about his appearance in the morning, Jo would barge into the makeup room at 4a.m. and give five hours to transforming herself into an indomitable backriver matriarch . . . Clift was a tenderhearted shell of a man, Jo as formidable and unyielding as the rock-ribbed country where we were working.

Kazan's idea of the weak versus the strong carried through to the love interest: 'I cast one of the finest young actresses I knew, Lee Remick, then at the top of her strength and confidence – but not without some official opposition. On one of my trips to the Fox studios . . . I'd had an absurd casting conference with the new head of production, Buddy Adler. He urged me to cast Marilyn Monroe in the role. Had he read the script. . .?'

The movie was shot in Cleveland, Tennessee, and Monty stayed at the Cherokee Hotel. Marge was not with him. She had accompanied him on four films and wanted a break. Her replacement was a young actress called Donna Carnegie, who promptly fell in love with him.

Mira, however, was with him, and endeared herself to Kazan from the start when she stationed herself beside the camera. '"Ah," I said to myself,' wrote Kazan in *A Life*, '"I have a co-director."' He went on:

> I couldn't check on what signals of approval or disapproval she was conveying to my hero, but I knew that a glance at the wrong time could make trouble for me, so I told Monty I didn't want her there and she disappeared . . . she continued, I was sure, to work with Monty at night. At least she kept him distracted until dawn, so I never enquired into what they did . . . He always showed up in the morning, quivering but ready and willing, and perhaps I have her to thank.

Lee Remick adored him and, unlike Elizabeth, did not have to protect him from the director as there was no animosity between Kazan and Monty. She confided to Robert LaGuardia, 'He did inspire in me, as he did in most women, I suppose, the feeling of wanting to look after him. He was like a wounded bird – so vulnerable. He was clearly a troubled soul. He made me feel needed.'

Kazan brought their personal relationship into the film.

> The contrast between her [Remick's] sureness and Monty's insecurity was what I wanted. In their love scenes she was dominant and Monty seemed sexually uncertain. He was. She was . . . sexually confident. And aggressive. This contrast was so strong that at first I was frustrated and disappointed. Then I decided to go with it. In one scene Monty, at the instant of arousal, slumped to the floor. I cursed him under my breath as a limp lover. Then I decided to play the scene as it happened, on the floor and at the very back of the room. I didn't move the camera closer. At twenty feet, the

lovemaking seemed spontaneous and heated. Still, Lee was taking him, not vice versa. Again the accident of personality turned to my advantage.' Their on-screen romance climaxed with Remick begging him to marry her, 'I just want you to marry me. I'll defend you for the rest of my life.'

Kazan kept the weak hero motif going even among the small part players. In her first film part, Barbara Loden, playing a clerk, had precisely the quality Kazan was seeking: 'When she stood next to Monty, the contrast I was reaching for, that reverse balance of strength between him and the natives of the region, was plain to see. The picture itself told the story – as it always should.'

Kazan knew of Monty's reputation as a drunk but had no problems on that score: 'Before agreeing to take him for the part, I'd extracted a solemn promise that he would not take a drink from the first day of work until the last. He kept his promise . . .' With Kazan and Remick's support, he did not need to drink so much. There was less to fear. He was a model actor, returning to his hotel after the shoot, learning his lines with Donna and studying his motivation with Mira. The locals rarely saw him.

Kazan and Monty's Method backgrounds created an empathy between them. Unlike Hitchcock, Kazan appreciated how Monty worked. As they sat, discussing their motivation, Monty would leap up, flowing with ideas, many of which Kazan used. Kazan encouraged improvisation, and much of the dialogue was made up as they went along.

Everyone was eager to be finished by Christmas, and it looked as though this might happen. Then Lee Remick's husband had a car crash and filming stopped while she went to him. Monty knew all about car crashes and she was touched when he hesitantly recommended Dr Kennamer, telling her how helpful he had been to him.

Filming was scheduled to resume a week later, but by then the weather had broken. Snow made continuity impossible for almost another week and, when the shoot resumed Monty broke his vow of abstinence: 'He kept his promise,' Kazan wrote in *A Life*,

surviving days of stress and physical discomfort without the help of a bottle until the very last day, when he arrived on the set swaying on his feet, then keeled over. When I got to him on the ground, he was asleep. I forgave him the lapse; I thought he'd done well by me. I knew I was handling a sick man, who was goodhearted and in no way evil. I can still recall the pathetic happy laugh that would burst out of him, then subside just as suddenly . . . As we went along, his confidence grew, and I believe he was easier to work with in films that followed. Despite all, I felt tender toward him. He was just a boy.

The film was released in July 1960. It is a lacklustre affair, worth watching only for Jo Van Fleet. Monty has no magic and, for all Kazan's enthusiasm, his scenes with Lee Remick are unconvincing. It received polite acknowledgement in most places except in France where for some reason it did exceptionally well and certain critics cited it as one of Kazan's best. But it did not attract much world attention, and Fox lost money.

'Some of his [Monty's] later films, such as Kazan's *Wild River*, miscast him or, like Joseph L. Mankiewicz's *Suddenly Last Summer*, called on him mainly to sacrifice himself in what were essentially secondary roles,' wrote a critic in the *Times* of 25 July 1966. Kazan himself summed up the film in *A Life* as

one of my favourites, possibly because of its social ambivalence. Jean Renoir's famous phrase, 'Everyone has his reasons,' was true here. Both sides were 'right'. *Wild River* is also a favourite of certain French film critics; one prominent fellow went so far as to name it as one of the twenty best films of all time – which it certainly is not. Skouras [President of Fox] and his sales force had an opposite view and treated the film deplorably; jerking it out of theatres before it had any chance to take hold and booking it thinly across the country. It was not exhibited in Europe until I staged a stormy scene in Spyros's office and shamed him . . . Money makes the rules of the market, and by this rule, the film was a disaster.

17

Monty's next film was guaranteed to bring in the punters. He was co-starring, for United Artists, with Clark Gable and Marilyn Monroe in *The Misfits*, the first screenplay by Marilyn's husband, Arthur Miller. Miller had written it specifically for his wife; previously he had despised screen writing.

Other cast members included Kevin McCarthy, Eli Wallach and Thelma Ritter – formidable competition or magnificent support, depending on how the star viewed them. The director was John Huston and, as he says in *An Open Book*, 'The cast alone made *The Misfits* the most expensive black and white film – above the line – which had been made until then.'* The budget was $3½ million, Gable's fee $800,000 and Monty's $200,000. There had been difficulty, again, insuring him, but with Miller on board and the bankability of Marilyn and Gable this hurdle was overcome.

Huston was a cultured and unpredictable troubadour. He had been born in 1906, the son of actor Walter Huston, and at an early age his father vouchsafed him the secret of success: 'Son, give 'em a good show, and always travel first class.' John Huston always did both things.

He was an Oscar-winner who had directed and written some of the

* *An Open Book* by John Huston, Macmillan, 1980

great Hollywood classics including *The Maltese Falcon*, *The Treasure of the Sierra Madre* and *The African Queen*. In 1984, three years before his death, he cracked, 'There is nothing more fascinating – and more fun – than making movies. Besides, I think I'm finally getting the hang of it.' Huston either liked people or disliked them. There was no halfway house.

His daughter Anjelica Huston, now a leading lady, clearly adored him. In July 1995 she told *OK* magazine: 'I'll never again see such glamour as I saw in my father. He was a pirate-like figure with a long, white beard who'd come from faraway countries bringing exotic gifts, telling stories of his great adventures . . . He looked quite beautiful, breathtaking – the most handsome man I had ever seen.' There was also a bullying side to his nature that was not so appealing, as Monty would discover some time later.

The story of his latest film at this time concerned a group of 'misfits' who meet in Nevada. Gable was Gay, the aging cowboy unable to come to terms with a changing world, Marilyn was Cathy, a dysfunctional stripper, and Monty was Perce, a concussed, mother-obsessed inadequate. There was much of Monty in Perce – for, although thirty-nine by now, he had still not come to terms with his sex drive and had recently asked his doctor if it was possible that he had started life as a female embryo.

Before leaving for the Nevada location he moved house. The smoke damage meant that the duplex needed extensive repairs and he was given notice to quit. This was traumatic and he panicked, begging, to no avail, to be allowed to stay on whatever the inconvenience.

Fortunately he found a brownstone for sale just a few doors away, still on East 61st Street. It had four storeys, six bathrooms and a garden with a maple tree. He fell in love with it, instructed decorators to renovate it, and moved in with Giles. He stayed there until his death. Today a tree covers the front of the house, its leaves masking a plaque which announces that he had once lived there.

Even though he loved the new house, the move disorientated him. This was aggravated by the presence of Giles. The affair was not working out and he wanted to be rid of the Frenchman. He behaved erratically, clearly under tension, startling Marge and Giles one day by reverting to one of his old tricks and hanging out of the window by his hands. Marge calmly tried to reason him to safety while Giles screamed. Very helpful.

Determined to be on form for *The Misfits*, he underwent a brisk treatment for alcoholism at Mt Sinai Hospital. In his more sober moments, Monty worried about his eyesight. Like many people with beautiful eyes he did not see very well out of them. His optician diagnosed the beginning of cataracts, but they were too unformed to operate. It scared Monty, who had a morbid fear of going blind. In 1957 he had been diagnosed as having a thyroid deficiency, requiring restorative medication, and the cataracts were a side-issue.

In July 1960, just after *Wild River* was released, he flew to Reno for *The Misfits*. Marge was no longer with him; she had sacrificed her entire personal life to accommodate him and had had enough. Eventually she went to work for Marilyn Monroe, which may have been out of the frying pan into the fire.

Monty checked in at Mapes Hotel, as did most of the cast with the exception of Gable, who rented a house with his wife, Kay. Gable loved the script of *The Misfits*, deeming it the best part he had had for years. In order to get fit he had gone on a diet, lost 35 lb, and played golf.

Gable was not, however, looking forward to meeting McCarthy, Marilyn or Monty. He was irritated by the very thought of Method actors. He did not have to worry about Marilyn just then, as she was on another film and joining them later, but the others were another matter. Producer Frank Taylor organized a dinner party for the cast to meet each other, and at first Gable declined to attend, 'I know it's gonna bug the hell out of me to work with those Method actors,' he had told Kay, 'but I don't have to socialize with them.'* In the end he went.

After dinner an intense Monty explained how he psyched himself up to become his character. An intimidating Gable had a simpler explanation; 'I gather up everything I was,' he told them, 'everything I am and hope to be. That's about it.'

'He didn't have to explain a damn thing to those kids,' Lew Smith, Gable's loyal stand-in, quipped. 'He won the battle the minute those amateurs saw him . . . If there was any doubt who the King was, Clark proved it that night by just being himself.'

Shooting began on 18 July, Monty took lessons in rodeo riding and badly cut his nose while helping a rider straddle a bull. The cut fitted his role and he refused to let make-up hide it. It can be clearly seen in the movie.

Monty did not respect Gable as an actor, feeling he had 'no range', but was nervous of him. The man had enormous presence. Huston, on the other hand, as he recorded in *An Open Book*, considered Gable

---

* *Clark Gable* by Jane Ellen Wayne, Robson Books, 1993

ideal; 'I saw very soon that Clark knew exactly what he was doing. Two or three times I thought I saw ways to improve his performance. I was mistaken. Each time I had him go back to his own way.' Gable is indeed magnificent. It was his last film and a fitting tribute.

Gable and Huston spent hours drinking together in Gable's trailer. When Huston was not with Gable he was gambling, losing and winning vast amounts.

Monty and Gable kept their distance, although there was one unfortunate professional encounter. During a scene in which they were driving through a crowd Monty, putting his heart into the business and nearly twenty years younger, punched an arthritic Gable too hard.

When they stopped for a retake Gable told Monty to lay off. But he was just as violent on the second take. There was a third take and still Monty was rough. Gable took the punishment, but when the shoot finished warned Monty, 'If you do that again, you little bastard, I'm going to land one on you.'

Monty burst into tears.

Gable turned incredulously to writer Michael Munn, who was on the set, 'What the fuck is the world coming to?' he asked.

Monty may have cried but that did not mean he was a coward. He did not shun the dangerous stunts, and both Gable and Eli Wallach cheered him on. On one occasion he had to throw a mare with a rope, and stayed with the task till his hands were raw and dripping blood.

Huston was particularly anxious for *The Misfits* to work as his previous film, *The Unforgiven*, had been a disaster. Dwight MacDonald had written: 'How much strain can a director's reputation take? Of late, John Huston seems to have been trying to find out . . .'

Huston was dreading the combination of Marilyn and Monty, nervous of their reputations. He knew Marilyn well, but she had changed since he had given her her first significant part in *The Asphalt Jungle* in 1950. However, he had no trouble with Monty, as Arthur Miller wrote in his autobiography *Timebends*:

Each day brought strange events, but some surprises were hopeful, like Clift's turning out to be so staunchly reliable . . . he was a pillar of the production. On his first day of work . . . he did his scene in the phone booth alongside the highway, a solid page of talk, without an error or a hesitation, and on the first take. Huston and I congratulated each other on our persistent confidence in him despite the insurance company's misgivings. I chose to see it as proof that when he had something to do that he respected and knew he was not simply being exploited, Monty could pull himself together . . .'

Elsewhere in *Timebends* Miller tells us more: 'He [Monty] was so pleased to be working with me and Huston and Marilyn . . . that I couldn't believe he would betray his responsibility. And indeed he never missed an hour's work: he had his entire part memorized before shooting began and was always on time despite the long delays in finishing the picture.'

Huston was not so lucky with Marilyn. Her reputation for temperament, lateness and missing days was at its peak. She was unhappy at the time as her marriage to Miller was failing. She was thirty-four years old, too, and worried that she was looking it. She was not helped by one of the worst wigs ever seen on screen.

She was drinking heavily, dependent on pills and insisted on sleeping late every day: 'I was very disturbed by her actions,' wrote Huston in *Any Other Business*. 'She seemed to be in a daze half the time . . . it was profoundly sad to see what was happening to her.'

Monty liked Marilyn and was patient with her, remembering the delays he himself had caused in the past. He held a trump card that she could never match: he was a trained actor with a formidable technique. She lacked confidence and relied on her drama coach, Paula Strasberg, Lee Strasberg's wife (Arthur Miller thought her 'comical'), and her natural talent. As Huston says, 'she never acted but actually lived all her scenes.' They were at opposite ends of their dramatic poles but the chemistry between them worked – better, in fact, than the chemistry between Gable and Marilyn.

'Montgomery Clift and Marilyn were extraordinary together,' writes Huston. 'Particularly in a long scene – several pages – behind a saloon, against a hill of beer cans and junk automobiles. It was a love scene that wasn't a love scene, and Arthur Miller at his best, too.'

Marilyn and Monty spent hours together, sometimes going off to small bars. She recognized that like her he, too, was lost and, in her befuddled way, did her best to find him.

On the set, her lack of punctuality drove Gable mad. As Huston says in *An Open Book*, 'He was non-plussed by Marilyn's behaviour. It was as though she had revealed some horrid fact of life that just couldn't be accepted in his scheme of things. 'What the hell is that girl's problem?' he demanded. 'Goddamn it, I like her, but she's so damn unprofessional. I damn near went nuts up there in Reno waiting for her to show.'

Filming was held up for ten days one one occasion when she was
taken to Westside Hospital, Los Angeles, after a suspected suicide
attempt. Gable furiously drove around the desert in his new Mercedes,
and Monty went to Los Angeles to see Ella Fitzgerald in concert.

Whatever her matrimonial problems, Marilyn had no cause to be
depressed about her finished work. Huston was delighted with the
rushes. The French philosopher Jean-Paul Sartre also admired them.
He visited the set to discuss a project he and Huston had been planning
for several years, the filming of the life of Sigmund Freud. Sartre was so
impressed that he wanted to cast Marilyn as Cecily, the female lead.

This never happened. According to Huston, Marilyn declined the
part the request of her analyst Ralph Greenson. Dr Greenson was a
close associate of Freud's daughter Anna, who strenuously opposed
any attempt to depict her father's life on screen. Rather than displease
her analyst, Marilyn refused the role.*

There were other visitors to the set, including Sinatra and Clifford
Odets, writer of *The Big Knife* (the original play upon which the film
was based) and *Sweet Smell of Success*. Libby visited him and noticed
a coolness in his attitude to Kevin. Everyone assumed he and Monty
would team up together. It never happened, and after *The Misfits* their
friendship seemed to fizzle out.

He spent his evenings quietly, sometimes having dinner with the
production team. His insomnia was bad and he and Marilyn, also a
chronic insomniac, would exchange sleeping pills – anything to try to
get a night's sleep. He even had his own bed transported from New
York to the hotel, but that was a last resort and did nothing to help.
As usual he spent the night making long-distance calls.

He sometimes flew to New York for the weekend and once went
to San Francisco. He spent much of the time sleeping there – to his
delight – on arrival he lay on the bed in his suite and went straight
off. He didn't see much of San Francisco, but it was worth the flight
just to sleep.

On his birthday, 17 October, Huston gave him a party at the Christmas
Tree Inn. Monty was among the quietest of the guests, while Huston
and his cronies drunkenly lived it up. Huston's stepmother was there
visiting; an interesting elderly lady, she and Monty formed a rapport.
They spent hours together, and she adored him.

Filming ended in November 1960. The film was half a million

---

* *Hollywood on the Couch* by Stephen Farber and Marc Green, William Morrow and
Co Inc, 1993

dollars over budget and forty days behind schedule. Considering Huston's difficulties, he had done remarkably well. Now he started to plan *Freud*, for which he wanted Monty in the name part.

Monty spent a few days at the Bel Air Hotel, Los Angeles, before returning to New York. He was interviewed by the press and enthusiastically chirped that he was now planning to direct. He did not mention *Freud*. He was fanatical to play the Father of all Psychiatrists, but too superstitious to say so.

Shortly after this it was announced that Marilyn was separating from Miller. She started another film in 1962 but died before it was finished. Gable died from a heart attack two weeks after *The Misfits* was completed. He was fifty-nine and justly proud of the film. Talking to Huston about the overspend, he said, 'If the studio's unhappy about the cost I'll buy the picture for $4 million. I think it's the best thing I've ever done.' Huston was ambivalent about *The Misfits*. Due to Marilyn's decline and Gable's death, his memories were 'mostly melancholy'.

Gable had insisted on performing some of the stunts himself, frightened that younger men might get the better of him. In one scene he was apparently dragged 400 feet by a lorry travelling at 35 miles an hour; in another he seemed to be tangling with a prancing horse. It has been widely reported in the press that his participation in these stunts brought about his death.

Huston is adamant this is not the case, and wrote in *An Open Book*: 'One of the myths attached to *The Misfits* was that Clark Gable died of a heart attack because of over-exertion in this film. That is utter nonsense. Toward the end of the picture there was a contest between Clark and the stallion the cowboys had captured. It looked like rough work, and it was, but it was the stunt men who were thrown around, not Clark.'

The real strain for Gable had been the interminable waiting for Marilyn. She herself was guilt-stricken about it. Gable would arrive on time and read a book, sometimes for hours, until she arrived. He appeared unflappable. Inside he was churning.

On 31 January 1961 Monty attended the premiere of *The Misfits* at New York's Capitol Theater. Marilyn was on his arm, doing what she did perfectly – posing for photographers. She and Miller had been divorced the week previously, on 25 January, and as author Donald Spoto writes in his biography of her, 'Beneath the brave, cheerful public exterior Marilyn's mood was dark as the New York winter.' The film was not the unqualified success which had been hoped for. Audiences were puzzled by it, but the critics in general approved. 'The theme with its implications of an essentially male savagery suits Mr Huston, and he has drawn extraordinary qualities from all his chief players,' wrote Dilys Powell. 'He [Monty] was perfectly cast in that underestimated and ill-fated production, John Huston's *The Misfits*,' said *The Times* on 1 June 1995.

While on holiday in Puerto Rico he learnt that producer/director Stanley Kramer wanted him to appear in *Judgment at Nuremberg*, a film version of the 1959 television drama by Abby Mann of a fictional account of the 1948 trial of judges who had relinquished their principles to Nazi authority. Kramer wanted Monty to play Rudolph Petersen, a retarded Jew who had been sterilized by the Nazis in their genocide programme. A brief description of the part over the telephone sold it to him. He could not wait to tell his father he was playing another Jew.

Kramer went to see him at the brownstone in New York and recalled in *His Place in the Sun*, 'He looked absolutely brutal, I mean terrible – he looked as though he had one foot in the grave . . . and this beautiful leading man had come to this point. He was perfect for the part.'

Kramer had memories of Monty as he had looked pre-*Raintree County* and, although he had certainly seen him in *The Young Lions*, this was his first face-to-face confrontation. It was a shock.

Peterson's part is a single protracted scene that lasts seven minutes on screen. Kramer had offered $50,000 but Monty's agents, MCA, would not accept less than $100,000. This was way over Kramer's budget, so he appealed to Monty directly. Monty agreed to waive the fee completely and appear solely for expenses. His reasoning was not entirely altruistic. If he reduced his fee word would spread that he was working cheaply, and he did not want to set a precedent.

Kramer had already assembled an impressive cast, including Spencer Tracy, Maximilian Schell (the only one of the principals who had been in the original TV play, and who had also been in *The Young Lions* with Monty), Marlene Dietrich, Burt Lancaster (replacing Laurence Olivier, who had dropped out), Richard Widmark and, for another cameo similar in style to Monty's, Judy Garland.

The film was shot at Universal Studios in Hollywood, and Monty stayed at the Bel Air once more; this time he took Giles with him. The film was generating enormous interest because of its starry cast, and several famous visitors came to pay their respects. Rather to his surprise they all seemed to want to meet him, and it did not occur to him that some of their interest was because he had become an object of curiosity. Everyone in the industry knew he was a drunken homosexual, which would not have raised an eyebrow, but this coupled with his alleged drug addiction made him something altogether more exotic.

As Kevin McCarthy said, after Monty's death, 'I never thought of him as being a drug taker – I don't know if he ever took drugs as we think of it today – cocaine and so forth – I doubt it.' But what has truth to do with rumour? Cocaine, and other drugs, had been used among the Hollywood set since the 1920s, but it was Monty's rumoured association with the drug rather than the drugs itself that struck Kevin as unlikely.

Monty's scene took place in the courtroom, with Spencer Tracy as the judge and Schell as the prosecutor. Most of the spectators were extras and the studio was crowded. He was unnerved, terrified of forgetting the lines he had spent hours analysing. He had had a deliberately bad haircut because he was sure Petersen would have gone to a barber before a court appearance, and could not have afforded a decent one. It was a complicated and rapid scene, full of three-handed exchanges between Tracy, Monty and Schell. His seven minutes amounted to ten pages of script, nearly as much as the whole of his part in The Misfits.

He did forget his lines, the whole time. He missed cues, forgot to give them and stumbled over monologues. On the verge of tears, he apologised to everyone. 'I told him, "Forget the lines," Kramer recalled in His Place in the Sun. "You know what it's about – your mother – the picture of your mother. Pull it out, show it when you feel you want to show it . . . when you feel it . . . It was a great actor to whom he was playing – Spencer Tracy – who told him, "Monty, forget the lines and play to me. Play to me", and they played eye to eye – and it was tremendous.'

Tracy steadied Monty and he went on to complete four takes, stumbling in his delivery and wandering from the script. It did not matter – he was brilliant. The fourth take was eventually used virtually in its entirety. Kramer described it as 'one of the best moments in the film', adding that it was 'a magnificent performance because he felt it here,' tapping his heart, 'and that's important.' Monty was to receive his fourth Academy award nomination for it.

Tracy was not in peak physical condition himself. His was an enormous part and he had had an attack of nerves before flying to Hollywood, actually getting off the plane in panic. Katharine Hepburn had made him get back on. He too had a reputation for temperament, and Monty was not the sort of man whom he would normally have cosseted, but he respected his talent. He did all he could to help him. Kramer told Tracy's biographer, Larry Swindell, that Tracy 'grabbed

Monty's shoulders and told him he was the greatest young actor of his generation, and to look into his eyes and to play to him, and to hell with the lines'.*

Monty was cooperative throughout – apart from the business of forgetting his lines – and, as usual, the crew became fond of him. So did another tormented and talented performer who was in the picture, thankfully on a high at the time. Judy Garland, by then a concert artist, had just had a success at Carnergie Hall and the Hollywood Bowl, where the rain had poured down on the thirty thousand people in the auditorium. No one had left; the entire audience hung on to her every note.

She had not made a film since *A Star is Born* in 1954, and since then had undergone various personal difficulties. She had accepted the cameo role in *Nuremberg* because she believed she was not up to carrying a whole film by herself. She played Irene Hoffman, a *hausfrau* who had had an affair with a Jew during the Third Reich. For this crime the Nazis had executed him and imprisoned her. She was now called upon to bear witness.

Kramer had been wary of temperament from her but, as with Monty, there was none. She had received a spontaneous round of applause when she arrived on the set and, visibly moved, gave a little bow in acknowledgement. She was required to look dowdy, and this did not go down well. It was her screen comeback after sixteen years and, though a touch overweight, she wanted to look her best. It was a battle to get her to accept the unflattering make-up and clothes.

Monty had finished his scene by the time she came to do hers, so he stood on the set and watched her. According to David Shipman's biography she had difficulty crying at first, 'Damn it, Stanley,' she said, 'I can't do it. I've dried up. I'm too happy to cry.'† Kramer called for a break while she mustered her resources, after which she cried superbly. Like Monty, she did several takes.

She moved Monty to tears and was still sobbing herself, now in Kramer's arms. In *Rainbow* Christopher Finch relates what happened next. 'She played that all wrong,' Monty said.‡ Neither Kramer nor Judy could believe their ears, and furiously rounded on him. They saw him laughing. Judy punched him, then disentangled herself from Kramer and fell into his arms.

He did not return to New York immediately but stayed on at the

* *Spencer Tracy* by Larry Swindell, WH Allen, 1969
† *Judy Garland* by David Shipman, Harper Collins, 1993
‡ *Rainbow* by Christopher Finch, Michael Joseph, 1975

Bel Air, enjoying the camaraderie. He was under no strain, knowing he had done well, and was proud to be in what he knew would be a fine film. When he did check out, his bill, which included Giles who had come with him although no one had seen him, was $15,000. It was paid for by Kramer, of course, and was considerably less than the $50,000 he had offered.

He now received an offer to appear on stage in the Actors' Studio's production of James Baldwin's *Giovanni's Room*. The novel was acclaimed, but the role was of a man with a homosexual past. Monty was not keen to play a homosexual. More darkly, he knew he would now never be able to remember the lines. His days as a stage actor were well and truly over. He did not reply.

That year, 1961, Warren Beatty was starring in his first film, *Splendour in the Grass*, directed by Elia Kazan. In his next he played a gigolo to Vivien Leigh's Mrs Stone in the adaptation of Tennessee Williams's only novel *The Roman Spring of Mrs Stone*. It was ten years since she had played Blanche and over twenty since Scarlett. Mrs Stone was an aging star coming to terms with her falling sexual allure. As with Blanche, the part could have been autobiographical.

Time magazine wrote of the handsome Beatty: 'With a facial and vocal suggestion of Montgomery Clift and mannerisms of James Dean he is the latest incumbent in the line of arrogant, attractive, hostile, moody, sensitive, self-conscious, bright, defensive, ambitious, stuttering, self-seeking and extremely talented actors who become a myth before they are thirty.'

Beatty admired Monty and, over twenty years later, spoke of him to his friend Leslie Caron: 'His conversation, she [Caron] recalled, centred around Marlon Brando, Montgomery Clift and himself. He saw all three of them as a trinity, equally gifted as actors.'*

By this time Monty was becoming increasingly worried about his sight. His cataracts were taking hold. Sunlight hurt his eyes and the thought of going blind continued to terrify him. All the same he was prepared to work in Spain should the offer come. He had learnt that David Lean was about to start shooting *Lawrence of Arabia* there, and telephoned him daily. He read *Seven Pillars of Wisdom* and found it tedious, but the man still fascinated him as did the aspects of homosexuality that clung to his character. Unlike those of the hero of *Giovanni's Room*, Lawrence's urges were sublimated.

* *Warren Beatty* by Suzanne Munshower, W.H. Allen, 1983

18

Monty did not play T.E. Lawrence, but he did receive a formal offer from John Huston to star as Freud in what Huston hoped would be his master work, a biopic entitled *The Secret Passion*. It was to be shot in Munich and Monty's fee was $200,000. Monty had known of the project since working with Huston on *The Misfits*.

Originally, Huston had had a far different Freud in mind. He had wanted Peter Sellers, who was suddenly big news. His 1959 film *The Mouse That Roared*, a farce in which a tiny duchy declares war on the United States, had taken over $2 million during its eight-month run in New York and Sellers himself had received rave reviews. Offers flooded in, including Mephistopheles to Olivier's Faust, Julius Ceasar in Elizabeth Taylor's *Cleopatra* and the title role in *I, Claudius*.

'I am jolly interested in the *Freud* idea for John Huston,' Sellers had told Roy Speer in March 1961, 'but I don't know how I can fit it in this year . . . I can't very well do *Freud* until the end of the year, but maybe Huston can't wait that long.'* Sellers had tried to move heaven and earth to rearrange his commitments to enable him to take the part. He saw himself heavily bearded as the enigmatic Austrian doctor. But, he was right, Huston could not wait that long. He had been working

* *The Life and Death of Peter Sellers* by Roger Lewis, Century, 1994

on the script with Jean-Paul Sartre for years and had finally managed to sell the project to Universal Pictures, who agreed to finance it providing there were no censorship problems.

To avoid this, Huston saw some officials of the Catholic Church in New York. If the Church objected to the script it had the power to ban Catholics from seeing the film. There are millions of Catholics in America.

There were some objections. As Huston wrote in his autobiography *An Open Book*:

> Freud's philosophy, they claimed, does not admit the existence of Good and Evil. Only a priest has the right to search into the soul of man. The very suggestion of sexuality in children was repugnant to them. I could not, of course, change *Freud* to suit such Catholic prejudice without completely destroying the picture – to say nothing of Freudianism – and the best I could hope for was a compromise . . . It wasn't easy but I managed to come to enough of an understanding with them for Universal to proceed with the project.

This was to be the first biopic of *Freud* and, taking into account the sexual voracity of the 1960s, the time was judged to be right. The story of psychoanalysis and sexual repression could now be told.

Huston had nurtured the idea of the film for twenty years, and for much of this time had worked with screenwriter Charles Kaufman. Kaufman had written a documentary on the hypnotic treatment of psychiatrically disturbed military personnel, called *Let There Be Light*, for the US War Department. Huston had directed it and become hooked on psychiatry, fascinated by the idea of dreams being interpreted under hypnosis via the libido. In 1957, Huston had also worked on the project with the existentialist philosopher Jean-Paul Sartre and screenwriter Wolfgang Reinhardt.

Sartre submitted a script to Huston which ran to ten hours of film time. This was ridiculous. Even if Sartre assumed the piece to be a serious work without commercial considerations, no one in their right mind would commission a ten hour-long film. Sartre must have known that; several of his works had already been filmed, including the much-praised *Huis Clos*.

When Huston read the script he was as appalled by its content as its length. There were blatant references to sexual deviation, child molestation, incest and other aberrations. As he later said in *Hollywood on the Couch*, 'What [audiences] wanted was "healthy" sex – the Marilyn Monroe kind of sex'.

The script did not square with what he had promised the Catholic censorship board, so he severed his connection with Sartre, and Kaufman prepared a new treatment. This did not satisfy Huston either, and Reinhardt took over. For six months Reinhardt and Huston worked together on a revised script. Much of Sartre's material was included and Huston sent him a copy. He read it, stated he wanted nothing more to do with it and instructed that his name should be removed from the credits.

Meanwhile Huston contacted other psychiatrists for their expert opinions. They included Dr David Stafford-Clark, head of the Psychiatric Clinic at Guy's Hospital London.

Monty was invited to Huston's script conferences, and this was the start of the real, destructive trouble between them. Monty was as fascinated by Freud as Huston. He would put his ideas forward and suggest changes. The policy backfired. As Rosalie Crutchley, who played Freud's mother in the film, says, 'Huston would never stand for an actor interfering with his lines.'

In *An Open Book**, Huston wrote:

> He [Monty] had been seeing psychiatrists since 1950 and fancied himself an expert on Freud. Monty would come into the room, take off his shoes and lie down on the floor. He said it was the only way he could think. He would interrupt at the wrong moments, and his remarks were largely incomprehensible. His presence served only to delay and confuse. One day I told him we couldn't include him any more, explained why, and shut and locked the door . . . Monty stood outside the door and cried. Then he turned to the bar and drank himself unconscious.

Crying men unnerved Huston, a man who hunted elephants. He said later that he should have 'dropped' Monty 'right then'. If he had done so, Monty's life might, perhaps, have been prolonged.

As it was, in August 1961 Monty flew with Giles to London where he was to attend costume fittings with designer Doris Langley Moore before continuing to Ireland, where Huston had a manor house, and then to Munich where most of *Freud* was to be shot. He was perfectly at home with Mrs Moore, a sophisticated, middle-aged woman. It was a pleasant stay.

At the end of August he flew to Huston's home at St Clerans in

Galway, to stay with the director while they discussed the film with Stafford-Clark. Monty and Giles shared a room. There is a legend that Huston unexpectedly came in one day and discovered them having sex. Huston was, allegedly, revolted as he had not realized Monty was homosexual.

Of course Huston knew Monty was homosexual. He could not possibly not have known – the entire film community knew, and he had just made a film with him. A variation of the rumour says that Huston discovered Monty having sex with one of his male staff; and sometimes it is a journalist.

Whatever happened during that visit, it was certainly not a happy occasion. Huston's attitude hardened during Monty's stay. It seems that the script was the basis of their trouble. 'They clashed over the script very early,' said production manager Doc Erickson in *His Place in the Sun*. 'At the time Monty visited John in Ireland they were arguing over certain points – the relationship went from bad to worse during the making of the film.'

Monty and Giles flew to Munich in September. Monty was rattled by Huston's attitude. He always drank when nervous, and did so on the flight. He refused to fasten his safety belt when the plane approached Munich, and the hostesses had to insist. He caused a scene and the papers were full of it the next day. Huston was disgusted.

The day after their arrival Monty and Wolfgang Reinhardt, the producer and writer, went to Huston's hotel suite for a conference. Huston asked Reinhardt to excuse them as he wanted to talk to Monty privately.

According to Reinhardt's account he returned to the suite almost immediately, having forgotten a letter which had been in his brief-case. He found the atmosphere tense. Monty was hyperactive – he had not been when Reinhardt had left – and went to extremes looking for the letter, tossing cushions off chairs and scrambling under tables. Whatever happened during that confrontation – and only Monty and Huston were there – did nothing to ease the strain.

Huston was shooting the film chronologically, as he wanted the cast to understand fully the development of Freud's train of thought. Monty's part was enormous and wordy, far more hefty than his role in *The Misfits*. He did his best to learn it, but it changed hourly. As Huston would not permit him to be present during the rewrites he had a great deal to relearn and could not always do it. The first scene had to be altered due to the number of holding shots that Monty fluffed. Huston writes in *An Open Book*; 'The opening scene between Freud and his mother was weak – reminiscent of the old biographical pictures. It was in fact a substitute scene ... and a poor replacement for the one that Monty hadn't been up to. So the picture got off to a bad start.'

Like Vincent Donehue with *Lonelyhearts*, and Mankiewicz with *Suddenly Last Summer* Huston had imagined long takes. Unlike Donehue and Mankiewicz, he was not prepared to compromise when his star was not up to the job. Donehue had done his best for Monty and an acceptable film had been the result. But Huston was an ultra-perfectionist. He did not want an acceptable film – he was looking for a masterpiece.

In his first outdoor scene, where the inevitable crowd had gathered to watch, Monty kept blowing his lines. Each time Huston insisted on shooting the scene again from the beginning. Eventually adaptations had to be made. Huston was bitterly disappointed.

Later, in the studio, Monty had a long, static scene lecturing to doctors and students. He had made notes, as would any lecturer, and intended to put these on the lectern in front of him. But Huston made him attempt the scene without notes. It was impossible. Huston was unrelenting, constantly making him go back to the beginning. After several hours Monty was a wreck and there was nothing in the can.

He spent a sleepless and drunken night shaking with nerves, frantically popping his painkilling pills, trying to learn his speech by heart. His head ached and he suffered from vertigo. Despite all this he was better next morning, but still not good enough for Huston. Each time Monty substituted a word he made him start again. A take that Huston finally found acceptable was made during the afternoon, but by then Monty's confidence was shattered.

Huston was determined to control him, to break his spirit until he obeyed orders unquestioningly. It was an old technique, but it was Monty who stuck to his guns. In his way he was as strong as Huston.

Both spent the nights in different quarters working on rewrites, which they would present to each other in the morning. In *An Open Book*, Huston complained:

What he produced was invariably infantile and absurd. Finally I realized this was primarily a stall for time. Monty was having difficulty memorizing his lines. I was surprised at this because he had done so well during *The Misfits*. The explanation is obvious, of course, in retrospect. Monty's lines in *The Misfits* had been simple, and he had had time to study them. His lines in *Freud* were quite difficult. There were many long speeches, the vocabulary was scientific and unfamiliar, and included words of Freud's own coinage. Monty's dialogue would have taxed the technique of a fine actor at his best; and Monty was far from being at his best.

His accident some years before had done him great damage . . . and there is no question in my mind that this included brain damage. His prior brilliance now came through in fitful flashes. His petulant and obstinate behaviour was an attempt to hide from me and the others – and probably himself – that he was no longer able to contend . . . There was a mist between him and the rest of the world that you simply couldn't penetrate. It must have been agony for him . . . I saw a crucified look on his face. But if the picture was hell for Monty, it was equally harrowing for me.

Elsewhere in his autobiography he wrote, 'He had deteriorated to a shocking degree since I had worked with him on *The Misfits*. He was supposedly on the wagon, so no one ever saw him with a drink in his hand, but I soon discovered that each time he passed a bar he'd pick up a bottle of whatever was handy, pick it up and drink directly from the bottle. He was also on drugs.'

Monty had made friends among the cast and they did not like what was happening. Rosalie Crutchley, playing his mother – although, to her amusement, she was actually a year younger than him – recalled in a conversation with the author, 'Huston was pretty awful. He gave Monty a new script to learn, ten minutes or a quarter of an hour before the take – new lines were arriving all the time. He learnt it and knew it and did a perfect take. Huston made him do it again, hoping he would forget the lines although the first take was quite acceptable. It was a long speech, eight to ten minutes of material. He did a perfectly good take again.'

In a separate conversation David Kossoff recalled Monty as 'a very dear man whom I remember with great affection'. He added, 'I can't think of a worse relationship than that of John Huston and Montgomery Clift. Huston was a big disappointment to me, I had been expecting someone remarkable. Monty had a boyfriend with him, who would sometimes come on the set. I felt he was taking advantage of Monty, as is often the case with gentle gay people, and I don't think this helped things.'

American actor Larry Parks, who was also in the film, was the sort of actor of whom Huston approved: efficient, word-perfect and non-combative. This was his first film since 1955 and he was trying desperately to resurrect a flagging career. He had shot to fame in 1946 with his portrayal of Al Jolson in *The Jolson Story* and, later, in *Jolson Sings Again*. Unfortunately he became unpopular after testifying to the Un-American Activities Committee. He was not only word-perfect, but his performances were unvarying from take to take.

Kossoff recalled, 'People were saying how wonderful Parks was, and that he knew all his lines perfectly. Monty needed several takes. "He's driving poor Mr Huston crazy,"' someone said. Kossoff continued:

> The film was shot in a sort of sepia colour which made the dream sequences seem not quite natural. As the processing was done in Hollywood it took some time for the rushes to arrive. When they did arrive, everyone was invited to see them. Monty's performance was genius. You couldn't take your eyes off him. It was decided to retake much of Parks's material.
>
> But Monty was not good first thing in the morning. Maybe he had had too much to drink the night before, but he was a bit catarrhal and he looked unwell. But there was something about that bruised face you couldn't take your eyes off. It was very sad.
>
> We stayed in the same hotel and as he was a retiring person we did not share confidences, but he would sometimes talk. For a star of his magnitude he was remarkably confiding. We shared a car to the set in the mornings and sometimes he would talk then. I think he took to me. I was aware of his difficulties and suffering.
>
> It was a very strange film. We shot one scene in Vienna, at the railway station where Freud is saying goodbye to his parents. There was a dressed crowd of the period of around 250 who were all rehearsed. There was lighting and sound. Just for Freud to say goodbye. It must have cost a fortune.
>
> As well as being strange it was a miserable film. The set was full of so-called psychiatric experts, some from Vienna. I said to one of them, 'What about Huston? He's had about four marriages, hasn't he?' He answered, 'What does that prove?' That made me thoughtful.

Believe me, on that film, Rosalie Crutchley saved everyone's sanity.
She has a marvellous self-mocking humour and she greatly cheered
up everyone.*

'Huston tried it on with everybody,' remembers Crutchley:

There was a scene where I had to hold a snake. I know he thought
I would scream and not do it, but I didn't. I hate snakes but
I did it.

He really made Monty suffer. There was another scene where he
had to climb up a slope using a rope. The rope burned his hands
and I think he had trouble with his hands after his accident. I know
they weren't right. He made Monty do it repeatedly although he
could see he was in distress. But Monty did it.

Huston was highly intelligent but sadistic and a bully, but there
was something masochistic in Monty that made him subject himself
to Huston's treatment. In a kind of way he asked for it.

Kossoff, too, noticed the masochistic side to Monty's nature. Huston
was tormenting him and getting satisfaction from it. So, it seemed, was
Monty. He had punished himself most of his life, and now Huston was
doing it for him. It did not lessen his suffering, which sometimes went
beyond his endurance. His tormented face told everyone that.

In another conversation Susannah York, Monty's leading lady,
endorsed the idea of the sado-masochistic relationship:

John Huston was guilty of bullying. More than that, he was guilty of
sadism. But there was something masochistic in Monty. He almost
looked to be the victim. What amazed me was Monty's resilience.
He reminded me of a rapier in the hands of an expert – he was
like quicksilver, parrying the blows. They were like David and
Goliath.

It was odd because in some ways Huston could be a very
cultivated, genial man. I think he was disappointed he had chosen
Monty and was almost willing it not to work.

It was one of the first films I'd done and I know I was nervous.
We had many scenes together and Monty was so wonderful, so
faithful, and I was devoted to him. He could be morose at times,
but I think that was when he had been drinking.

* Conversation with the author

'We would shoot a scene, then, two or three days later, there would be a reshoot of the same scene. I think John Huston was rewriting it and the dialogue got more and more purple as we went along and we had to say different things.

This is difficult for an actor. Monty would put it in his own words, as would I. Film people do that. But John Huston would not have it. Sometimes we would have three or four different versions of the same scene.

Monty had great problems with his memory and so did I with mine, because I learnt my lines in a different way and it was all so purple. We might do twenty or thirty takes, then he might blow a line – but it was not always him, sometimes it was me. Huston would go mad. An actor who went wrong? This angered Huston.

In the dream sequence, where Monty has to climb using a rope, it would have been right for Freud to have used gloves. Gloves were a part of Freud's costume. Huston would not let Monty have gloves. By the end his hands were bleeding. Huston's attitude was to punish him physically.

Monty took it all. He had great courage and he was a perfectionist. He had such generosity of spirit towards other actors it was inspiring – he would never let you get away with second-best. We had to do a scene in which Freud finds me in a brothel and I tear the bodice of my dress and jump on a parapet. We did this in Vienna and I think the whole of Vienna was watching.

The language was so purple I couldn't get the words out. They stuck in my throat, or I would start to laugh. I just couldn't manage it. We tried seven or eight times. John Huston was getting madder and the crowd was thinking, 'Who is this idiot?' Suddenly Monty said my lines – he let rip in a very un-Freudian way. He so shook me that I said them just as he had said them. He was very brave and didn't mind making himself look a fool in front of the others to help me.

He had real humour and a quality of fun, a gaiety. We had some of our best evenings sitting around a table laughing. We laughed a lot together.*

They also worked together on the script. Huston brooded about this, writing in *An Open Book*: 'Under Monty's influence she became convinced that she was entitled to scientific opinions regarding a subject of which she was woefully ignorant.'

Monty had never been treated in such a high-handed way before,

---

* Telephone conversation with the author

and under the strain his damaged memory began to falter even more. In desperation, and against his principles, Huston wrote Monty's lines on boards: 'At that time the idea of having an actor read lines from a board was abhorrent to me,' he wrote. 'During this picture Monty was in some ways the male equivalent of Marilyn Monroe, and at about the same stage in his deterioration as she had been during *The Misfits*.'

Huston made his contempt for Monty plain, and Monty was often in touch with Silverberg about how to cope with this attitude. Their sado-masochistic relationship reached its height one day when Huston stormed into Monty's dressing room. According to Wolfgang Reinhardt Monty taunted Huston to hit him, proffering his jaw. Huston – who would have taken a swipe at any man if challenged and could have flattened Monty with one hand tied behind his back – could not cope with this. He wanted a two-way fight, such as he might have had with Bogart, not this fey, quasi-sexual, almost flirtatious taunting. Another reason he did not punch Monty was that it crossed his mind that a lawsuit could ruin him and put paid to the film.

Reinhardt tells us Huston destroyed the furniture instead. Robert LaGuardia writes that Monty is alleged to have come out of his room when the crashing stopped and said, pointing to Huston, 'I pity this man.' 'I sure taught the little bastard a lesson,' Huston is then alleged to have told Reinhardt. 'I had him trembling in a corner. Maybe he'll start to remember his lines a little better now.'

In *An Open Book* Huston denies Reinhardt's account: 'Recently I have read remarks made by Wolfgang concerning incidents that supposedly occurred during the making of the picture. They are either complete fabrications or sadly twisted versions of what really happened.'

He provides his own version of the dressing room incident:

> I . . . decided I would get rough with him. I went to his dressing room, opened the door and slammed it behind me so hard that a mirror fell from the wall and shattered, showering glass shards all over the room. Monty looked up at me with a blank expression. I stared back at him – hard. I wanted him to feel my anger. Finally he said, 'What are you going to do . . . kill me?' I said, 'I'm seriously considering it!' Monty shrugged; it didn't make any difference . . . I have read recent accounts of this incident that have me going into Monty's room and smashing chairs, breaking mirrors, tearing the couch apart. It simply didn't happen that way.*

---

* *An Open Book* by John Huston

Huston explained to Michael Munn, who included it in *Hollywood Rogues*:

'It was a tactic. I've read accounts of that incident in which I was supposed to have smashed everything up in his room. There's a story also of how I supposedly made him do take after take of a scene in which he slides down a rope until he was rope-burned so badly he had blood pouring from his hands. What really happened was that he had to climb a length of rope which had mattresses underneath it so that at the end of each take he could simply drop to the ground in safety. But for some reason each time I yelled "Cut" he slid down the rope, holding very tightly, causing him severe rope burns . . .

No, I was never cruel to Monty. He was just 'non compos mentis' most of the time and there were times when you could be forgiven for forgetting he was a woefully sick man . . . I would rather make *The Roots of Heaven* again, with all its hardships, than go through a single week of what I went through with Monty on *Freud* . . . My reputation for cruelty appears to stem directly from this one picture . . . I find this impossible to understand. That simply isn't me; it isn't the way I work . . . I go about trying to build an ego, not destroy it. Apart from Montgomery Clift and – through association – Susannah York, I don't think I've ever had a conflict with an artist . . .

It is over thirty-five years since *Freud* was made, but Susannah York, Rosalie Crutchley and David Kossoff, who were there at the time, remember Monty with affection and Huston's treatment of him with distaste.

Monty could still attract fans, some frighteningly devoted. One of these was an Austrian woman, Irmgard Gassler, who cajoled her way on to the set. She fell in love with him and, after the film was made, followed him back to New York begging him to marry her. Monty's success with women, particularly beautiful ones like Susannah York, infuriated Huston, who felt he hid behind their skirts. It annoyed him that Monty could make so much headway without even trying.

The film was by now over budget, over-long and and weeks behind schedule. By this time no one, including Huston and Monty, believed it would amount to anything other than a disaster. An executive from Universal was sent to try to sort things out. Huston regarded Monty as being directly responsible for this humiliation. *Freud* should have been his master-work, and his dislike intensified. 'John was relentless,' said Doc Erickson, the production manager, in *His Place in the Sun*. 'He would not give an inch. He would not see that what he was doing was only aggravating the situation. He would not try to modify his behaviour . . .'

Then Monty flew to London to see an eye specialist. During a film sequence in which a scuffle develops, his hat had been accidentally knocked into his eyes. Paranoid about losing his sight, on a Friday evening, after the week's filming, he flew to London for advice. Half-hardened cataracts were now finally diagnosed.

Susannah York had gone away for the weekend, too. When she arrived back on the set on the Monday morning the first thing she saw was Doc Erickson and Huston laughing together. She recalled to the author:

> I was so pleased to see some levity that I went up to them and asked what was the joke? Doc said, 'Shall we tell her?' and Huston said, 'Why not, she's a big girl now . . . We're taking up a collection to buy Monty a seeing-eye dog for Christmas.' I was so mad I went for him physically. I think I hit him two or three times on the chest. Then I stamped off the set. Monty was always terrified about his eyes so he had panicked and rushed to see his eye doctor.

Huston, who at the time did not know that cataracts had been diagnosed, recalls the incident in his memoirs: 'I was guilty of a remark in very bad taste. I had thought Monty's insistence on seeing an eye doctor at our expense was simply another bit of malingering. The holidays were approaching, and I said, "I suppose now we'll have to get Monty a seeing-eye dog for Christmas, to lead him around the set." As it turned out, that was not so funny.'

Monty returned, clearly worried by the diagnosis. According to Huston,

> He insisted the studio was responsible . . . There was no reasoning with Monty. He was faced with incontrovertible evidence that the problem with his eyes was a long-standing one, but he insisted the damage had been caused by the falling silk hat, and he wanted to sue the studio. In fact, all he was legally entitled to – in the event that his claim was a just one – was $75 a week disability pay. But

Monty wouldn't listen when this was explained to him. He wanted to sue.*

There were several heated long-distance telephone conversations between Monty and his agent, Lew Wasserman of MCA. His inability to concentrate was now worse, if that were possible. Monty told friends that the film would shorten his life by ten years.

On 13 December 1961 he took official leave to attend the West Berlin premiere of *Judgment at Nuremberg*. He had happy memories of the film and he hoped he might meet some friends there. It was just good to get away from the stifling atmosphere of *Freud*.

He was in good company. Garland also turned out, as did Dietrich, Tracy, Schell and Widmark. Stanley Kramer invested heavily in promotion and spent $150,000 just in ensuring that VIPs attended. The publicity blared; 'Once in a generation . . . a motion picture explodes into greatness.' It was not far from the truth.

Before the screening Mayor Willy Brandt gave a speech reminding the Germans of their personal responsibilities. After the film there was a standing ovation. Monty was warmly congratulated and it was a welcome tonic. But he became a little over-enthusiastic and thumped Spencer Tracy too hard for comfort. For a while their friendship was tested. The critics, as ever, varied in their response. 'Stanley Kramer is one of the few men in Hollywood with the courage to face, to discuss and risk his time and money on pictures that have something to say,' trumpeted *Cue* magazine. Stanley Kauffmann carped: 'Some believe that by tackling such themes Kramer earns at least partial remission from criticism. How much? 20% for effort?'

Back on the Munich set it was the usual misery. Huston had given up hope of salvaging the movie. He lacked the energy to torture Monty further, though, and was now content to express his contempt by reading while Monty performed. But he no longer insisted on retakes of whole scenes and compromised by cutting away in the middle of a sequence when Monty dried up.

But this came too late for Monty, who had fallen too low. He would miserably flounder for his words, clearly lost, to Huston's indifference. Sometimes, when things became too rough, he broke down and cried, running off the set. The cast and crew watched aghast. For many, time has not dimmed the vileness of this memory.

Universal was now threatening to sue for delays, and most of the

---

* *An Open Book* by John Huston

accusations seemed to be levelled at Monty. If the studio successfully sued him, his career would be over. It was already difficult to insure him, and a court action would make it impossible. Whatever the outcome, his reputation would be ruined. The industry was rife with rumours of what was happening, or supposedly happening, on the set of *Freud*. It still is.

In 1980 Huston wrote in *An Open Book*:

> Monty collected a small group of protective converts and supporters around him who professed to be aghast at the 'brutal' manner in which I was treating him. In fact, I was doing everything I knew how simply to get a performance out of him, but Monty had the knack of making even the most reasonable requests look like persecution.
>
> His group of protectors included Susannah, the woman who furnished the period clothing [Doris Langley Moore] and a few other members of the company, mostly female. I could understand this. Although you often felt like strangling Monty, there was at the same time something fundamentally appealing about him. He called forth your pity and your sympathy, and you'd suddenly feel like embracing and comforting him.

For all his frustration, Huston is forced to pay homage to Monty's talent: 'In spite of all these things, it was impossible not to marvel at and admire his talent. Monty's eyes would light up, and you could actually "see" an idea being born in Freud's mind. Monty looked intelligent. He looked as though he were having a thought. He wasn't, Christ knows.'

Filming dragged morosely on until February 1962. Universal had Monty examined by doctors and psychiatrists to determine his physical and mental condition in connection with the possibility of suing him for causing delays and forcing the film into overtime. The film's insurance company – Fireman's Fund Insurance, who had paid out over the delays to *Raintree County* – also arranged for him to be examined. This barrage of experts finally came up with the diagnosis that he was suffering from anxiety due to worry about his cataracts.

Monty's solicitor, Benet Polikoff – the firm of Polikoff and Clareman still administer the Clift estate – flew to Munich to assist him. His memory was tested and found to be slightly below par – many had expected a far worse diagnosis. But, as Susannah York endorses, he was able to learn many of Huston's rewrites immediately before a shoot. It was the ensuing tension that threw him. And, of course, a professional actor needs a memory that is well above par, not slightly below.

He remained in Munich for three weeks after the shoot had finished. He dreaded the return to New York and the legal furore that awaited him there. He and Giles broke their journey to America with a stay in London as a house guest of Doris Langley Moore, an invitation which she came to rue.

She had put on a welcoming dinner. He and Giles arrived drunk with Monty's driver, who, Monty announced, was staying to eat. Miss Moore was distinctly put out, as an extra place had to be crammed in at table. Then something else unexpected happened which made her entirely forgive him. During the meal he got up, stood behind her and, without a word, put a diamond necklace around her neck. She burst into tears.

Long after the guests had gone he stayed downstairs, playing records. Ella and Sinatra boomed through the house. He made no concessions to the lateness of the hour and the fact that the rest of the household was in bed. When Mrs Moore came down and gently remonstrated, he jumped up and down on the floor in a rage.

She began to long for him to leave, but there was quite a haul ahead yet. She invited friends round to meet him, including Michael Redgrave and his daughter Vanessa, whom he liked, but these were oases of calm in a stormy visit. She was treated to the experience, which all who spent a night in Monty's company underwent, of him tramping around the house at night and sometimes sleep-walking. When he did nod off, the night would be rent by screams as his nightmares took over. He would confide his problems to her at times and, like Arthur Miller and others, she came to the conclusion that guilt over his sexual orientation had ruined his life.

She was outraged, though, by his drunken behaviour and claimed she did not know he drank. Yet she had worked on the set of *Freud* and, if he had been drinking as much as Houston claimed, she would surely have already seen him drunk several times.

While being driven around Soho he had a nasty fright. Some people recognized him and he started to talk to them. But they were louts who rocked the car and scared the life out of him.

He visited Rosalie Crutchley and behaved impeccably. 'He came round for a cup of tea and met my two children – they were ten and thirteen then. He was charming . . . I was very fond of him.'

While working on *Freud* he had made friends with English cameraman Desmond Davis. Ella Fitzgerald was in London and, knowing how Monty adored her, he took him to see her. Like Doris Langley Moore, he came to regret his generosity. During Miss Fitzgerald's performance Monty wandered on to the stage. She was forced to stop and introduce him to the audience. In his painkilling drug- and alcohol-induced haze he had lost touch with reality and forgotten he was in a theatre, for he would not knowingly have embarrassed her for the world. He had just wanted to get close to her.

Worry about the court case, and his possible expulsion from the movie industry, was driving him demented and turning him to even greater consumption of alcohol and amphetamines. Universal had already withheld what remained of his fee in lieu of possible damages.

He disrupted the Moore household so much that eventually Doris's daughter, seeing the effect on her mother, suggested he move to a hotel. He and Giles checked into the Savoy, after which he reluctantly flew back to New York.

He soon patched up his friendship with Doris, who sent him astrological forecasts in New York. He had to stop her: he was frightened of what the stars might predict.

19

By spring 1962 Elizabeth Taylor was in Rome's Cinecitta Studios making *Cleopatra* for the record-breaking fee of $1 million. She was in love with her co-star Richard Burton. Within weeks the press announced that she and Eddie Fisher were to split. The newspaper coverage was enormous. In Kitty Kelly's biography of Elizabeth, Burton is said to have announced in amazement: 'She knocks Khrushchev off the bloody front page'. Monty was equally amazed by the amount of publicity accorded her: 'Bessie Mae is now the most famous woman in the world,' he said.

On 9 April 1962 the annual Oscar ceremony was held at the Santa Monica Civic Auditorium. It was to be simultaneously televised.

Judgment at Nuremberg was nominated on several counts. 'So many stars have been squeezed into *Judgement at Nuremberg* wrote the *New Yorker* 'that it occasionally threatens to run into a judicial *Grand Hotel.*'

Maximilian Schell, tipped for an award, came to Los Angeles for the event. He had tough opposition up in Paul Newman, nominated for his role in *The Hustler*. Monty was up for Best Supporting Actor, but did not attend. He had no desire to spend an evening on display to millions of television viewers while his future was being judged. It meant too much to him, particularly now when he was on the verge of being blasted out of the industry. It was a matter of life and death.

As always, it was a glittering affair. The press went hysterical when

Cesar Romero arrived escorting Joan Crawford; the Queen Bee herself, shimmering with half a million dollars' worth of diamonds. She was to present the Best Actor award. Natalie Wood and Warren Beatty showed up, too, looking darkly gorgeous together and echoing the effect that Monty and Liz had created after *A Place in the Sun* twenty years before. Shelley Winters, also from that film, was draped in mink and escorted by Ty Hardin, then starring in his TV series *Bronco*. Paul Newman and his wife Joanne Woodward were also there.

Audrey Hepburn, who was up for Truman Capote's *Breakfast at Tiffany's*, was not at the ceremony. She had flown in from Switzerland but gone down with a virus, so she saw it on her hotel television. Judy Garland was doing the same thing – her son had a throat infection and she would not leave him.

Even before the voting started it was announced, to universal approval, that Kramer would receive the Thalberg Award for *Nuremberg*. Both Abby Mann, who had written *Nuremberg*, and Schell received Oscars. In addition to Garland and Monty (it was his fourth nomination, but again, he did not win) nominations were accorded to Kramer, cinematographer Ernest Lazlo and Spencer Tracy (his eighth).

Hedda Hopper, steeped in Hollywood to the roots of her dyed hair, was enraged by Monty and Judy. She fumed that stars should not lower themselves by appearing in cameo roles. There were a hell of a lot more changes awaiting to outrage Hedda. Meanwhile, unknown to anyone, Monty was sobbing his heart out alone. An Oscar would have been life blood to him.

Stars did not come much bigger than Marilyn Monroe, and Monty was shattered on the morning of 6 August 1962, when he learnt of her death. To this day it is unsure whether she committed suicide, died by accident or was murdered. She kept pretty racy company.

As Monty digested the news Anthony Summers writes in *Goddess** that the corpse of the great lady herself was stretched out naked on a stainless steel operating table in the Los Angeles Hall of Justice, covered by a sheet of plastic. A surgical saw would soon divide her skull and a scale for weighing human organs was nearby; some of hers would soon be in it. An autopsy was being performed on one of the most voluptuous bodies in the world, a body that had aroused millions of men. The autopsy revealed that for all her alleged drug dependency she was in fine physical form at the end, and drugs had not contributed to her death.

Monty did not know the details, but the news made him physically sick. At thirty-six she was six years younger than him.

* *Goddess* by Anthony Summers, Sphere, 1986

Around this time he made the only television appearance of his career. *Freud* was about to be released, and he agreed to do an interview to promote the film. He mentions nothing about his disputes with Huston and is urbane, sophisticated and charming; clearly neither drunk nor under the influence of any substances. Asked about the accident, he admits that he fell asleep at the wheel. 'I had a blink too many,' he says self-deprecatingly.

As he dreaded, *Freud* was released to little praise and much ridicule. 'It is impossible, I would think, for any educated person to sit through *Freud* without bursting into laughter at least once,' wrote Ernest Callenbach in *Film Quarterly*. It has since been re-evaluated and is now a cult film. As Rosalie Crutchley says, 'It turned out to be better than we thought it might.'

Although the Swinging Sixties had begun the world had not swung enough to accommodate the unadulterated teachings of Dr Freud. *Dr Kildare* was about as far as medical viewing went then, and Huston had had to temper many of the sexually explicit dialogues. The *Evening News* commented:

> Here, I think, couches should replace the regulation cinema seats for John Huston's elaborate tribute to Sigmund Freud, the father of psychiatry, virtually psycho-analyses its audience as well as its characters ... I gather that the Freud family has disassociated itself from the film but, whatever its objections may be, the film comes over as the familiar story of the scorned pioneer, the prophet without honour in his own times. We see him, in the dour, bearded and strangely subdued person of Montgomery Clift unravelling his own complexes through the hysterical stresses of a woman patient ... On this tortured mass of inhibitions the film concentrates its emotional fireworks and Susannah York, in her most demanding role to date, lets them off with an impressive frenzy of exploding fears and delirious dreams ...
>
> The accompanying screams and paroxysms, the dreams and erotic fancies photographed through a mist, the pitiful sight of the girl painting herself like a prostitute and compulsively stealing out by night to her father's favourite brothel – all these achieve a high drama. Considered generally, however, as an animated treatise on the darker mysteries of the mind (and in its contrived lecture hall scenes not so very animated either) it is unlikely to mean as much here as in America, where the psycho-analyst seems to be as essential as the grocer.

The dream sequence certainly did not go down too well. In the words of critic John Simon, 'photographed mostly in negative or overexposure, they belong not on the couch of Dr Freud but in the Cabinet of Dr Caligari'.

But there were compliments about Monty's performance. 'There is an impressive stillness in the man when he acts ... Whether he understands more of his lines than other actors do, only he could tell you. But he seems to.' That was *The Times* in London. Across the Atlantic, *Time* magazine said, 'Montgomery Clift has the singular ability to make his eyes light up. This is an enormous convenience in *Freud*. Thinking, after all, does not lend itself to visual representations ... With Clift's odd physiological talent, however, Huston can show the instant of young Freud's conception of the theory of infantile sexuality, the theory of repression, and the theory of dreams ...' While in the *New York Times* Bosley Crowther called Monty's performance 'eerily illuminating'. In 1963 he listed it among the year's best ten movies.

By 1980 Huston too had re-evaluated his work, and wrote in *An Open Book*, 'I saw *Freud* again recently. There are some good things in the picture. In spite of the difficulties I had with Monty, his genius shows through, and in the end I think he gives quite an extraordinary performance.'

While Monty had been in Munich, Libby had remarried. Her husband was Louis Schanker, a painter. He drank a great deal and is now best remembered for the part he played at one of her dinner parties, when he collapsed in a drunken stupor and his head rolled into the mousse, splattering his elegant wife. She merely wiped it from her face and asked 'Would anyone like coffee in the library?'*

Schanker disliked homosexuals. As many of Libby's friends were gay, this presented a problem. She had introduced him to Monty and he had not approved. When, some time later, he learnt that she planned to invite him for a weekend to Treetops, he made her cancel the invitation. Monty and Libby never saw each other again although she often thought of ringing him, and even coming to see him, but never did so for fear of upsetting her husband. It was an inglorious end to a close and mutually beneficial friendship.

Meanwhile, the balance of his Universal salary was still unpaid and he felt he might never get it unless he counter-sued. He was reluctant to do so but could see no option. He needed the money.

Universal then intensified its suit against him and put in a claim against the Fireman's Fund Insurance Co. In support of this the insurance company took statements concerning Monty's alleged incompetence

---

* Account taken from *Dreams That Money Can Buy*

from Huston and his supporters. Others, among them Susannah York and Rosalie Crutchley, supported Monty. Crutchley still recalls speaking to 'tough American lawyers'. It took courage to support Monty. His supporters were all professional people who needed work; not only were they alienating Huston, an important director, but they were also making an enemy of the powerful Universal studios.

In November 1962 he was formally questioned by representatives of Universal, and of the Fireman's Fund, on his part in the delays which had caused the film to over-run. He admitted he had not bothered to learn any lines until they had passed Huston's approval, stating that as re-writes were arriving constantly there was no point. He was unequivocal about this, despite objections from his defence. The case dragged on for months. The *Evening News* of 1 June 1963 brought Londoners up to date.

Film star Montgomery Clift is being sued for $686,000 – £244,902 – by Universal Pictures because, it is said, he 'failed to memorize his lines' in the film *Freud* and caused delays in production. The suit against the star became known when the studio filed a counter claim in New York State Supreme Court against an action by Clift for $131,000 – £46,757 – against Universal Pictures. Clift said the studio had agreed to pay him a basic salary of $200,000 – £71,000 – plus other benefits for his role as the world-famous psychiatrist.

The heartbreak contained in the story escaped most of its readers. The sums were unreal; £15 was a good weekly wage in Britain, £20 excellent. What did the average reader know of thousands of dollars or care about drunken stars, Universal Pictures or Dr Freud? It was all the cock-eyed realm of the movies.

But to Monty it was vital. He eventually won his case and Universal surrendered the balance of his payment. He was going to need the money, for his reputation was now shattered and he was considered unemployable. His name in a film had long ceased to guarantee full houses. No one disputed that he was a fine actor, but fine actors did not pull in the crowds. Stars did that.

His health broke under the strain. He had recently had a hernia repaired, and he blamed the rupture on the activity he had put into the *Freud* scenes, notably the rope sequence in which his hands had been burned. His jaw, never free of pain since the accident, flared up again, necessitating an increase in his dosage of painkillers. He drank in proportion.

In this state he took Dr Silverberg to see *Freud*. He was still infatuated by his psychiatrist, and some people said, erroneously, that Monty had made the film as a tribute to him. Although their relationship was certainly not sexual it far overrode the patient-doctor link. Silverberg was co-dependent now, and in their sessions together he would spend as much time discussing his own problems as he did listening to Monty. On the screen Monty was sure he could see the cataracts in his eyes, and eagerly pointed them out to Silverberg. He had been told it would take a couple of years yet for them to harden sufficiently to have them removed.

Before the court case had been settled his agents, MCA, with whom he had been for his entire movie career, had taken over Universal Pictures. He was suing his own agency, the very people upon whom he relied to find him work. He had no option other than to leave, putting his representation in the hands of Robert Lantz. But Lantz soon found that trying to find work for him was an uphill struggle.

In one way Monty was relieved: he had rarely enjoyed making movies, and he despised himself for being a movie star, particularly a failed one. He had never explored his full potential on stage and would never do so now. But the perks of stardom had become a way of life, and he needed to act. Since the stage was out of the question he could only act in movies.

His friend, actor Jack Larson, came to stay with him for a while. Larson's career was not in the same league as his, but Monty felt jealous of him. Larson still had a career, he was still working. A part of Monty would still like to have gone out to work. He spent most of his time in front of the television, which gave him too much leeway to think. Larson often saw him crying.

Larson took him to the theatre once and Monty fell asleep. Due to his insomnia he nodded off anywhere where it was comfortable – cars, restaurants or theatres. He woke up with a shout so loud that it startled not only the audience but the actors. Heads turned. His name reverberated in whispers around the theatre. There were a few covert sniggers. Friends rarely stayed now – Larson was an exception. Monty became a recluse, shuffling around the streets in the daytime and buying food at delis. Giles was still there, but they had separate lives. The nocturnal phone calls continued, as they always would, and another pastime was cruising. This provided excitement. All cruisers were loners; groups never attracted trade – they were too dangerous, either muggers or plain clothes cops.

He was impotent by now but loved the thrill of the chase. Although he could not sustain an erection he still felt lust. That he was a movie star had great pulling power, particularly with out-of-towners who sometimes could not believe who they had netted. Those whose customary beat coincided with his were not always so impressed. He was too regular a sight, slouching through the night and disappearing into the shadows with other equally nebulous characters. On many nights he skulked through alleys, bars and parks, coming home in the mornings having survived another night which otherwise might have been spent in a vain attempt to sleep. In a way cruising was his salvation.

Then another scandal, nothing to do with his nocturnal ramblings, reared its head and sucked him in. Brooks's twenty-one-year-old pregnant daughter, Suzanne, shot and killed her lover. The newspapers had a field day, running headlines on her family relationship to Monty. He refused to comment, although he could well have used the publicity to his own advantage.

But it brought the Clifts, long estranged, together. Sunny and Bill both came to see Monty, although separately, and he had not seen them for quite a while. When Bill came he met Giles. News of Monty's homosexuality had reached even his ears by now, and he could not fail to recognize their relationship for what it was. In his view homosexuals were pitiful. Nothing was said, but Bill knew. And Monty knew he knew.

He spent much time fretting about the future, which seemed to hold nothing. Then he joined Alcoholics Anonymous, which was a real breakthrough. Brando had tried to persuade him to join years earlier but had failed. Billy Le Massena, himself an alcoholic who had received help from AA, succeeded.

Monty's privacy was not jeopardized as all AA meetings are conducted in an atmosphere of anonymity. All members have to pull their weight, and he would take his turn to make coffee and hand it out. But the comradeship that is essential to successful meetings did not appeal to him. He felt uncomfortable. It was intensely difficult for him to take the first step and declare, 'My name is Monty and I am an alcoholic.' He was convinced he was not an alcoholic. He was drinking because he enjoyed it. He believed he could stop at any time.

Now and then he and Billy would discuss whether or not Monty wanted to end his life. Monty was adamant he did not want to. Billy would try to make him see that the amount of liquor he was downing, coupled with the pills, was an invitation to death. But there were no suicide attempts, even though he had enough pills in his medicine chest to end his life any time he chose. He knew about medicines and would have known precisely what to take. He was sometimes careless about living, but had no wish to die. What he needed was a job – anything to get him out of the house and force him to pull himself together.

He continued to consult Silverberg. Sunny had never been happy with his relationship with the psychiatrist and now, of her own volition, arranged a meeting to confront him about his treatment of her son. She took a lawyer and a medical doctor. The psychiatrist saw her but could see no problem with Monty's behaviour.

Much of the time Silverberg and Monty must have been discussing homosexuality. The guilt was always on Monty's mind. Being homosexual himself must have placed Silverberg in a dilemma. It was not until ten years later, during the 1970s, that homosexuality ceased to be regarded as an aberration by the American Psychiatric Association. Before then it was thought to be an undesirable and sometimes curable condition.

Record producer Ben Bagley, a friend of Monty's who had helped him decorate his house and had fixed orange awnings outside to give a Continental effect, was setting up a compilation disc of well-known actors singing famous songs. Monty was no Sinatra, but he could put over a number in his charming, hesitant way and so Bagley asked him whether he would be interested. He could not make up his mind, so Bagley, a patient man, got in touch with Anthony Perkins and asked him to persuade his fellow actor. They had met several times since he had seen Monty in The Seagull, and Perkins himself had made a few reasonably successful records.

The gangling Perkins, then an attractive thirty-two-year old who was to die of AIDS in 1992, did his best. He went to the brownstone and tried out some songs with Monty. Eventually he built up Monty's confidence – he was frightened he would make a fool of himself – and he agreed to record Jerome Kern's 'I Have the Room Above'.

Pleased with himself, Bagley gave the tidings to his recording company executives. But they rejected Monty on the spot. As far as they were concerned his name would have a negative effect on sales. He was yesterday's news, a totally fallen star. The contract was made over to Perkins instead, and he went on to record several other songs for the label.

Monty had high hopes for a while when it was mooted that he might play Singer, the deaf-mute in Carson McCullers's The Heart is a Lonely Hunter. There would have been no lines to remember and he would have expressed the deaf man's frustrations through mime. It was ideal casting and he immediately made arrangements to study sign language.

Unfortunately it was a waste of time. He was uninsurable and the idea was dropped. It broke his heart.

20

The new year of 1964 did not have the most promising start. Monty's body was starting to crumble as a result of the years of abuse, and he was on a course of calcium injections to counteract his thyroid condition. Without these he would shake uncontrollably. That, coupled with the cataracts and DTs, put him in real trouble. On top of this he had varicose veins, which needed to be operated upon, and phlebitis, a painful inflammation of the veins. This meant that he could not walk without help, and even then he staggered. People assumed he was drunk.

But there was a positive side. He had split from Giles after the Frenchman had made a couple of attention-seeking suicide attempts. Giles's departure was the best thing for him because, after a short, disastrous period of living by himself, it opened the door for another man to live with him, this time someone special.

The black Lorenzo James was a former actor turned nurse recommended by Monty's doctor, Arthur Ludwig, after consultation with Billy Le Massena and Sunny. He proved himself loyal and devoted to the end: if angels came in human form, he was one.

Initially he retained his own apartment, but after a few months he moved into the brownstone. Under his surveillance the number of free-loaders whom Monty attracted diminished drastically. When

Giles tried to get back with Monty, Lorenzo allowed him in to collect his possessions but no more. He also changed the telephone number so that the constant dubious incoming calls ceased.

Monty was happier and looked it. He drank less and ate more. Lorenzo took him to cinema matinees, helping him along like an old man as his painful legs forced him to hobble. Lorenzo would try to get him into the back seats so that he would not disturb other patrons if he yelled out.

That February Bill died, but there was no display of grief from Sunny or Monty. Sunny spent several hours alone with her husband before he died, so perhaps they made up their differences. Whatever Monty felt, if anything, he did not show much. According to Barney Hoskyns in his biography of Monty, Lorenzo found the Clifts 'isolated, closed off, remote and suspicious of each other – except for Monty and his twin sister'.* That was the way Sunny had brought them up. Like royalty, they did not show their emotions in public.

Worried that she might have difficulty making ends meet without Bill he arranged for an allowance to be paid to her – not that he was flush with cash himself, but the fees from *Freud* had now been settled. It was not easy to get Sunny to accept the money; she viewed herself as the provider and was fiercely independent. As always in times of hardship she found herself a job – despite the fact that she was now in her seventies. This time she was employed collating the papers of famous writers. She grudgingly accepted the allowance, however, more to placate Monty than anything else.

That spring Elizabeth Taylor and Richard Burton were in town. Burton was on Broadway in the outrageously successful *Hamlet* directed by Gielgud. It played for seventeen weeks to standing room only. Monty was not so impressed. He saw Brooks shortly after seeing Burton's performance and enacted almost the entire play for him, telling him how he thought Burton should have done it.

By now Burton and Elizabeth were married. Love suited Elizabeth and she looked radiant. She came to the theatre often, each time wearing a different stunning outfit. The crowds outside filled the street. They got a wonderful show, particularly when the couple left together.

She was shocked by his appearance: 'When Elizabeth saw Monty in New York in the Spring of 1964 she was appalled,' writes Kitty Kelley in her biography of Elizabeth. 'Sickly and malnourished, he weighed barely 100 lbs . . . Worst of all was the fact that he had not worked

---

* *Beautiful Loser* by Barney Hoskyns, Bloomsbury, 1991

in four years. Elizabeth was convinced that it was the professional inactivity that was killing him as much as his own self-destruction. 'If he doesn't work soon, he'll die,' she told a friend.' She could not fail to notice the cataracts on both his eyes and the fact that his poor face was ravaged by drink.

He attended a $100-a-seat charity event at the Lunt-Fontanne Theatre, where Burton and Elizabeth, with purple flowers cascading through her hair, read poetry to raise funds for the Musical and Dramatic Academy of New York. He met several old friends including Lee Remick and Myrna Loy. Lauren Bacall, one of the few stars who came to his funeral two years later, was also there.

Truman Capote told Elizabeth how worried he was about Monty – this was before Lorenzo had moved into the brownstone. She arranged for him to move into a hotel near her, where she could keep an eye on him.

He did not want to go, but Capote persuaded him it was for his own good. Within three days he was back. 'I can't stay in a hotel,' he told Capote, as recorded in Gerald Clarke's biography of the writer. 'I have to be at home.' In truth he was better there: his house was his security.

He took solace from his garden and planned to plant silver birches there as a tribute to Chekhov. He fancied he would sit under them reading, like a character from *The Cherry Orchard*.

He stayed in contact with old friends such as Roddy McDowall and Nancy Walker; in February 1963 he had been on a holiday to the Virgin Islands with Nancy. Truman Capote, too, continued to keep in touch – Capote was not one to lose contact with a star, albeit a tarnished one. Just before Christmas 1963 they had lunch together and then went Christmas shopping. Capote noted, again quoted by Gerald Clarke:

[He seemed] perfectly normal and full of good humour and we were laughing and having a fine time. No one could have been more charming. Everyone in the street kept stopping and turning – they recognized him, me or both of us . . . the whole thing had a sort of jolly, jingling quality about it.

When we finished eating we went to an Italian store that specialized in beautiful, expensive sweaters. At lunch he had had just one drink – one drink! But he must have shot up or taken pills in the men's room, because suddenly he went utterly, completely, to pieces, just like an insane person.

He pointed to the counter, where all the sweaters were stacked, and counted one, two, three, four, five . . . sixteen.

'How much are all those?'

The salesman told him, and Monty picked up all of the sweaters in one huge bundle – there were so many they were falling out of his arms – and somehow got the door open. It had begun to rain by this time – in fact it was pouring – but he walked out and threw them all in the gutter.

When he came back, the salesman just asked, 'And to what address do I send the bill, Mr Clift?' I've never seen anyone so cool in my life as that salesman.

Monty wouldn't speak to him, but I gave his address and made him sign the bill.

'Monty, you've got to go home,' I said when we were outside.

'I'm not going anywhere!' he replied, and we began to have a struggle in the street. I shoved him into the back seat of a taxi, but he got out, walked round the back and got into the front seat, where he tried to grab the wheel away from the driver, who told us to get out or he would call the police.

'Oh, please God, do anything except that!' I said. 'This man is very ill. Take us to this address, and I'll give you a big tip, please!' So he did, through all the Christmas traffic, while I was holding onto Monty, who was screaming and shouting. It was a nightmare. When we got to his house, his coloured houseman managed to get him inside and called his doctor who gave him an injection. After this experience something went snap in our relationship.'

Capote says they had just one drink together, that he doesn't know whether or not Monty took pills that day, but assumes from his behaviour that he did. This was not necessarily the case. The effect of just a single drink on his saturated system at that time could tip him over the edge.

Giles had still not given up on Monty, his meal ticket, and, high as a kite one night, rang the fire brigade and reported that Monty's house was on fire. He then waited outside hoping that Monty would rush out and that he would be able to get to him. It never happened.

On another occasion he waited until he saw Lorenzo leave, then knocked on the door. Monty let him in but Giles did not have the push-over for which he had hoped. Lorenzo had been able to stabilize Monty's condition and he calmly told Giles that their affair was over and he was to go away.

He spent that summer with Lorenzo in a rented house on Fire Island, joyous haunt of promiscuous homosexuals. The news that he was there, albeit having to be helped along by Lorenzo, spread like wildfire. He accepted a few invitations to parties. He couldn't stand, so he sat, and it was not unusual for him to fall off his seat. It was precarious replacing him on the chair, from which he would be likely to fall again, so he was considerately left on the floor, with his back propped against the wall, where he could not hurt himself. People would squat down and chat to him.

Incredibly, on Fire Island, he began to pull himself together. He started by cutting down his drinking. This was not so much voluntary but a case of self-defence. He was taking yet another new medication to relieve the pain in his shoulders, legs and jaw. The new painkiller, DMSO (soon to be withdrawn from the market due to its doubtful side-effects) gave him relief but reacted against alcohol, causing him to vomit. With the decrease in alcohol came a lessening of its accompanying depression, so there was less need for pills.

He planned a come-back. Monty wanted to return to his first love, the stage, though only in small cameo roles at first. He thought he might also direct, something he had always fancied. He did not rule out the possibility of more film work, should it come his way. He would take anything to get back where he felt he belonged – anything was better than inactivity.

A return to the stage at that point in his life would of course have been physically and mentally impossible. His legs had improved but he still had only limited mobility, his arthritic shoulder made any quick movement painful and his memory could not cope with learning any length of lines.

He was, however, optimistic. In fact, in time his mobility did improve and he was convinced he could retrain his memory. Most positively, his cataracts could soon be removed – that opened the floodgates to all sorts of possibilities. For the first time in years he saw a goal for which to aim – for which he wanted to aim, however remote.

Inspired by Burton's success in *Hamlet*, he started rereading the play. He already knew most of it by heart, and now he practised the speeches as he stumbled about Fire Island. He cut an eccentric figure among the other men, who were mostly there for sex. He made plans for his own production, which he would star in and direct, and in which Myrna Loy would be Gertrude. She was still in his thoughts after he had bumped into her at the Taylor-Burton charity affair.

Back home, he started to work. Caedmon Records contracted him to play Tom, the leading male character, in a record set of *The Glass Menagerie*. Julie Harris was Laura, his crippled sister, and Jessica Tandy Amanda, their mother.

Set in Depression-riven America, *The Glass Menagerie* is autobiographical. Tom is a thinly disguised young Tennessee Williams. His role as narrator/brother consists of lengthy poetic rhetoric often addressed directly to the audience.

Monty was able to use a script, so the length of the speeches was no problem. Sitting in the studio, in congenial company, with two fine actresses, his glasses perched on the end of his nose, he poured his heart into it. His characteristic voice is ideal, stirring memories of Prewitt and Noah Ackerman. This is a yearning Tom, eager to cut loose before he is dragged into Amanda's eddy. He is the perfect Williams actor.

After this, also using a script, he provided the voice-over for novelist William Faulkner's *Mississippi*, a two-hour television documentary for which he again played the narrator. He received an Emmy nomination.

He saw John Huston's Oscar-nominated *The Night of the Iguana*, and his reflections must have been bitter as his own career was floundering and Huston, who had done so much to make that happen, had now received a nomination. Who had come out best from the *Freud* battle? *Freud* had been a nightmare from which Monty had never recovered, rating with the car accident as one of the great tragedies of his life. But the past was the past, and now he had to build the future.

He continued to see his family and would even telephone Sunny at times, and invite her round, something he had rarely done before. He invited his niece Suzanne, too; she had been judged unbalanced at the time she had shot her lover and had undergone psychiatric treatment. Monty knew all about mental troubles. Suzanne's baby would happily crawl around the floor as she and Monty commiserated.

His brother Brooks got married for the fourth time. Monty was the best man and hosted the reception at his brownstone. He spent a fortune on flowers and catering. Sunny made mounds of sandwiches and greeted the guests as if she were royalty. Even there his sense of humour broke through. When the minister asked if there were any objections he quipped, 'He smokes.'*

In August 1964 he felt sufficiently together to make a lightning visit to London. Olivier was appearing in *Othello* and he did not want to

---

* Brooks Clift's Foreword to *The Films of Montgomery Clift* by Judith M. Kass

miss it. He dined with Olivier's party afterwards, then went to see the play again, taking Susannah York with him.

This time he did not stay at the Savoy but checked into the exclusive and subdued Brown's Hotel. He took the opportunity to look up other old friends, including Sybil Burton, to whom Richard Burton had been married for twelve years before marrying Elizabeth.

He tried to shun publicity, but that was a lost cause and he reluctantly agreed to be interviewed. His reputation may have dwindled in America, but to the British he was still a star. His very Quixoticness made him hot property. Although he was cooperative with the reporter, the essence of the piece shows that he was still emotionally delicate.

'Quietly, surreptitiously, even furtively into town slips that lotus eating actor, Mr Montgomery Clift,' read the *Daily Sketch* for 7 August 1964.

> And, judging from his appearance, lotus leaves are all he does eat
> . . . Mr Clift is an actor who drives his agent not only up all four walls but halfway across the ceiling. Compared to Mr Clift, who has an arrant disregard for folding money, a beachcomber on Papeete would resemble an undertaker in the middle of a typhoid outbreak.
>
> Mr Clift wishes to see no one. Not even himself in a mirror. Which is why he books into a quiet hotel that knows how to cope with hunt balls and jolly hockey stick debs rather than dedicated actors . . .

The reporter referred to the accident, then continued:

> Since then Mr Clift, talented and tormented, has seemed to one and all hell-bent for destruction. We talk together as Mr Clift shelters in his hotel and he says: 'The one reason I came to London just now was to see Larry in *Othello*. Life is far too short to miss an experience like that. I guessed he wouldn't bring it to Broadway, so I thought it would cost me nothing to make the trip over here. What is money compared with experience? So now I've seen it – twice . . . and all I can say is that Larry is head and shoulders above any living actor.'

He began to weep. Silently. 'I never got a chance to tell him,' he went on. 'There was always someone else at the table, you know how it is.' He cleared his throat. 'Did you see me in *Judgment at Nuremberg*? he asked. 'There was only seven minutes of me – did

you see it? I turned down a part worth $300,000 to play in that
picture. And I did it for nothing. You know why? Because it was
a hurdle. I don't want to know about anything that isn't a hurdle,
don't you see? That's why I've done nothing since *Freud*.'

'Your agent must be gnashing his teeth,' I said.

'Oh, you can afford to coast a little and still be a star,' said
Mr Clift. 'My agent understands that I only enjoy going over real
hurdles. You see, I don't have to prove anything to people any
more – but I have to prove things to myself . . .

'I read so much garbage . . . no challenge. No hurdles. Tell me,
did you see me in *The Young Lions*'? He began to weep again. 'I
was so very proud of that performance,' he said. He was silent
again and then: 'You know, one pays a very high price to be a
public figure. That's why I don't like to talk to anybody except
the few friends I have. Maybe work is the only thing. I want to
work – oh yes – I want to work and I believe they've got something
for me to look at when I get back. I just hope it's a hurdle. I really
do. That's what I need right now.'

Although much of the piece was brouhaha (his agent had nothing for
him to look at – nothing that was worth seeing, anyway – and he had
not turned down $300,000 to play in *Nuremberg*), his pride in his films
comes through. He may have despised the industry, but he knew he
had done it proud.

Before leaving London he had an unexpected encounter with film
critic Alexander Walker. It took place in Rank's screening room in
Wardour Street where Walker had gone to see Peter Finch in *The Girl
with Green Eyes*. He recalls in a letter to the author:

I was aware of someone slipping in shortly after it started, but I
didn't see who it was until the lights went up – then I recognized
Clift. Why he was there, I have no idea to this day. Maybe he
wanted to see Finch, or maybe just kill time. Anyhow, I went up,
introduced myself and started to discuss *Freud* with him . . . that,
probably, wasn't a good idea, given its turbulent history and lack
of success. But after a minute or two I sensed that Clift had been
backing away from me, inch by inch, and all unconsciously, I had
been advancing on him – until his back and curiously hunched head
were flat against the . . . wall. He quite visibly resembled a man under
torture! I hadn't, of course, seen his last . . . film, *The Defector*, but
when I did I realized I was witnessing the reflex he had adopted

through most of it, and it was of a terribly vulnerable man shrinking into himself. To this day, I have the impression that I must have seemed to him like someone whom Amnesty International would condemn. Movie making had been a torture-chamber to him.

On 8 August 1964 he flew back to New York. There were some offers of work, including an Italian Western, but nothing he could seriously consider. He had not made a film for over three years, but would not lower his standards.

Judging from its title, the projected horror film *The Last of the Late Great Jellie Bellies* might have been trash, but he did consider this for a while as the writer had told him Shelley Winters had agreed to do it. In the end he turned it down, as had Miss Winters.

Then Lee Strasberg offered him *The Three Sisters*, a highly acclaimed production about to open in London. Monty had to say no, not because he thought Strasberg a phoney but because he knew he was not yet up to it. But the offer boosted his morale. He hoped to do all the great Chekhov plays one day.

For want of something more productive to do, he decided to decorate the house. The blinds that Ben Bagley had put up cast a restful golden glow throughout the street-facing rooms and he wanted to ensure that the decor was similarly calm. He spent hours shopping for fabrics and wallpapers and bought some new furniture – there was always one place in the house that was in chaos. Impatient for a builder, one day he took an axe and demolished the wall of a bathroom he was converting into a bar.

By early 1965 he had had his cataracts removed, a process which involved two separate operations. Sunny came to see him in hospital but, moodily, he would not talk to her. She carried on regardlessly. In the end he rounded on her, crying out that he wished he had her strength. The doctor later remarked that he had seldom seen such a resolute old lady. His face looked less haunted now that he could see clearly again, and he could also read, which was a great comfort. He had missed his books.

The operation, however, left his eyes sensitive to light. A photographer flashed a camera at him at close quarters one day and he screamed, throwing his hands over his eyes. It was reported that he had attacked the man. The accompanying photograph showed him with his hands raised to protect his eyes, but it looked as though he was squaring up for a fight.

He was still wiry, despite all he had gone through, and was now

beginning to regain a little much-needed weight. He took up swimming
again and went on a boating trip with a friend, frequently diving into
the water. It washed away the haze of the city and sleeping pills. For
the first time in months he was clear-headed. He liked the sensation.

21

Elizabeth Taylor had not forgotten how ghastly he had looked when she had seen him at the charity appeal. She had meant it when she had said she believed he might die if he did not work soon. His face had haunted her.

At her instigation they met to discuss a suitable film in which they could appear together. She was the world's highest-paid star and could choose whatever suited her – 'If someone's dumb enough to offer me a million dollars to make a picture, I'm certainly not dumb enough to turn it down.' She had the final word, too, on her co-star.

For a while they toyed with *The Owl and the Pussycat*, which was eventually made in 1970 with Barbra Streisand and George Segal. They liked the idea of doing a comedy, but it never came about. Later in the year, however, she agreed to do a film, at a date yet to be set, for Warner Brothers/Seven Arts, that was far removed from comedy – Carson McCullers' story of hothouse passions set in the Deep South, *Reflections in a Golden Eye*.

Miss McCullers, lesbian and unwell, had written a story, or rather a series of detached incidents, of repressed homosexual lust, nymphomania and sexual mutilation set in an army camp in Georgia. A young soldier is discovered riding naked through the countryside and spied upon by his latently homosexual officer, who fantasizes about him. The major is impotent and his wife (Elizabeth) has an affair with a neighbour whose wife is repelled by sex and, as a deterrent, has amputated her nipples with shears. Judith Crist dismissed it as 'nothing more than nutty people and pseudo porn'. It was considerably more than that.

Elizabeth thought Monty would be right as the major. As Alexander Walker puts it in his biography *Elizabeth*: 'This was a part that Elizabeth's instinct told her Clift could align with his own self-loathing and craving for affection.' Although Monty had nothing at all on offer, and was an admirer of Carson McCullers, he would not agree to do the film until he had read a draft script. He accepted as soon as he had.

It would be the first time he had played a homosexual, albeit a latent one. Perhaps his acceptance of the part was a final acceptance of his own nature? As Jack Babuscio put it in *Gay News*, No. 104:

Not only could the part revive a dangerously flagging career . . . but might it not also enable him to return, via the route of his art, to a more secure reality – to face up to the fact of his homosexuality? . . . For the actor apparently had, at long last, though only at the very end of a most difficult life, seemed to really understand that most poignant line of Private Prewitt's: 'If a man doesn't go his own way, well, he's nothin!'

But it was not as simple as that. No company would insure Monty. Any film starring Elizabeth Taylor was expensive, and the risk of bankruptcy if Monty failed to deliver was too great. It looked as though the offer would have to be withdrawn.

Elizabeth, however, would not hear of this. As Monty's guarantor she put up her entire fee as collateral, a genuinely selfless act unparalleled in the annals of film-making. 'We got them by the balls, baby,' she is reported to have reassured a trembling Monty.

No sooner had Monty learnt he was still on board than he faced another problem. Of all the directors in the world, the director of *Reflections* was to be John Huston. Elizabeth again came to the rescue and persuaded him to accept Monty. He was far from keen to do so, but he knew, as the cast of *Suddenly Last Summer* had known, that Monty was more stable when Elizabeth was around. He also knew that, if Monty failed to deliver, Elizabeth could lose a million dollars. Surely he would not do that to a friend?

She then persuaded Monty to accept Huston. The role of the major was less demanding than his part in *Freud*. There were certainly a lot fewer lines to learn. He had no option other than to bite the bullet.

'Miss Taylor was determined to have Monty in *Reflections* and to make another picture with an actor she greatly admired and loved as a friend,' said Robert Lantz, as reported in Kitty Kelley's biography of Elizabeth. 'Her immense devotion to him was not only responsible for the acceptance of Clift by John Huston, but she also overcame certain insurance problems.'

Meanwhile Elizabeth and Burton travelled to England where, at Oxford University, they appeared in Marlowe's *Doctor Faustus*, she in a four minute silent part as Helen of Troy. The production was later filmed. They then went to Rome where they filmed *The Taming of the Shrew*, followed by Graham Greene's *The Comedians*.

While Elizabeth crammed one movie after another into her whirlwind international schedule, Monty sat at home and waited for a start date on *Reflections*. He telephoned her constantly, wherever she was, terrified that the deal might fall through. She repeatedly confirmed that it would not.

It was finally agreed that filming would start, in Rome for tax reasons, in September 1966. His fear of Huston bubbled up again, but she assured him there would be no problems. She was a match for Huston any day.

He was the happiest he had been for years. This was truly a new beginning, and he was going to make sure he was ready for it. The frightened, lonely days of obscurity were over. He had a year and a half to prepare – quite a time, and he was going to fill it well.

The Burtons returned to New York in the summer of 1965 and checked into the Regency Hotel. Monty spent much time with them, Burton good-naturedly tolerating his babbling. Monty found things to appreciate in him, and Burton discovered he quite liked Monty.

Monty decided to improve his appearance, the first real interest he had taken in his looks since the accident. He had minor plastic surgery, not a full face-lift, but just the bags removed from under his eyes. It was a decided improvement.

On 20 August 1965 Monty made a will: 60 per cent of his estate was to go to Ethel and the remaining 40 per cent to Sunny. This excluded certain legacies, such as one to Brooks who was to receive $12,500, others to Mira and Marge Stengel, $5000 each, to Lorenzo $3000 and to other friends $500 each.

Jack Larson came to stay with Monty again and instantly, and with relief, noted the improvement. But Monty could regress at any time, and Jack knew that these lapses occurred when Monty was idle, so he tried to keep him occupied as much as possible.

Monty had never lost touch with Salka Viertel, Garbo's writer, who now lived in Switzerland. Larson was also a friend and they telephoned her together one day. She spoke of the call, and her friendship with Monty, to French movie producer Raoul Lévy. Lévy was strangely interested.

He had made an impact on the world in 1957 when he had co-written and produced *And God Created Woman*, starring Brigitte Bardot and the beach at St Tropez. The Catholic Legion of Decency denounced both as 'an open violation of conventional morality', and in doing so put Bardot and St Tropez on the map. Bardot kept her feet firmly on the ground: 'I started out as a lousy actress and remained one,' she is recorded by Halliwell as having said, adding, 'I didn't throw myself off the balcony only because I knew people would photograph me lying dead.'*

Lévy had made a few other successful movies, but nothing since *The Truth* in 1960. He needed a hit as much as Monty and he had planned his come-back, a low-budget spy movie to be called *The Defector* which he would direct and shoot in Munich. He had already made an offer to Monica Vitti, the sexy Italian actress, to star in it. Monty would be the perfect leading man to bring the film Hollywood kudos.

After speaking to Lévy, Salka Viertel telephoned Monty. He was very interested. Although *The Defector* was a small-budget affair he wanted to prove to the world that he was a responsible actor. Without the prospect of *Reflections* he would probably have dismissed it out of hand. Now, however, he could use it as a rehearsal to get back into training and show everyone he could still do it.

The script was sent to him, by which time Monica Vitti was out of the frame. But, excitingly to Monty, Leslie Caron was interested. He detested the script but, for the first time in his life, put that aside. It was more important that he worked. Not, however, before ensuring that Lévy would permit him to change his lines as he thought fit. He made contact with Caron and found that she too was dissatisfied with the script. They decided to get together in London to work on their parts.

He flew there early in 1966, after a skiing holiday with Ethel in New Mexico. Although never free of pain, he was getting fitter. He injected himself daily with Demerol, which kept the worst at bay. By now, apart from infrequent binges, he was barely drinking. Fitness was his aim. *Reflections* was the nirvana that was going to heal all.

He worked on the script with Caron, who was keeping company

* *Filmgoer's Companion*, Grafton Books, 1965

with Warren Beatty at the time, and was mortified when she too had to tell him she could no longer do the film. According to Patricia Bosworth, she felt she would be unable to work constructively with Levy. Another French actress, Simone Signoret, was in town, working on *The Sleeping Car Murders*. He tried to persuade her to take over the role, but with no luck. In the end the part was taken by actress Macha Méril.

On the plus side Levy had signed up Hardy Kruger, a blond German beefcake who happened to be a useful actor; Monty's friend Roddy McDowall – it would be the first time they had worked together; and director Jean-Luc Godard in an acting role. Monty went out of his way to see Godard's films.

Monty played a physicist who is sent to East Germany and spies for the CIA. While there he has a love affair with a foreign spy. *Dr No*, the first Bond movie, had opened in 1962 and *The Defector* was trying to jump on the bandwagon.

The script called for Monty to do stunts: he had to leap into moving boats, scale walls, jump fences and swim in freezing water. Although he had been skiing he was no Sean Connery, and put these athletic feats out of his mind until he reached Germany. He could sort them out there.

He searched the script for sub-texts, hoping to give his character more depth, but there were none that he could find. Finally he rang Mira and, loyal as she was, she agreed to go to Munich with him. They started on rewrites immediately.

Lorenzo went too, and the three of them checked into the Ambassador Hotel. It was freezing. He had made *Freud* in Munich, and the city held unhappy memories. He had been a star then, having just made a film with Marilyn Monroe – directed by Huston. Now he was going to work with him again. There was an icy wind. On the other hand he had also made *The Search* in Munich, the first of his films to be released, and that had brought the world to his feet. He had been young then, full of promise, the first post-war teen idol.

He was no one's idol now, just a burnt-out figure of lost opportunity trying to hang on. *The Search* had been a low-budget film too, but a lifetime's experience was sandwiched between that and *The Defector*. He had been full of hope on *The Search*, and he was full of hope again, despite the fact that the beautiful young man was now a worn-out roué.

Typically, he refused a stunt double for the action scenes and they nearly killed him. Like Gable on *The Misfits*, he was terrified anyone might think he was past it. Careful editing would make these shots usable and he was delighted. Mira was more sceptical: 'I remember he fought with the director that he wanted to go into the cold water with some kind of rubber suit,' she recalled in *His Place in the Sun*. 'They wanted to persuade him not to, but I don't know why he wanted to make such a big point that he could do it all.'

Roddy McDowall was impressed by the way Monty had taken himself in hand: 'It was very cold,' he remembered in the same documentary. 'He didn't have the physical resources left any more to protect him. But [he was] totally committed, totally there and totally responsible . . . he still had this wonderful way, he drew out of you what you should be doing.' Burt Lancaster had said much the same about *From Here to Eternity*.

There are some off-set shots of him strolling in his donkey jacket, hands in pockets, hunched against the wind. He cuts a lonely – but appealing – figure. Most photographs of Monty make him appear lonely even when he is with people. He was able to project this into his movies – an unenviable talent.

As usual he got on with his leading lady. In the *Sunday Telegraph* of 28 June 1966 Macha Méril was to say, after his death, 'He reminds me of Marilyn Monroe' which was what Huston had said. She added, 'He gives so much it is painful. Almost as though he were acting to destroy himself.'

He welcomed the attention of the press, knowing he needed every favourable column inch he could get. He spoke of his earlier time in Munich making *The Search*. The *Sunday Telegraph* reported:

'So I became', and Clift shut his eyes as though to obliterate the concept, 'a star! Public property. Yes, it was exhilerating for a bit, I remember the first time I tried to push the door open and I couldn't, as if it had snowed, fan mail was so deep. But, quickly I got the aggression. You have never, never seen anything like it.' Suddenly his fist bunched, his fine-boned face thrust forwards. 'You – are Montgomery Clift, aren't you?' It spat out like a threat.

'I could never play a part like *The Search* again. Too much innocence. One grows cynical . . . I am not a good judge of my own work. Some things I have done I like. *Young Lions*, maybe, and *Nuremberg*. I saw one on television the other day. It must be twenty years old. But there is so little good screen acting. Ah! To be jealous of an actor. This is the highest compliment – jealousy . . . to loathe an actor for his performance, to say, 'I wish I had done that.' How often do I feel like that? . . . so seldom . . . Laurette Taylor. And now Simone Signoret, and Larry Olivier, of course.

And Marlon, in his early roles ...' And Clift was unclenched: soaking up fruit juice from a flask; patting a passing script girl on the rump; flicking that smile, brilliant as a gas jet ... But now the next scene, and he tightened up visibly, almost painfully ...

The writer of the film was Robert Guenette, later to produce the TV documentary *His Place in the Sun*. They had worked together on Faulkner's *Mississippi*. Guenette retains an affection for him and, when he learnt this biography was to be written, warned the author, 'Do good by him. He was a gentle soul and a gifted artist.'

As always when filming, Monty was tense, aware how much depended on it. But he remained on good terms with everyone and it finished on time and within budget. This was the main reason he had done it – to prove that he could, stunts and all. He had to go to Paris for the dubbing, so he parted from Mira in Munich with thanks and promises to see her soon in New York.

Raoul Lévy died shortly afterwards, a death as eccentric as his life. He had a row with his girlfriend and went to her home to sort her out with a loaded rifle. He hammered on the door and the gun went off, shooting him through the stomach. He never saw *The Defector*.

From Paris Monty and Lorenzo went to London. They stayed at the Royal Garden Hotel, overlooking Kensington Gardens. He went to Stratford-on-Avon for the theatre and visited the set of Fred Zinnemann's *A Man for All Seasons*, in which Susannah York was appearing. Zinnemann was delighted to see him but shocked by the deterioration in his appearance. Zinnemann was not to know that, compared to how Monty had looked just six months previously, he was now the epitome of good health.

It was humiliating for Monty to visit the set of this quality film and explain to the man who had directed him in one of his finest performances that he had been working on a cheap-budget German movie. No one treated him as less than a star, though. Paul Scofield came over specially to pay his respects.

He went to a party given by Leslie Caron and Warren Beatty. Richard Harris told him how much he admired him and Barbra Streisand, clearly in awe, cornered him for most of the evening.

John Huston's production manager, Doc Erickson, was in London to do preparatory work for *Reflections*. Although the film was to be shot in Rome, some work would be carried out in England. Erickson could barely believe that Monty had agreed to work with Huston again. But then he did not know the depths to which Monty had sunk since *Freud*:

'I was setting up . . . and ran into him,' Erickson recalled in *His Place in the Sun* 'I said, "Monty, how are you?" "I feel great" [he said], you know, and we threw our arms around each other and so forth and I, laughing, said, "You're really a glutton for punishment – how could you do this thing?" He almost threw himself on the floor – Monty would get very energetic when he got hyped-up a bit and he laughed, "Yeah, yeah, yeah – it'll be alright, You'll see, you'll see."'

He returned to New York in July and became depressed. Part of this was nerves, as he would soon have to work on *Reflections*. He was pondering on the wisdom of having done *The Defector*, a poor film which would do nothing for him artistically. He wished he had never agreed to it. It was even more important now that *Reflections* put him back where he belonged.

Idleness increased his depression. He had nothing much to do until filming started. Ben Bagley came round and they started working on the decor of the brownstone yet again, but he could not do too much as he was exhausted after the physical exertions of filming.

He began to get snappy with Lorenzo, accusing him of not looking after him properly and spying on him. He was a bag of nerves, dreading *Reflections* yet impatient to start. *The Misfits* was on television on the night of 22 July 1966. Lorenzo asked him if he wanted to see it. 'Absolutely not,' he replied.

He died during the night. His glasses were still on when Lorenzo found him naked in the morning. He had been reading. He always preferred books to films.

22

Lorenzo called Dr Ludwig. He was away and so a colleague of his, Dr Klein, came to the house. Then Lorenzo called Monty's attorney Jack Clareman, who also arrived. They were followed by the police.

It appeared to be a straightforward death by natural causes, with no evidence of foul play or signs of suicide. But Monty had locked his bedroom door, something he had never done before. He had cut down his drinking for weeks beforehand but increased his intake of Demerol. As a result he had started to hallucinate and, in fear of *Reflections*, had imagined he was being persecuted. That was the reason for his short temper with Lorenzo, and possibly why he had locked his door. Lorenzo had had to break it down to get in.

An ambulance took the body to the Medical Examiner's Office, where an autopsy was performed by Dr Michael M. Baden. No traces of alcohol or narcotics were found, but the examination revealed he had been suffering from advanced arteriosclerosis – hardening of the arteries consistent with angina – and occlusive coronary artery disease or myocardial infarction. In plain words, Monty had died from a heart attack.

It was apparent that he had suffered a milder attack some days previously, probably as a result of the strain of stunts called for in *The Defector*. He had withstood alcohol and drug abuse for years, but exercise had killed him.

Sunny could not be located at first and actually heard of Monty's death on the radio. It was almost as though she had expected it; when she reached the brownstone she was controlled and in command. Yet again people marvelled at her strength of will. Ethel flew in from Texas.

Someone, clearly eager to waste no time, had put the house on the market and, in the midst of the turmoil over funeral arrangements and press questions, a family arrived to view it. They were shown in and, agape, watched the mayhem. It was the sort of anecdote Monty loved.

The funeral took place on 26 July when an Episcopalian service was held at St James' church on Madison Avenue, after which he was to be buried. Sunny had wanted a Quaker service but was over-ruled by Ethel.

Sunny, Ethel, Brooks and Lorenzo were at the front of the church. Libby Holman was at the back, sitting grim and gaunt with her sons Tim and Tony. Roddy McDowall had telephoned her with the news before she had the chance to hear it on the radio or read it in the papers.

Libby's ninety-three-year-old mother Rachel had died recently and she was racked with guilt, which merged with the guilt she felt for abandoning Monty. She knew she should never have lost touch with him – they were kindred spirits and had been loyal to each other. She wrote to Sunny, as quoted in *Dreams That Money Can Buy*, 'He will always be like a bright shining sun to my family and me.'

When Monty's coffin was brought into the church she rose to her feet, sobbing, hands outstretched. She was too upset to attend the burial afterwards, and her grief never lessened. She went to Japan for a while, where she entered a Buddhist retreat near Mount Fuji called the Temple of the Swamp Dragon. There, surrounded by snowy slopes, she read *The Three Pillars of Zen* and sought peace of mind. She never found it. Five years later she killed herself.

Lauren Bacall was also in the church, as were Nancy Walker, Mira and other friends who had stood the test of time. For others, life had to continue. Myrna Loy sent flowers; Kevin McCarthy was on the road, touring; Roddy McDowall was in Hollywood, filming; Elizabeth Taylor was in Rome, also filming. She sent two wreaths of white chrysanthemums. Her card read, 'Rest, perturbed spirit.'

She too had heard the news from Roddy, who had phoned Burton in the early hours of 23 July. Burton had told her when they were alone. She told reporters, 'I loved him. He was my dearest friend. He was my brother.' Privately she told friends she had been dreading the news for some time. For years afterwards she would get upset when his name came up. Truman Capote remarked, 'In his last years nobody, not even Elizabeth Taylor, could have helped him.' She certainly did more than most.

A spirited crowd of autograph hunters jostled the coffin as it left the church. Lauren Bacall was asked for her autograph and there were hopeful shouts for Elizabeth. It was everything Monty abhorred.

His burial took place at the Friends' Cemetery in Brooklyn. In the Quaker manner a small granite headstone was placed over his body, simply bearing his name and dates. The following spring some scarlet tulips bloomed there, making the stone look, from a distance, as though it were daubed with blood.

The value of his estate came to half a million dollars, not a great deal by movie star standards. Ironically, a poll recently conducted by *Variety* magazine revealed that, based on the takings from his films over the years, he was one of the world's top money-making stars. He would have preferred to have been remembered as a good actor.

At the end of August a small Quaker memorial service was held, a warm-hearted affair in which friends and family bore testimony to his friendship. That he would have liked.

The Defector was released four months after the funeral. If the intention was to cash in on his much-publicized death, it backfired. It did poor business and, in Britain, did not get a major West End showing. Reviews were sparse: David Shipman called it 'mechanical, somnambulant, with no hint of his former charm and ability'. Judith Crist commented: 'All that we are finally left with is the cliché, a relatively new one, along with the triple-viced hero, that spying is not a nice profession but the good guys have to go in and win for our team.' Halliwell's *Film Guide* dismisses it as 'Disenchanted espionage 'realism', not very well styled and hampered by a star at the end of his tether.'

Reflections in a Golden Eye went ahead. Both Richard Burton and Lee Marvin were considered for Monty's part, but in the end it went to Brando for a million dollars – more than Monty had ever earned. It was as if fate was mocking him by casting Brando at a vast fee as a replacement for his desperate come-back attempt. Brando was his inspiration and his despair.

Brooks died in 1986, the husband of four wives and father of eight children, his problematical life a testimony to Sunny's upbringing and Monty's shadow. He, and Ethel, had been shocked by much that has been written about Monty, particularly his alleged hard drug addiction which Brooks dismissed in the *Washington Post* as 'over-exaggeration'. Monty was in contact with Brooks and Ethel throughout his career, and they saw him regularly. If he was into hard drugs neither saw any signs of it. Nor did Jack Clareman, Monty's attorney and executor to his estate. 'I think he drank too much,' says Clareman. 'But I never saw him take drugs.'

Ethel, now widowed, still lives in Texas. She is vulnerable and hurt by some of the things that have been written about her brother. The drug-obsessed Monty who sometimes appears in print is not the brother she knew. Listening to her frail voice on the telephone, it is hard to believe she is the twin of one of the most explosive, if involuntary, sex symbols ever to hit the screen.

Brooks said of Monty in the *Washington Post* that he had 'a dedication, a fierce concentration to his work. He was the most aware person. A man without a skin.' Monty was Brooks's hero. He would have loved to have been a star himself, and in his early years tried to become one. Unlike some other stars, Monty never insisted that a part for his brother should be written into his contracts. He could easily have done so, and probably Brooks would have loved it, but he was too much of an idealist. Acting was a sacred trust to Monty.

After Monty's death Brooks did everything he could to ensure the continuation of Monty's fame. He became the professional dead star's brother, converting a room of his Washington DC house into a shrine. On 6 August 1979 journalist Myra MacPherson wrote in the *Washington Post*: 'His [Monty's] beautiful/handsome face, captured like a butterfly under glass on the cover of *Life* magazine 31 years ago, stares from one wall.'

Also in the room were the duffle bag that Monty had used as Prewitt, items of clothing, film costumes, cans of movies, an ashtray he made as a child, tapes and signed cheques, even the neck brace he had used while recovering from the accident. There was also an X-ray of Monty's broken jaw, which had never healed properly and had forced him to take so many analgesics – painkillers to which his system reacted so badly and to which he had become addicted. Most are now off the market.

Brooks welcomed everyone to his shrine, from kids with a crush to film researchers. All were allowed to handle Monty's possessions, listen to tapes of his telephone conversations that Brooks had made and read his letters. He referred to himself as 'Keeper of the Flame'.

Plans were made for two biopics based on Monty's life. Sidney Lumet was to direct one based on Patricia Bosworth's biography, and Silva Productions of New York planned another based on the earlier biography by Robert LaGuardia. So far neither has been made.

His inconspicuous headstone, which has to be sought out, with its scarlet poppies blooming in the spring is his memento.

Films

The Search: MGM. Produced by Lazar Wechsler, directed by Fred Zinnemann, 1948.

Montgomery Clift
Aline McMahon
Jarmila Novotna
Wendell Corey
Mary Patton
Ewart G. Morrison
William Rogers
Ivan Jandl
Leopold Borkowski
Claude Gambier

Red River: United Artists. Produced and directed by Howard Hawks, 1948.

John Wayne
Montgomery Clift
Joanne Dru
Walter Brennan
Coleen Gray
John Ireland
Noah Beery, Jr.
Chief Yowlachie

Harry Carey, Sr.
Harry Carey, Jr.
Mickey Kuhn
Paul Fix
Hank Warden

The Heiress: Paramount. Produced and directed by William Wyler, 1949.
Olivia de Havilland
Montgomery Clift
Ralph Richardson
Miriam Hopkins
Vanessa Brown
Mona Freeman
Ray Collins

The Big Lift: 20th Century Fox. Produced by William Perlberg, directed by George Seaton, 1950.
Montgomery Clift
Paul Douglas
Cornell Borchers
Bruni Lobel
O. E. Hasse
Danny Davenport
Fritz Nichlisch
Capt. Dante V. Morel
Capt. John Mason
Capt. Gail Plush

A Place in the Sun: Paramount. Produced and directed by George Stevens, 1951.
Montgomery Clift
Elizabeth Taylor
Shelley Winters
Anne Revere
Raymond Burr
Herbert Heyes
Keefe Brasselle
Shepperd Strudwick
Frieda Inescort
Ian Wolfe
Lois Chartrand

Fred Clark
Walter Sande
Douglas Spencer
John Ridgley

I Confess: Warner Brothers. Produced and directed by Alfred Hitchcock, 1953.

Mongomery Clift
Anne Baxter
Karl Malden
Brian Aherne
O. E. Hasse
Dolly Haas
Roger Dann
Charles André
Judson Pratt
Ovila Legare
Gilles Pelletier

From Here to Eternity: Columbia Pictures. Produced by Buddy Adler, directed by Fred Zinnemann, 1953.

Burt Lancaster
Montgomery Clift
Deborah Kerr
Frank Sinatra
Donna Reed
Philip Ober
Mickey Shaughnessy
Harry Bellaver
Ernest Borgnine
Jack Warden
John Dennis
George Reeves
Tim Ryan
Barbara Morrison
Kristine Miller
Jean Willes

Indiscretion of an American Wife: Columbia Pictures. Produced and directed by Vittorio De Sica, 1954.

Montgomery Clift
Jennifer Jones

Gino Cervi
Dick Beymer

Raintree County: MGM. Produced by David Lewis, directed by Edward
Dmytryk, 1957.
Montgomery Clift
Elizabeth Taylor
Eva Marie Saint
Nigel Patrick
Lee Marvin
Rod Taylor
Agnes Moorehead
Walter Abel
Jarma Lewis
Tom Drake
Rhys Williams
Russell Collins
DeForrest Kelley

The Young Lions: 20th Century Fox. Produced by Al Lichtman, directed by
Edward Dmytryk, 1958.
Marlon Brando
Montgomery Clift
Dean Martin
Hope Lange
Barbara Rush
May Britt
Maximilian Schell
Dora Doll
Lee Van Cleef
Liliane Montevecchi
Parley Baer
Arthur Franz
Hal Baylor

Lonelyhearts: United Artists. Produced by Dore Schary, directed by Vincent
J. Donehue, 1959.
Montgomery Clift
Robert Ryan
Myrna Loy

Delores Hart
Maureen Stapleton
Frank Maxwell
Jackie Coogan
Mike Kellin
Frank Overton
Don Washbrook
John Washbrook

Suddenly Last Summer: Columbia Pictures. Produced by Sam Spiegal, directed by Joseph L. Mankiewicz, 1959.

Elizabeth Taylor
Katharine Hepburn
Montgomery Clift
Albert Dekker
Mercedes McCambridge
Gary Raymond
Mavis Villiers
Patricia Marmont
Joan Young
Marie Britneva
Sheila Robbins
David Cameron

Wild River: 20th Century Fox. Produced and directed by Elia Kazan, 1960.

Montgomery Clift
Lee Remick
Jo Van Fleet
Albert Salmi
J. C. Flippen
James Westerfield
Barbara Loden
Frank Overton
Malcolm Atterbury

The Misfits: United Artists. Produced by Frank E. Taylor, directed by John Huston, 1961.

Clark Gable
Marilyn Monroe
Montgomery Clift
Thelma Ritter

Eli Wallach
James Barton
Estelle Winwood
Kevin McCarthy

Judgment at Nuremberg: United Artists. Produced and directed by Stanley
Kramer, 1961.
Spencer Tracy
Burt Lancaster
Richard Widmark
Marlene Dietrich
Maximilian Schell
Judy Garland
Montgomery Clift
William Shatner
Ed Binns
Kenneth Mackenna
Werner Klemperer
Alan Baxter
Torben Meyer
Ray Teal
Martin Brandt
Virginia Christine
Ben Wright
Joseph Bernard
John Wengraf

Freud: Universal. Produced by Wolfgang Reinhardt, directed by John
Huston, 1962.
Montgomery Clift
Susannah York
Larry Parks
Susan Kohner
Eileen Herlie
Eric Portman
Ferdinand Ledeux
David McCallum
Rosalie Crutchley
David Kosoff
Joseph Furft
Alexander Mango
Leonard Sachs

The Defector: Seven Arts. Produced and directed by Raoul Levy, 1966.
    Montgomery Clift
    Hardy Kruger
    Roddy McDowall
    Macha Meril
    David Opatoshu
    Christine Delaroche
    Hannes Messemer
    Karl Lieffen

INDEX

Films and plays are listed under titles; books under authors' names